GREEK MEDICINE

GREEK MEDICINE

From the Heroic to the Hellenistic Age

A Source Book

James Longrigg

Routledge
New York

First published in 1998 by
Gerald Duckworth & Co. Ltd.
The Old Piano Factory
48 Hoxton Square, London N1 6PB
Tel: 0171 729 5986
Fax: 0171 729 0015

Published in the United States by
Routledge
29 West 35th Street
New York, NY 10001

A catalogue record for this book is available
from the British Library

CIP data is available from the Library of Congress

ISBN 0 415 92087 6

Printed in Great Britain

Contents

FOR NANCY WITH AFFECTION & GRATITUDE

Preface

I should like to express my great gratitude to the Principal and Fellows of Wolfson College, Oxford for the award of a Charter Fellowship in the History of Science in 1994 which enabled me significantly to advance this work; to the Principal and Fellows of Brasenose College, Oxford and the Hellenic Fund for the award of a Fellowship in Hellenic Studies in 1997 which enabled me to bring it to completion, and to the University of Newcastle for granting me study leave on both occasions.

I should also like to acknowledge the great kindness of Vivian Nutton of the Wellcome Institute and my colleague, Philip van der Eijk, both of whom read an early draft of this work and whose comments proved invaluable. Last, but by no means least, I should like to express my gratitude for help in preparing the indices and for other assistance to my wife to whom this book is affectionately dedicated.

Hamsterley Mill
Durham
1997

Introduction

One of the most impressive contributions of the ancient Greeks to Western culture was their invention of rational medicine. Up to now this important subject has been difficult to study because of the inaccessibility of source material, which, in addition to being written in the Classical languages, is highly diverse, widely scattered throughout a multiplicity of ancient authors, frequently lacking a modern edition, and, at times, fragmentary and distorted. This *Source Book* seeks to help to alleviate this problem by providing a collection and translation of some of this fascinating material covering several of the most important aspects of ancient Greek medicine from Homer to the Alexandrians and assembling it in a form where it is more readily accessible to researchers, teachers and students alike.

The primary aim of this book is to set Ancient Greek medicine within its historical and intellectual context by presenting a selection of passages (not all of them, of course, strictly medical, or even Greek) in English translation. Such a policy, it is hoped, will enable one to reveal where, when, and how developments occurred; to trace the fortunes and modifications of individual theories, and to reveal the attitudes and beliefs of individual doctors on particular issues (which is not easily done on the more conventional approach).

It should be stressed that this work is not intended to serve as a General Reader. Nor is it primarily an attempt to illustrate the manifold virtues of Ancient Greek medicine by presenting, in conventional fashion, a selection of texts of outstanding merit or interest. Several such attempts have already been made. Again, it must be pointed out, it is not the aim of this collection to cover the whole of Ancient Greek medicine. (Restrictions of time and space would, in any case, preclude such an ambition.) Comparatively little emphasis, for example, has been accorded to social and practical aspects of Greek medicine – not because these aspects are regarded as lacking in importance and interest, but because the desire here is to concentrate most especially upon that aspect of Greek medicine that set it apart from other medical systems – its rational and theoretical nature.

The Greeks invented rational medicine. It was they who first evolved rational systems of medicine for the most part free from magical and religious elements and based upon belief in natural causation. The importance of this revolutionary innovation for the subsequent history of medicine can hardly be overstressed. The strikingly rational attitudes introduced here into medicine resulted in a radically new conception of disease, whose causes and symptoms were now accounted for in purely natural terms. These are the elements I wish to accentuate. In this latter connection, I have sought, where appropriate, deliberately to provide overlap with my earlier book, *Greek Rational Medicine*, in the hope that it might prove helpful to augment the contexts now assembled with the longer commentaries supplied in that earlier work, and, conversely, to augment the latter with the more numerous contexts provided here.

It is inevitable that an author's choice of contexts in a *Source Book* will not always coincide with that of his readers; inevitably, it will sometimes be felt that better choices could have been made. Frequently, too, this author has himself been unable to include all the passages he would have liked. Again, the actual topics selected may not be to the taste of every reader. Indeed, since Greek medicine was not itself sub-divided into the various specialisms of its modern counterpart, it may be objected that to present this material under a diversity of headings is, strictly speaking, anachronistic. The validity of this objection is freely acknowledged and, by way of atonement, frequent cross-references have been introduced to serve as reminders of the more unitary nature of Greek medicine. Readers are, therefore, cordially invited to add further contexts where they will and, should they wish, to re-arrange the numbers of the passages translated here to form topics of their own choice. It is, in any case, most earnestly hoped that readers will not be content to confine themselves solely to the passages presented here, but that, whenever they are able, they will study them within the larger literary context from which they have severally been drawn.

Finally, a short synopsis covering the subject-matter and cross-referenced to the contexts selected has been added at the end of each chapter.

With the exception of the Near Eastern material all the translations are by the author.

Abbreviations

CIG = *Corpus Inscriptionum Graecarum* (Berlin, 1828-77).
CMG = *Corpus Medicorum Graecorum* (Berlin/Leipzig, 1908-; Berlin, 1947-).
CML = *Corpus Medicorum Latinorum* (Berlin/Leipzig 1915-).
Di. = Diller, H. *Hippokrates. Über die Umwelt* (= *CMG* I.1, 2 (Berlin, 1970).
DK = *Die Fragmente der Vorsokratiker*, 8th edn., 3 vols., ed. H. Diels & W. Kranz (Berlin, 1956).
Fr. = Fragment.
Heib. = Heiberg, J.L. (ed.) *Hippocratis Opera* Vol. I.1 (*CMG* I.1), (Leipzig & Berlin, 1927).
Ilb. = Ilberg, J. *Sorani Gynaeciorum Libri IV. De signis fracturarum. De fasciis. Vita Hippocratis secundum Soranum* (*CMG* IV) (Leipzig & Berlin, 1927).
Jo. = Joly, R. *Hippocrate: Du Régime* (*CMG* I.2, 4) (Berlin, 1984)
Jou. = Jouanna, J. 1975. *Hippocrate: La Nature de l'Homme* (*CMG* I.1, 3) (Berlin, 1975).
K = Kühn, C.G. *Claudii Galeni Opera Omnia*, 20 vols. in 22 (Leipzig, 1821-33; repr. Hildesheim, 1965)
L = Littré, E. *Oeuvres complètes d'Hippocrate*, 10 vols. (Paris, 1839-61).
SIG[3] = *Sylloge Inscriptionum Graecarum*[3], ed. W. Dittenberger, Leipzig, 1915-24
SVF = *Stoicorum Veterum Fragmenta*, 4 vols., ed. H. von Arnim (Leipzig, 1903-24; repr. Stuttgart, 1964).

I

Pre-rational and irrational medicine in ancient Greece and neighbouring cultures

ANCIENT EGYPT AND MESOPOTAMIA

In both of these ancient societies diseases were held to be manifestations of the anger of the gods. The physician's role was to appease the god and drive out the demon possessing the sick person's body.

Disease in ancient Egypt

I.1. *Ebers Papyrus* 1 (Trans. Majno, 1975, p. 127)

This medical papyrus here records an appeal to the goddess Isis in the recital of a spell accompanying the removal of a bandage.

O Isis, great in sorcery! Mayest thou loosen me, mayest thou deliver me from everything evil and vicious and red,[1] from the spell of a god or from the spell of a goddess, of a dead man or of a dead woman, of a fiendish man or of a fiendish woman who will be fiendish within me, like thy loosening and thy delivering thy son Horus.

[1] The prayer is that the skin beneath the bandage will not turn out to be bloody or inflamed.

I.2. *Hearst Papyrus* 85 (Trans. Sigerist, 1951, Vol. I, p. 275)

Coprotherapy is here employed to drive out the possessing spirit.

O ghost, male or female, thou hidden one, thou concealed one, who dwellest in this my flesh, in these my limbs – get thee hence from this my flesh, from these my limbs. Lo, I brought thee excrements to devour! Beware, hidden one, be on your guard, concealed one, escape!

I.3. *Papyrus Medicus Londinensis* 22 (Trans. Sigerist, 1951, Vol. I, p. 285)

Here the eye of Horus, son of Isis and her brother Osiris, is invoked to drive out malignant demons.

This Eye of Horus created by the spirits of Heliopolis, which Thoth has brought from Hermopolis – from the great hall in Hermopolis, – in Pe, – in Dep, – sayest thou to it: 'Welcome, thou splendid Eye of Horus – brought to drive out the evil of the God, the evil of the Goddess, the demon, male and female, the dead, male and female, the enemy, male and female, who have insinuated themselves into the eyes of the sick under my fingers. Protection, behind me protection, come, protection!'

Disease in Mesopotamia

I.4. Sumerian incantation. (Trans. Campbell Thompson, 1903-4, Vol. I, pp. 60-3 with slight modification)

This cuneiform text preserves a procedure for the elimination of a possessing spirit. The demon is threatened that it will find neither food nor drink.

> Until thou art removed, until thou departest
> From the man, the son of his god,
> Thou shalt have no food to eat,
> Thou shalt have no water to drink,
> Thou shalt not stretch forth thy hand
> Unto the table of thy father Enlil, thy creator.
> Neither sea water, nor sweet water,
> Nor bad water, nor Tigris water,
> Nor Euphrates water, nor pond water,
> Nor river water shalt thou drink.
> ...
> Come not nigh, Get thee hence.

I.5. Sumerian incantation. (Trans. Campbell Thompson, 1903-4, Vol. II, p. 101)

Here Marduk, the city god of Babylon, is told to make a clay figure in the image of the sick man and utter a ritual incantation to drive out the plague demon.

> Go, my son < i.e. Marduk>,
> Pull off a piece of clay from the deep,
> Fashion a figure of his bodily form and
> Place it on the loins of the sick man by night,
> At dawn make the 'atonement' for his body,
> Perform the Incantation of Eridu,
> Turn his face to the west,
> That the evil plague-demon which hath seized upon him
> May vanish away from him.

The usual practice was for the clay model to be carried out of the house and destroyed, bearing away with it the demon which had been transferred into it by the magical formulae.

I.6. Sumerian incantation (Trans. Campbell Thompson, 1903-4, Vol. II, p. 109)

On this occasion the model is fashioned from dough.

> Fashion a figure of him in dough,
> Put water upon the man and
> Pour forth the water of the Incantation;
> Bring forth a censer (and) a torch,
> As the water trickleth away from his body
> So may the pestilence in his body trickle away.

I.7. *Sakikku* 12-26 (Trans. Wilson & Reynolds, 1990)

Epilepsy is a disease which, because of its sudden, dramatic and frightening symptoms, has been regarded with superstitious awe. A recently translated cuneiform text preserves invaluable evidence of Babylonian views regarding the nature of this disease. Here we are presented with an accurate and comprehensive description of many familiar features of an epileptic seizure which provokes comparison with the well-known account in the Hippocratic treatise, *On the sacred disease* ch. 7 (VI.372-5L). Whereas the Hippocratic author accounts for epilepsy upon the basis of purely natural causes, our unknown Babylonian unequivocally maintains: 'If epilepsy falls once upon a person [or falls many times], [it is (as a result of) possession] by a demon or a departed spirit.'

12. [If at the time] of his fit [the patient] loses consciousness and foam comes from his mouth, it is *miqtu* [diurnal epilepsy].

13. [If at the time] of his fit he loses consciousness and his arms and legs bend round to the same side as his neck, it is *miqtu* ...

14. If at the time of his fit ... takes hold of him and foam comes from his mouth, an [unfulfilled] vow made by his father has seized him. He [the child] will die.

15. If at the time of his fit after it has taken hold of him foam comes from his mouth, – hand of *Lilü*.

16. If at the end of his fit when his limbs become relaxed again his bowels are sometimes seized and he has a motion, it is 'hand of ghost' [nocturnal epilepsy].

17-18. If at the end of his fit his limbs become paralysed, he is dazed [or dizzy], his abdomen is 'wasted' [sc. as of one in need of food] and he returns everything which is put into his mouth – hand of a ghost who has died in a mass killing. He will die.

19-22. If at the end of his fit his limbs become paralysed, [the demon] 'pouring out' upon him so much that he loses control [of his functions]; if when he thus 'pours out' upon him his eyes are red and his face expressionless; if his *ser'anu*-vessels pulsate at a quickened rate and he cries although the tips of his fingers and toes remain cold; if when the exorcist asks the sick person to repeat [a prayer] he repeats what he says to him, but after [the demon] has let him go he does not know what he said, – hand of *Lilü-la'bi*.

23. If before his fit a half of his body is 'heavy' for him and pricks him, and afterwards he has a fit with loss of consciousness and he loses control [of his functions], it is *miqtu*. At midday it will be most serious for him.

24-5. If before his fit he suffers from frontal headaches and is emotionally upset, and afterwards he ... [..] his hands and feet, [and] rolls from side to side [on the ground] without deviation [of the eyes] or foam[ing at the mouth], it is a fall due to emotional shock, or 'hand of Ishtar'. He will recover.

26. If when he has his fit [the fallen person] is looking sideways or the whites of his eyes deviate to the side, and blood flows from his mouth, for female [patients] it is *Lilü*, and for male, *Lilîtu*.

ANCIENT GREECE

Disease in Greek epic

The gods as cause of disease

I.8. Homer, *Iliad* 1.46-53

In this extract Apollo sends a plague upon the Greek army investing Troy.

The arrows rattled on the shoulders of the angry god when he moved and his coming was like the night. Then he sat down apart from the ships and let fly a shaft. Terrible was the twang of the silver bow. He attacked the mules first and the swift dogs, but then he loosed his piercing shafts upon the men themselves and shot them down and continually the pyres of the dead thickly burned. For nine days the missiles of the god ranged throughout the host ....

I.9. Homer, *Iliad* 24.758-9

Hecuba addresses the corpse of Hector:

You lie like one whom Apollo of the Silver Bow has slain, coming upon him with his gentle darts.

I.10. Homer, *Iliad* 21.483-4

The goddess, Artemis, kills women.

Zeus has set you <Artemis> as a lion against women and given you the privilege of killing whomsoever you wish.

I.11. Homer, *Iliad* 24.605-7

Artemis and her brother Apollo kill the children of the unfortunate Niobe.

Her sons Apollo in his wrath against Niobe slew with shafts from his silver bow, and Artemis the shooter of arrows slew her daughters because Niobe made herself the equal of fair-cheeked Leto.

I.12. Homer, Odyssey 9.407-11

The Cyclops Polyphemus is deluded by Odysseus's stratagem and told by his kinsmen that his blinding is a malady sent by Zeus.

Then from the cave mighty Polyphemus answered them: 'My friends, Nobody is killing me by guile and not by force'. And they, speaking winged words, answered him: 'If no one is assaulting you in your solitude, you must be sick. It is impossible to avoid the sickness sent by great Zeus ....'

I.13. Hesiod, *Works and Days* 238-45

Zeus sends famine and plague which kills men and makes women barren.

But for those whose hearts are set on violence and cruel deeds far-sounding Zeus, the son of Cronos, ordains punishment. Often even a whole city suffers for a bad man who sins and devises wicked deeds. The son of Cronos from heaven inflicts upon the people great misery, famine and plague together. The men perish, the women are barren and their homes become few through the cunning of Olympian Zeus.

I.14. Hesiod, *Works and Days* 100-4

Although diseases are described here as attacking spontaneously, they are still the deadly gift of the gods.

Countless plagues wander among men; for the earth is full of evils and the sea is full. Diseases spontaneously (*automatai*) come upon men continually by day and by night silently bringing mischief to mortals; for wise Zeus took away speech from them.

I.15. Homer, *Odyssey* 11.171-3

Odysseus meets his dead mother in the Underworld and seeks to learn the cause of her death.

But come now, tell me this and give me an accurate answer. What doom of death that lays men low has been your undoing? Was it a long sickness, or did Artemis, shooter of arrows, come upon you with her grievous shafts and destroy you?

Not all diseases, it appears, were the result of divine agency.

I. Pre-rational and irrational medicine

The gods also cure wounds and disease

I.16. Homer, *Iliad* 5.114-22

Diomedes has been hit by an arrow and is bleeding profusely.

Thereupon Diomedes prayed: 'Hear me, child of aegis-bearing Zeus, unwearied one. If ever with kind thoughts you stood by my father's side in dreadful battle, now, likewise, be kind to me, Athena. Grant that I might slay this man and that he might come within the cast of my spear, who smote me first and is boasting over me and says that I shall not long behold the bright light of the sun.'

So he spoke in prayer and Pallas Athena heard him and made his limbs nimble.

I.17. Homer, *Iliad* 5.445-8

Aeneas's hip has been crushed by a stone hurled by Diomedes.

Apollo set Aeneas apart from the throng in sacred Pergamus, where his temple was built. There Leto and Artemis, shooter of arrows, healed him in the great shrine and glorified him.

I.18. Homer, *Iliad* 16.527-31

Glaucus's arrow wound is healed by Apollo.

So he spoke in prayer and Phoebus Apollo heard him. Straightaway he made his pains cease and staunched the black blood that flowed from his grievous wound and put strength in his heart. Glaucus knew in his mind and rejoiced that the great god had swiftly heard his prayer.

I.19. Homer, *Odyssey* 5.394-8

The relief of the ship-wrecked Odysseus at the sight of land is compared to that of children who see their father cured by the gods of a critical illness.

As welcome as is the glimpse of returning life in a father to his children, when he has lain sick, suffering strong pains, and wasting long away, and the loathsome *daimon* has assailed him, but then, and it is welcome, the gods delivered him from his sickness, so welcome appeared land and forest to Odysseus.

I.20. Homer, *Odyssey* 19.455-8

The sons of Autolycus, when Odysseus is wounded at a boar hunt, bandage his wound and employ magic to stop the bleeding.

Then ... the wound of the noble, god-like Odysseus they bound skilfully and checked the dark blood with an incantation.

Healing cults

Among the many gods and demi-gods skilled in the art of healing the following are especially noteworthy for their healing-cults.

The cult of Amphiaraus

Important centres of the chthonic cult of Amphiaraus, one of the Seven against Thebes, were established at Thebes, Athens, and Oropus, where the god gave advice to suppliants during their incubation upon the earth beneath which he resided.

I.21. *Inscriptiones Graecae* VII.235 (= *SIG*[3] 1004)

This inscription stipulates that the priest of Amphiaraus should spend some time each month at his Sanctuary near Oropus to care for it and to serve his worshippers. Rules for incubation are prescribed.

From the onset of winter until the spring ploughing-season the priest of Amphiaraus is to go into the sanctuary, when winter arrives until the sowing-season with no greater interval than three days between visits. He is to be in residence there not less than ten days in each month. He is to require the temple attendant to care for the sanctuary in accordance with the law and also for those who visit the sanctuary ....

When someone comes to be healed by the god, he is to donate a first-fruit offering of at least nine obols of silver and deposit it in the treasury in the presence of the attendant. When present, the priest is to say prayers over the sacrifices and place the victim on the altar; when he is absent, the one making the sacrifice is to do this. During the public sacrifice each person should say the prayers for himself, but the priest should say them over the public sacrifices and he should receive the skins of all the victims sacrificed within the sanctuary. Each person may offer whatever sacrifices he wishes. No portions of meat are to be carried out of the precinct. Sacrificers should donate the shoulder-portion of each victim to the priest except during a festival; at that time he should receive the shoulder-portion only from the public victims.

Rules for incubation: the attendant should record the name and city of the person undergoing incubation when he deposits his money and display it on a notice-board for anyone to read. In the sanctuary men and women should lie separately, the men to the east of the altar, the women to the west.

The cult of Asclepius

The most influential healing-cult in ancient Greece was that of Asclepius, the son of Apollo, whose worship became much more widespread from the last third of the fifth century BC. In addition to existing shrines at Tricca and Epidaurus new ones were established at Athens and the Piraeus. Subsequently his cult spread to the Aegean, Asia Minor and Egypt.

I.22. Pindar, *Pythian* III.47-55

Pindar enumerates the various types of patient resorting to Asclepius in the hope of a cure in an ode addressed to Hiero, tyrant of Syracuse, which he seems to have composed *c.* 473 BC.

And whosoever came suffering from the sores of nature, with limbs wounded by grey bronze or far-hurled stones, or with bodies wasted by summer's heat or winter's cold, he delivered them, different ones from different pains, tending some with kindly incantations, while he set others on their feet again with the knife.

I.23. Aelian, *Nature of animals* IX.33.1

A miraculous cure is effected by Asclepius.

A woman had a worm and the cleverest of the physicians despaired of curing her. So she went to Epidaurus and begged the god to free her from the parasite. The god was not there, but the attendants made her lie down where the god was in the habit of healing the suppliants and she lay quiet as she was enjoined. But the servants of the god began to treat her and removed her head from her neck. Then one of them inserted his hand and drew out the worm, a great brute of a beast. But they were no longer able to fit the head in place and restore it to its usual fitting. Then the god arrived and was angry with them for undertaking a task beyond their wisdom and he himself with the irresistible power of a god restored the head to the body and raised up the suppliant.

I.24. *Inscriptiones Graecae* IV². 1 Nos. 121-2, pp. 70-3, ll.113-19
      (= Edelstein, *Asclepius,* Vol. I, No. 423 A XVII, p. 224)

A 'cure' *(iama)* from the temple of Asclepius at Epidaurus. Aelian tells us that his source is the Sicilian historian, Hippys of Rhegium, who is said to have lived at the time of the Persian Wars. Thus, if this assessment is correct, we would have here an early view of the practice of this healing cult.

A man had his toe healed by a snake. The man, in a terrible state because of a malignant ulcer on his toe, was carried outside in the daytime by the attendants and he sat down upon a seat. When sleep overcame him, a serpent came out of the sanctuary and healed his toe with its tongue. When the patient awoke, he was healed. He had seen a vision: it seemed that a beautiful youth was spreading a potion upon his toe.

I.25. *Inscriptiones Graecae* IV². 1 Nos. 121-2, pp. 70-3, ll.113-19
      (= Edelstein, *Asclepius,* Vol. I, No. 423 B XXVII, p. 226)

Another miraculous 'cure' from a votive column found at Epidaurus. See also **XV.9** below for Asclepius's successful treatment of Ambrosia's diseased eyeball.

A man with an abscess in his belly. This man while sleeping in the Temple had a dream. It seemed to him that the god ordered his attendants to seize and hold him so that he might cut open his belly; he tried to escape but they seized him and bound him to a door-knocker. Then Asclepius cut open his belly, excised the abscess, sewed him up again and released him from his bonds. Whereupon he walked out sound, but the floor of the sanctuary was full of blood.

1.26. *Palatine Anthology* VI. 330

A defaced inscription records how the orator, Aeschines, having lost confidence in human medical skill, turned successfully for help to Asclepius and was cured.

No longer counting upon mortal skill, I placed all my hope in divinity. I left Athens ... I came, Asclepius, into your sacred wood and I was cured in three <nights?> of a wound that I had in my head for a year.

1.27. *Inscriptiones Graecae* II². 4960a (= Edelstein, *Asclepius*, Vol. I, No. 720, pp. 374-5)

Asclepius is brought to Athens in 420 BC.

The god came up during the Great Mysteries and was escorted into the Eleusinion. From his home he summoned the snake in a chariot. Telemachus went out to meet him. Hygeia came along and thus was founded the whole sanctuary in the year of the archonship of Astyphilus, the son of Cydantides [420/19 BC]. In the archonship of Archias [419/18 BC] the Heralds laid claim to the property and <prevent>ed some work ... In the archonship of Teisandrus [414/13 BC] the wooden gateway was constructed and the rest of the sacred furnishings were installed. In the archonship of Cleocritus [413/12 BC] the planting was done and he completed the decoration of the whole precinct at his own expense.

1.28. Aristophanes, *Plutus* 659-738 (= Edelstein, *Asclepius*, Vol. I, No. 421, pp. 214-16)

In the following extract from his comedy performed in 388 BC Aristophanes burlesques the rites of the cult of Asclepius. Here a slave, Carion, describes the greed of the priests and the cure of Plutus, the blind god of wealth.

Carion: Then we went to the precinct of the god. When the cakes and offerings were dedicated as food to Hephaestus's flame, we laid Plutus down in the customary manner. And each of us arranged a pallet for himself .... The attendant of the god extinguished the lamps and ordered us to sleep, saying that if anyone should hear a noise, he should keep quiet. We all lay down in an orderly fashion. I was unable to sleep. A pot of porridge, which stood a small distance from an old crone's head, aroused my desire. I had a wondrous urge to creep towards it. Then, looking up, I catch sight of the priest stealing the cakes and figs. After this he went circling round all the altars in the hope that a cake might have been left behind. Then he consecrated these into a kind of sack. I considered that the deed had full sanction and got up after the pot of porridge.

Wife: Most wretched of men, did you not fear the god?

Carion: Yes, by god, I did – lest he might get to the pot first, garlands and all. For the priest warned me of him beforehand. When the old crone heard the noise I made, she put out a stealthy hand. Then I hissed and took it between my teeth like a sacred snake and she immediately drew it back. She wrapped herself up in her bedding and lay quiet, farting through fear more pungently than a polecat. I, by that time, was gobbling up a lot of the porridge ....

Carion: The god visited every patient in a very orderly manner, examining their diseases on his round. Then a servant placed beside him a stone mortar and pestle and a little medicine chest .... The god sat down beside Plutus. He first took hold of his head and then took a clean napkin and wiped all round his eyes. Panacea covered his head and the whole of his face with a scarlet cloth. Then the god whistled. There then darted out from the temple two serpents of monstrous size.

Wife: O dear god.

Carion: The two of them slipped quietly under the scarlet cloth and licked his eyes, as it appeared to me ... Plutus arose his sight restored.

1.29. *Corpus of Inscriptions at Delphi* (Inv. 6687A & B & 8131)

Here an inscription of the first half of the fourth century BC shows how the association of the Asclepiads of Cos and Cnidus reserved certain privileges in connection with their consultations of the oracle.

It has pleased the association (*koinon*) of the Asclepiads of Cos and Cnidus: that if the Asclepiad on arriving at Delphi desires to consult the oracle or to sacrifice he should swear among the Delphians before consultation that he is an Asclepiad ... that he who infringes these rules should not have access to the oracle in his capacity as an Asclepiad and if any other privilege is granted to the Asclepiads by the Delphians that it should not be accorded to him any longer if there is no question of conformity with the previous arrangements.

*

Although our evidence of early medicine in ancient Egypt and Mesopotamia is in an incomplete and fragmentary state, it is nevertheless possible to draw some general conclusions from it. It is clear that the physician in these societies considered diseases to be signs of divine displeasure and caused by the intrusion of a demon. The primary purpose of the physician was to appease the god or drive out the demon which had 'possessed' the sick man's body. To do so he employed prayers, supplications, spells and incantations. The ancient Babylonians lived in a world haunted by evil spirits. Whenever they fell ill they believed that they had been seized by one of these spirits. Those afflicted sought for aid to bring about a return to their previous condition. The healer's function was to help them achieve this end by removing the cause of their illness. Patients were required to atone for their sins and the angry god had to be placated. The treatment involved the employment of ritual involving sacrifice and incantations [I.4-7]. The outlook of the more prestigious and influential Egyptian medicine is not dissimilar. The ancient Egyptian, too, seems to have believed that sickness was caused by evil spirits or by the anger of the gods [I.1]. Surviving Egyptian medical papyri, such as the Hearst and Ebers Papyrus, consist largely of prescriptions of drugs interspersed with magical spells which were believed to impart efficacy to the prescriptions they follow.[1] Many of the remedies prescribed contain noxious or offensive ingredients to make them as unpalatable as possible to the possessing spirit and so give it no inducement to linger in the patient's body [I.2].

Our earliest literary sources for the history of Greek medicine are the epic works of Homer and Hesiod which clearly reveal that the views of the Greeks of the Heroic Age regarding disease and the operation of remedies employed to effect a cure were, like those of their ancient Egyptian and Mesopotamian counterparts, permeated with belief in magic and the supernatural. As Celsus says, 'morbos ... ad iram deorum immortalium relatos esse' (*On medicine*, Proem, 4), diseases were attributed to the wrath of the gods – although here the gods, for the most part, act directly and not through the intermediary of demons or evil spirits. In the first book of the *Iliad*, for example [I.8], the plague which attacks the Greek army besieging Troy is sent by Apollo[2] as punishment for Agamemnon's arrogant treatment of his priest Chryses, who had come to the Greek camp to try to ransom his captured daughter. On a more individual level, the arrows of Apollo are held to cause the death of men [I.9], whereas his sister Artemis kills women [I.10]. Together they killed the six sons and the six daughters of the unfortunate Niobe, who had boasted that she was superior to their mother Leto, who had produced only two children [I.11]. Elsewhere in Greek epic, other gods are held to be the cause of disease and death. In the *Odyssey* the Cyclops Polyphemus, deluded by Odysseus's stratagem, is told by his kinsmen that his blinding is a malady sent by almighty Zeus [I.12] and in Hesiod's *Works and Days* it is Zeus again who sends famine and plague which kills men and renders women barren [I.13]. (It is maintained by some scholars that, earlier in this work (vv. 100-4) [I.14], Hesiod puts forward a rather different conception of disease from that found elsewhere in Greek epic when he describes diseases attacking men spontaneously (*automatai*); but it should not be overlooked that these diseases were originally the (deadly) gifts of the gods and that the object of the Olympians' combined wrath is mankind as a whole and not any particular group or individual. The form of the myth explains the lack of specificity here.) Not all diseases, however, were attributed to divine agency, and a distinction seems to have been drawn between sudden and often dramatic diseases sent by the gods and other ailments [I.15].

In addition to causing death and disease, the gods also cured disease and healed wounds, When Diomedes is hit by an arrow and bleeding profusely, Pallas Athena answers his prayer by healing him immediately and restores him to the battle [I.16]. Aeneas, when his hip is crushed by a stone hurled by Diomedes in his turn, is rescued first by Aphrodite, then by Apollo, and is finally nursed back to health by Artemis and Leto [I.17]. Glaucus's haemorrhaging arrow wound is also healed by Apollo, who staunched the black blood [I.18]. The same belief in divine cures is found in the *Odyssey*. In a metaphor employed to illustrate the shipwrecked Odysseus's relief at the sight of land [I.19], his feelings are compared to the reaction of children who see their father relieved of a serious illness by the gods. The *Odyssey* also provides evidence of the use of magic in the treatment of wounds.

I. Pre-rational and irrational medicine

In the nineteenth book [I.20] the sons of Autolycus bandage Odysseus's wound and stop the bleeding with an incantation, which was evidently employed to constrain the deity to perform his healing function.

The earliest Greek god of healing was Paeon, who is depicted in Homeric epic as the physician of the gods. Subsequently his name became an attribute of other gods and was used to denote their healing function – for example, of Zeus at Dodona and Rhodes, of Apollo, of Dionysus, of Asclepius, and of Helios. Goddesses came to be regarded as the tutelary deities of women. Hera, for example, was considered to be the patroness of marriage and of female sexual life generally. She assisted women during childbirth. Eileithyia, the divine midwife, was identified with her but on other occasions was regarded as her daughter. Artemis performed a similar role as birth-goddess and served as the protector of young girls. Healing functions were also attributed to Athena. At Oropus she was worshipped as Athena Paeonia and at Athens as Athena Hygieina.

Many demi-gods were also regarded as skilled in the art of healing. The Centaur Chiron acquired a considerable medical reputation both as a healer and a teacher and is credited with the discovery of the medicinal properties of many herbs [XV.2-4]. Included among his disciples were the seer Melampus, Jason, Aristaeus, Achilles and Asclepius himself. Melampus's most remarkable feat was his successful treatment of the daughters of Proteus, who had been driven mad and were wandering about the countryside believing themselves to be cows. These he cured by administering to them black hellebore – a drastic and cathartic, indeed, potentially lethal potion that fully earned its description in antiquity as the 'Great Concitator' [XIII.15]. According to Theophrastus, this remedy was thereafter called 'Melampodium' [see XIII.12B]. A sanctuary was built for Melampus at Aegosthena in Attica and an annual festival instituted in his honour. A descendant of Melampus, Amphiaraus, one of the Seven against Thebes, also became famous as a seer and divine physician. According to legend, while fleeing from the city in defeat, he was saved from his pursuers by Zeus, who engulfed him, chariot and all, in a cleft in the ground made by his thunderbolt. Important centres of his chthonic cult were established at Thebes, Athens, and Oropus [I.21]. At these sanctuaries suppliants were required to sleep upon the earth in which the deity resided and during their incubation were advised as to the best course they should follow to be rid of their afflictions. According to Pausanias (I.34.4) it was the custom at the Amphiareion at Oropus for the cured to throw gold and silver coins into the spring near the temple to express their gratitude.

Of all the gods and demi-gods who are depicted in Greek mythology practising the art of healing, Apollo became the god of healing *par excellence*. But even he was subsequently eclipsed by his own son Asclepius [I.22-8]. In the last third of the fifth century BC the latter was transformed from a minor cult hero into a major god. His influence was doubtless considerably increased as a result of the impact of the Great Plague of Athens. Although, as Thucydides records [X.6], that dreadful epidemic led to disillusionment with conventional religion, since it was thought to make no difference whether one worshipped the gods or not, as believer and non-believer perished alike, others were clearly driven to seek a more powerful magic. In 420 BC, during the Peace of Nicias, Asclepius was solemnly inducted into Athens in the form of his sacred snake [I.27] and lodged at the house of the tragedian, Sophocles, until a shrine could be built for him. This cult, too, adopted the practice of incubation, the ritual act of sleeping within the precincts of a temple in the hope of receiving a dream-vision of the healing god, who would bring about a cure of the sleeper's affliction. Details of many miraculous cures have survived [I.23-5]. Pausanias records that on his visit to Epidaurus he saw six votive columns upon which were engraved 'the names of men and women healed by

16

Asclepius, together with the disease from which each suffered and how he was cured'. Similar steles could be seen at the sanctuary at Cos and at other sanctuaries as well. Archaeological excavations at Epidaurus have disinterred three of the four columns seen by Pausanias together with fragments of a fourth. They contain seventy case-histories, 'cures' (*iamata*) of Apollo and Asclepius inscribed in the fourth century BC, and provide valuable information of the different types of patients who sought healing within the temple and the kinds of cures achieved [**I.24 & 25**]. Once firmly established at Athens the cult spread swiftly and its widening popularity in the early fourth century BC is clearly evidenced by the fact that Aristophanes presents a farcical account of the procedures in the temple of Asclepius in his comedy, *Plutus* [**I.28**]. More than four hundred shrines and sanctuaries were dedicated to Asclepius all over the ancient western world and some of these were still actively engaged in his worship until as late as the sixth century AD.

[1] The *Edwin Smith Surgical Papyrus,* however, is organised in a systematic manner and seems to be mainly free from the magical elements which pervade other Egyptian medical papyri. Breasted (1930) has claimed that the treatise is in the true sense scientific. But this belief stems largely from the fact that, unlike the physician, the surgeon had to deal with observable physical causes that had little or no connection with the malignant demons of disease.

[2] The plague which is described attacking Thebes in Sophocles's *Oedipus Tyrannus* is there held also to have been sent by Apollo (see, generally, **X.1 & 2**).

II

The rise and development of rational medicine in ancient Greece

The ancient Greeks were the first to evolve rational and theoretical systems of medicine free from magical and religious elements and based upon natural causes.

SUPERNATURAL CAUSATION IN THE HEROIC AGE

II.1. Alcaeus, Fr. 4

Initially even comparatively mundane phenomena are attributed to supernatural agency.

Zeus rains upon us, and from the sky comes down enormous winter.

Aristophanes exploits the comic potential of this traditional belief in the *Clouds* when the old peasant, Strepsiades, describes his earlier belief that the rain was caused by Zeus urinating through his 'chamber-pot sieve' (*Clouds* 373).

II.2. Homer, *Iliad* 20.56-8

Zeus and Poseidon respectively cause thunder and earthquakes.

The Father of Gods and Men thundered terribly from on high and from below Poseidon caused the boundless earth to quake and shook the lofty mountain peaks.

II.3. Homer, *Iliad* 21.198-9

Zeus is the cause of thunder and lightning.

... even Okeanos fears the lightning of great Zeus and his terrible thunder when it crashes from heaven.

II.4. Archilochus 74.3 (Diehl)

Zeus is also the cause of eclipses.

Zeus, the Father of the Olympians, made night at noon when he concealed the light of the shining sun ....

THE MILESIAN PHILOSOPHERS REJECT
SUPERNATURAL CAUSATION

II.5. Seneca, *Natural questions* III.14 (DK 11A15)

Here Thales dispenses with two Olympian gods – Atlas, who supports the earth, and Poseidon, the 'earthshaker'.

<Thales> said that the Earth is held up by water and rides like a ship and when it is said to 'quake' it is then rocking because of the movement of the water.

II.6. Aëtius, *On the opinions of the philosophers* III.4.1 (DK 13A17)

Here, according to our doxographer, Anaximenes implicitly rejects the traditional belief that Zeus sends the rain and deduces instead from his first principle (*aêr*) the natural explanation that it is 'squeezed out' from the clouds.

Anaximenes said that clouds are formed when the air is thickened further; when it is compressed further still, rain is squeezed out; hail occurs when the descending water condenses, and snow, whenever some portion of the air is included within the moisture.

This mode of explanation is parodied at *Clouds* 367-9:
Strep.: What do you mean 'there is no Zeus?' Who sends the rain? First of all tell me this.
Soc.: The Clouds do, of course. I'll prove it to you by strong evidence.

II.7. Aristotle, *Meteorologica* 365b6ff. (DK 13A21)

In this passage Anaximenes attributes earthquakes to natural causes – not to Poseidon, the 'earth-shaker god'.

Anaximenes said that when the earth becomes soaked or parched it breaks and is shaken by the high ground that is broken off and falls. It is for this reason, too, that earthquakes occur both in times of drought and during heavy rains; for in droughts, as has been said, the earth becomes dried up and breaks, and when it becomes excessively wet by the rains it falls apart.

A similar theory is attributed by Ammianus to Anaximander (XVII.7.12 (DK 12A28).

II.8. Aëtius, *On the opinions of the philosophers* III.3.1 (DK 12A23) & III.3.2
   (DK 13A17 = Diels, 1879, pp. 367-8)

Thunder and lightning are no longer attributed to the agency of Zeus. Here and in the following contexts a natural cause is put forward.

With regard to thunder, lightning, thunderbolts, waterspouts and whirl-winds: Anaximander says that all these are caused by wind. When it is enclosed in thick cloud and forces its way out by reason of its fine texture and lightness, then the tearing makes the noise and the rent in contrast to the blackness of the cloud produces the flash. Anaximenes is of the same opinion.

II.9. Aëtius, *On the opinions of the philosophers* II.20.1 (DK 12A21)

Zeus is no longer regarded as the cause of eclipses.

According to Anaximander, the sun is a circle twenty-eight <twenty-seven?> times the size of the earth and resembles a chariot wheel. The felloe is hollow and filled with fire. At a certain point it allows the fire to shine out through an orifice, as though through the nozzle of a pair of bellows.

II.10. Aëtius, *On the opinions of the philosophers* II.24.2 (DK 12A21)

The cause of a solar eclipse.

According to Anaximander, the sun is eclipsed when the orifice of the blow-hole of fire is closed.

II.11. Aëtius, *On the opinions of the philosophers* II.25.1 (DK 12A22)

A similar explanation is put forward to account for a lunar eclipse.

According to Anaximander, the moon is a circle nineteen <eighteen?> times the size of the earth, resembling a chariot wheel with its felloe hollow and full of fire like that of the sun. It lies oblique also like the sun and has one blow-hole like the nozzle of a pair of bellows ....

II.12. Aëtius, *On the opinions of the philosophers* II.29.1 (DK 12A22)

It, too, is caused by the blockage of its 'blow-hole'.

According to Anaximander, the moon is eclipsed when the orifice in the wheel becomes blocked.

NATURAL EXPLANATIONS ARE USED IN MEDICINE

Just as the Natural Philosophers had sought to explain in natural terms frightening meteorological phenomena, so the same outlook was applied by medical authors to explain frightening manifestations of disease.

Epilepsy

As a result of its striking and alarming symptoms epilepsy was regarded with superstitious awe throughout antiquity and given the title the 'sacred disease'.

II.13. [Hippocrates], *Sacred disease* 1 (VI.352,1-9L)

Here this Hippocratic author attacks the superstitious awe with which epilepsy is regarded.

I do not believe that the so-called 'Sacred Disease' is any more divine or sacred than any other disease. It has its own specific nature and cause; but because it is completely different from other diseases men through their inexperience and wonder at its peculiar symptoms have believed it to be of divine origin. This theory of divine origin is kept alive by the difficulty of understanding the malady, but is really destroyed by the facile method of healing which they adopt, consisting as it does of purifications and incantations. But if it is to be considered divine on account of its remarkable nature, there will be many sacred diseases, not one.

II.14. [Hippocrates], *Sacred disease* 1 (VI.354,12-20L)

Our Hippocratic author then attacks as charlatans those who claim that epilepsy has a sacred character.

In my opinion those who first attributed a sacred character to this disease were the sort of people we nowadays call witch-doctors, faith-healers, charlatans and quacks. These people also pretend to be very pious and to have superior knowledge. Shielding themselves by citing the divine as an excuse for their own perplexity in not knowing what beneficial treatment to apply, they held this condition to be sacred so that their ignorance might not be manifest. By choosing suitable terms they established a mode of treatment that safeguarded their own positions. They prescribed purifications and incantations ....

II.15. [Hippocrates], *Sacred disease* 2-3 (VI.364,9-15;366,5-6L)

He claims that it has a similar nature and cause to that of other diseases.

I believe that this disease is not more divine than any other disease; it has the same nature as other diseases and a similar cause. It is also no less curable than other diseases unless by long lapse of time it is so ingrained that it is more powerful than the drugs that are applied. Like other diseases it is hereditary .... [3] The brain is the cause of this condition as it is of other most serious diseases.

II.16. [Hippocrates] *Sacred disease* 18 (VI.394,9-15L)

Like other diseases epilepsy is susceptible to treatment.

This so-called 'Sacred Disease' is due to the same causes as other diseases, to the things that come to and go from the body, to cold and sun and changing restless winds. These things are divine so that there is no need to put the disease in a special class and to consider it more divine than the others; they are all divine and all human[1]. Each has its own nature and character; none is irremediable or unsusceptible to treatment.

[1] It is at first sight surprising to find here that, although supernatural explanation is firmly ruled out, the notion of the divine is not entirely excluded. According to our author the whole of nature is divine, but this belief does not allow any exception to his rule that natural effects are the result of natural causes. Here again may be seen the continuing influence of Ionian natural philosophy. The Milesians, in rejecting supernatural causation, did not reject the notion of divinity altogether, but regarded their own first principles as divine. According to this medical author, diseases, too, share in this divinity in the sense that, as parts of the cosmos, they also possess their own individual *physeis* (natures), which display in the regular pattern of their origin, development and operation the same intelligible laws inherent in the world about them. [See below **II.26 & XI.1**.]

II.17. [Hippocrates], *Airs, Waters, Places* 3 (II.18,2-7L)

Here an attempt is made to account for certain diseases, including epilepsy, as due to the effect of particular climatic and topographical factors. It is maintained that all these diseases are endemic in cities 'exposed to hot winds and sheltered from the north'.

The women are unhealthy and prone to fluxes. Again, many of them are barren through disease and not naturally so, and frequently miscarry. The children are liable to convulsions and attacks of asthma and to what is thought to cause the disease of childhood and to be a sacred disease <i.e. epilepsy>. The men suffer from dysentery, diarrhoea, ague, chronic fevers in winter, pustules and haemorrhoids.

*The same rational outlook is carried over into
fourth-century medicine*

II.18. Plato, *Timaeus* 85A-B

Plato agrees with the author of *Sacred Disease* that epilepsy is an affection of the brain and caused by phlegm (with, in his case, an admixture of black bile). He retains the use of the term 'sacred disease' but justifies it upon a non-supernatural basis.

When <white phlegm> is mixed with black bile and is diffused over the most divine circuits in the head and throws them into confusion, the visitation, if it comes during sleep, is comparatively mild, but when it attacks those who are awake it is harder to throw off. As an affliction of the sacred substance <i.e. the brain marrow> it is most justly termed the 'sacred disease'.

II.19. *Anonymus Parisinus* 3 = *Anecdota medica* 3 (p. 541 Fuchs = *Diokles* Fr. 51 Wellmann = *Praxagoras* 70 Steckerl)

Both Diocles and Praxagoras employ a similar natural explanation and hold epilepsy to be due to the blocking of the psychic *pneuma*.

Praxagoras says that epilepsy occurs in the region round the thick artery <aorta> when phlegmatic humours aggregate within it. These, being formed into bubbles, block the passage of the psychic *pneuma*, from the heart and thus the *pneuma* makes the body shake and convulse. Again, when the bubbles have been settled, the condition ceases. Diocles also believes that there is an obstruction in the same region and concurs in other respects with Praxagoras.

Apoplexy

Apoplexy is another disease with a dramatic and terrifying onset. The very Greek term used to denote this sudden affliction carries the connotation of being struck by violence.

II.20. Cornelius Celsus, *On medicine* III. 26 (*CML* I, p. 141 Marx)

This passage in Celsus reveals a connection between the heavens and some incidences of the disease.

We also see on rare occasions some who have been struck (*attonitos*), stupefied in mind and body. It comes about sometimes by lightning stroke, sometimes by disease: the Greeks call the latter *apoplexia*.

As Clarke has pointed out (1963a, p. 303), the Latin terms for apoplexy, *attonitus* and *sideratio*, preserve the belief in the celestial origin of this affliction.

II.21. [Hippocrates], *Breaths* 13 (VI.110,6-9L = *CMG* I.1, p. 99 Heib.)

Like epilepsy, apoplexy is held in the Hippocratic *Corpus* to be due to natural causes.

Apoplexy, too, is caused by breaths. For whenever cold and frequent breaths pass through the flesh and puff it up, those parts of the body lose the power of feeling. If, then, many breaths rush through the whole of the body, the whole patient suffers an apoplectic seizure.

In Ch. 14 of this treatise the 'Sacred Disease' is attributed to an identical cause.

II.22. [Hippocrates], *Diseases* II.21 (VII.36,1-6L)

This Hippocratic treatise provides a succinct description of apoplexy.

A healthy subject is taken by a sudden pain in the head; he suffers immediate loss of speech, breathes stertoriously and his mouth gapes open. If someone calls him or shakes him, he only groans and understands nothing. He urinates copiously without being aware of it. If fever does not supervene, death ensues within seven days, but if fever does supervene, he usually recovers.

Similar natural explanations of apoplexy were put forward by doctors in the fourth century

II.23. *Anonymus Parisinus* 4 = *Anecdota medica* 4 (p. 542 Fuchs = *Diokles* Fr. 55 Wellmann = *Praxagoras* Fr. 74 Steckerl)

Here Diocles and Praxagoras attribute apoplexy to phlegm inhibiting the passage of *pneuma*.

Praxagoras and Diocles say that this condition originates in the area around the thick artery <aorta> due to cold and thick phlegm with the result that no *pneuma* whatsoever can be admitted within it and thus there is danger of complete suffocation.

Delusions

Like epilepsy and apoplexy, delusions, too, were frequently regarded as due to supernatural causation.

II.24. [Hippocrates], *Diseases of young girls* 1 (VIII.466,4-470L)

Here delusions, which afflict especially young women of marriageable age, causing them to imagine that they see evil demons and even contemplate suicide, are held to be caused by retention of menstrual blood. Thus there is no necessity to follow the advice of diviners and seek to propitiate Artemis.

First of all I shall deal with the so-called 'Sacred Disease' and with apoplexy and with terrors which people fear exceedingly – to the extent that they become deranged and imagine that they see hostile demons, sometimes at night, sometimes in the daytime, sometimes both. Because of such visions many already have hanged themselves: more women than men; for the female is more fearful and weaker by nature. Young girls, who remain unmarried when ripe for marriage, suffer this affliction more at the descent of the menses. Before this time they are not much distressed by these matters. For later on the blood streams into the womb to flow away outside the body. Thus when the orifice of the exit is not open and more blood keeps on flowing in, then, having no outlet, the blood, because of its quantity, wells up into the heart and diaphragm. When these parts were filled, the heart became stupefied. Then, from this sluggishness came numbness and from numbness delirium took hold ... shivering coupled with fever starts up ... the patient is driven mad by a violent inflammation; she becomes murderously inclined because of the putrefaction; fears and terrors are aroused by the dark; the compression around the heart causes these girls to hang themselves; their spirit, being distraught and in anguish through the corruption of the blood, brings an evil in its train. It is an evil of a different sort and it specifies fearful things. These delusions bid the girls to leap and fall into wells and hang themselves, on the grounds that these actions are better and offer all kinds of advantage. When the girl is not affected by visions, she experiences a certain pleasure, which makes her fall in love with death as though it were something good. When she has come to her senses, the women dedicate to Artemis, among many other objects, their costliest garments. They are ordered to do so by diviners; but they are thoroughly deceived. Release from this malady comes about when there is nothing hampering the outflow of blood. I order young girls, when suffering such an affliction, to marry as soon as possible. For, if they become pregnant, they regain their health. If a girl does not marry, then immediately at puberty, or a little later, she will be afflicted by this or by another disease. Among married women, the sterile are more prone to suffer from these conditions.

Impotence

Impotence was superstitiously held by some to be a divine affliction.

II.25. Herodotus, *Histories* 1.105

In this passage Herodotus records that according to some this affliction was the result of the anger of an affronted goddess.

Thence <the Scythians> marched against Egypt and when they were in the part of Syria called Palestine, Psammetichus, the king of Egypt, met them and sought to dissuade them with gifts and prayers from advancing any further. They withdrew and came on their way back to the city of Ascalon in Syria. The majority of the Scythians passed by without doing any harm, but a few of them were left behind and they pillaged the temple of Heavenly Aphrodite .... The goddess sent upon those Scythians, who plundered the temple at Ascalon and upon all their descendants a 'female' disease; in consequence the Scythians say that this is the cause of their disease and that those who come to Syria can see the plight of those men whom the Scythians call 'Enareis' ....

II.26. [Hippocrates], *Airs, Waters, Places* 22 (II.76,12-78,19L = *CMG* I.1,2, pp. 72-4 Di.)

The attitude of this Hippocratic author stands in marked contrast to that described by Herodotus.

Very many Scythians become impotent, do women's work, live like women and talk in the same way .... The Scythians themselves lay the blame upon a god and revere and worship such men, each fearing for himself. I myself hold that these and all other afflictions are divine and so are all others, none being more divine or more human than another; all are alike and all divine.[1] Each of them has its own nature and none happens without its natural cause. I will explain how, in my own opinion, this condition arises. As a result of riding, they develop arthritis because their feet are always hanging down from their horses. Then those who are severely afflicted become quite lame and drag their hips. They treat themselves in the following way. At the onset of the disease they cut the vein behind each ear. In their weakness caused by loss of blood they become drowsy and fall asleep. Then, when they wake up, some are cured and some not. In my opinion the semen is destroyed by this treatment. For there are vessels beside the ears which, if cut, cause impotence.[2] After this, when they come to women and are unable to have intercourse, they do not take it seriously at first but keep it quiet. But when, after the second, third and even more attempts, the same thing happens, they consider that they have offended in some way against the deity whom they hold to be the cause of their affliction. Then, judging themselves unmanly, they put on female attire, act as women and join with women in their work.

[1] On the significance of this remark see **II.16 n.1** above.
[2] The author here evidently believes that the brain is the source of the semen and cutting this vein disrupts the link between brain and genitals.

II.27. [Hippocrates], *On generation* 2 (VII.472,5-16L)

The author of this Hippocratic treatise also seeks to account for impotence upon a natural basis and here in the second chapter he puts forward several explanations to account for the plight of eunuchs, including this belief that it is caused by impairment of the spermatic vessels that run beside the ears. Here again the disability is held to be due to purely natural causes.

Eunuchs do not have intercourse because their seminal passage is destroyed. This passage goes right through the testicles themselves. From the testicles to the penis extend numerous fine ligaments by which it is raised and lowered. These are severed in the operation for castration. In consequence eunuchs are impotent. In the case of those whose testicles are destroyed, the seminal passage is obstructed, for the testicles become calloused; and the ligaments, having become hard and insensitive, because of the callus, are unable to stretch and relax. Those who have had an incision made beside the ear are capable of intercourse and emitting sperm, but the amount is small, weak and sterile. For the greater part of the sperm goes from the head past the ears into the spinal marrow; but this passage becomes obstructed when the incision has formed a scar.

Madness and mental disease

Madness and mental diseases generally were regularly attributed to the agency of
the gods. However, in Presocratic philosophy, in the Hippocratic *Corpus*, and in
later philosophy and medicine, madness and mental diseases are regarded as not
essentially different from diseases of the body and the same kinds of purely
natural causes are put forward to account for them.

II.28. [Hippocrates], *Sacred disease* 1 (VI.360,10-362,6L)

This Hippocratic author attacks here as charlatans those who diagnose manifestations of mental disease as due to supernatural causation.

Men in need of a livelihood contrive and embroider many fictions of all
sorts with regard to this disease and many other matters, putting the
blame for each kind of complaint upon a particular god. If the patient acts
like a goat, if he roars, or has convulsions on his right side, they say that
the Mother of the Gods is responsible. If he utters a higher-pitched and
louder cry, they say he is like a horse and blame Poseidon. If he should
pass some faeces, as often happens under stress of the attack, Enodia is
the name applied. If the stools are more frequent and thin like those of
bird, it is Apollo Nomius. If he should foam at the mouth and kick, Ares is
to blame. In the case of those who are beset during the night by attacks of
fear and panic and madness and jump out of bed and rush out of doors,
they speak of attacks by Hecate and assaults by the Heroes.

II.29. Caelius Aurelianus, *On chronic diseases* I.5 (= DK 31A98 in part
= Drabkin, 1950, p. 534 = *CML* VI,1, Vol. 1, p. 516 Bendz)

In contrast to the beliefs of the charlatans described above madness is here
described as due to bodily affliction.

Likewise, following Empedocles, they say that one form of madness comes
about from the purification of the soul and another from mental aberration
arising from a bodily cause or indisposition. It is this latter form of
madness that we shall now consider. The Greeks call it *mania*, because it
produces great mental anguish (which they name *ania*); or because there
is excessive relaxation of the soul or mind. (For they call that which is
relaxed or soft *manos*.)

*These attitudes toward madness are continued into
the fourth century*

II.30. Plato, *Timaeus* 86B-E

Plato, too, believes that madness has a corporeal cause.

Diseases of the soul are caused by the body in the following way. Granted that folly (*anoia*) is a disease of the soul; and of folly there are two kinds: madness (*mania*) and stupidity (*amathia*). Therefore, every affection one suffers, which involves either one of these conditions, must be termed a 'disease'. Excessive pleasures and pains must be regarded as the greatest of the soul's diseases. For, when a man is in great joy or, conversely, in great pain, in his immoderate desire to seize the one and avoid the other, he is unable to see or hear anything correctly and is mad and is at that time least able to participate in reasoning. When the seed in a man's marrow is plentiful and strongly-flowing, and, like a tree that has become burdened with an over-abundance of fruit, he brings upon himself individually many pains and many pleasures in his desires and their issue. He becomes for the greatest part of his life maddened on account of these very great pleasures and pains, and keeps his soul diseased and senseless by the actions of his body, and is supposed to be voluntarily wicked and not diseased. But the truth is that this sexual intemperance has come about as a disease of the soul primarily through the condition of a single substance, <i.e. the marrow, or that part of it which forms the seed> which owing to the porousness of the bones floods the body with its moisture. Almost all that is called, by way of reproach, 'incontinence in pleasure', as if men were voluntarily wicked, is wrongly censured. For no one is voluntarily wicked,[1] but the wicked man becomes wicked on account of some evil disposition of the body and an uneducated upbringing. These are hateful things that happen to every man against his will.

[1] For this well-known Socratic dictum see, too, *Protagoras* 345Dff. & *Laws* 731Cff.

II.31. *Anonymus Parisinus* 17 (= *Anecdota medica* 17 p. 548 Fuchs = *Praxagoras* Fr. 72 Steckerl)

Praxagoras also subscribes to this belief that madness has a physical cause.

Praxagoras says that madness (*mania*) comes about through a swelling of the heart, where he believes thinking also takes place.

*

It was the Greeks who first evolved rational systems of medicine free from magical and religious elements and based upon natural causes. The importance of this revolutionary innovation for the history of medicine can hardly be overstressed. Here for the first time is displayed an entirely different outlook towards disease, whose causes and symptoms are now accounted for in purely natural terms. This emancipation of medicine from superstition, paving the way for its subsequent development as a science, was the outcome of precisely the same attitude of mind which the Milesian Natural Philosophers, Thales, Anaximander and Anaximenes, were the first to apply to the world about them. Their attempts to explain the world in terms of its physical constituents, without having recourse to supernatural agency, brought about the transition from mythological conjecture to rational explanation. Rain, for example, which was previously attributed to the activity of Zeus [II.1] is now held to be squeezed out from the clouds by compression [II.6]. Moreover, just as the natural philosophers had sought to explain in purely natural terms such frightening phenomena as earthquakes [II.5 & 7], thunder and lightning [II.8], and eclipses [II.10-12], which had previously been regarded as the manifestations of supernatural powers [II.2, 3 & 4], so the same outlook was applied by medical authors of Hippocratic treatises to explain in terms of natural causation such frightening diseases as epilepsy (the 'sacred disease'), apoplexy, delusions, and even impotence [II.13-17, 21, 24, 26-7], which had all previously been attributed to divine action. Evidence of this relationship between philosophy and medicine may be seen in the fact that the medical literature of the fifth and early fourth centuries BC is written in the Ionic dialect. Although both Cos and Cnidus, whence the bulk of the treatises in the Hippocratic *Corpus* seem to have emanated, were both Dorian settlements, the *Corpus* itself is written throughout in Ionic, which became at this time the standard literary medium not only for philosophy but for medicine and science generally. Similar explanations of the causes of these diseases continued to be employed at a later date and can be paralleled in Plato [II.18], Diocles [II.19 & 23], and Praxagoras [II.19, 23]. [See, too, IX.17-18.]

Madness and mental diseases, too, were regularly attributed to supernatural agency. Greek tragedy, especially, affords abundant evidence of this and there is no good reason to disbelieve that the views expressed here do not widely reflect popular Greek contemporary beliefs [see II.28]. In Sophocles's plays, for example, Herakles is afflicted by Hera's malevolence with a delusional rage that culminates in the murder of his own family; Ajax is driven mad by Athena to prevent him from killing Odysseus and the sons of Atreus; Orestes is hounded to madness by the Furies after the murder of his mother, and, in Euripides's *Bacchae,* both Pentheus and Agave are driven mad by Dionysus. However, in Presocratic philosophy, in the Hippocratic *Corpus*, and in later philosophy and medicine, madness and mental diseases are regarded as not essentially different from diseases of the body and the same kinds of purely natural causes are put forward to account for them. Afflictions of this type, no less than their physical counterparts, are here regarded as investigable and treatable. There is no suggestion that their origin is in any way supernatural.

These explanations of the causes of madness, epilepsy and other mental disturbances, by purely natural causes [II.28-31] stand, then, in marked contrast with the belief in the supernatural causation of these afflictions found in contemporary works of Greek tragedy as well as with the diagnoses of those charlatans who, as the author of *Sacred disease* points out [II.28], attribute one type of epilepsy to Poseidon, another to Apollo, a third to Ares, a fourth to Hecate and still another to the Mother of the Gods. Yet it might be objected, and not without some justification, that his own standpoint is hardly less speculative than the theories under attack. Although in the opening chapter of *Sacred disease* our author criticises his opponents for 'pretending to have superior knowledge about what causes and what cures disease', he is himself susceptible to this same charge since the particular treatment recommended by him, dietetic control of temperature and humidity, in fact afforded no greater possibility of cure. While his establishment of a naturalistic basis for the understanding of madness and his rejection of any reference to the divine or demonic marks a release from one sort of mystification, he achieves this at the cost of the substitution of another.[1] His manifest confidence that salutary effects are to be derived from the anti-bilious or anti-phlegmatic diet he recommends is itself clearly a matter of faith. Our author is patently over-confident in his assessment of the procedures he advocates. Although they are, in principle, capable of being subjected to further tests with a view to their verification, in practice, they remain speculative and untested.

[1] See, especially, Lloyd, 1987, p. 28.

III

Philosophy and medicine in the fifth century I: Alcmaeon and the Presocratic philosophers

COSMIC JUSTICE IN IONIAN NATURAL PHILOSOPHY

III.1. Simplicius, *Commentary on Aristotle's Physics* 24.13 (DK 12B1 see 12A9)

The Milesian philosopher, Anaximander, conceives the universe to be a balance maintained between opposing forces.

Anaximander said that the first principle <*archê*> and element of existing things was the *apeiron* <indefinite/infinite>. He was the first to introduce this name for the *archê*. He says that it is neither water nor any other of the so-called elements, but some other *apeiron* nature, from which come into being all the heavens and the worlds in them. Things also pass away into those things out of which they come into existence *according to necessity; for they pay penalty and retribution to one another for their injustice according to the assessment of Time*, as he puts it using somewhat poetical terms.

Alcmaeon's theory of health

Alcmaeon of Croton is the first doctor to reveal the influence of Ionian Natural Philosophy upon medicine.

III.2. Aëtius, *On the opinions of the philosophers* V.30.1 (DK 24B4)

This cosmic theory is adopted by Alcmaeon as the basis of his theory of health.

Alcmaeon holds that what preserves health is the equality <*isonomia*> of the powers – moist and dry, cold and hot, bitter and sweet and the rest – and the supremacy <*monarchia*> of any one of them causes disease; for the supremacy of either is destructive. The cause of disease is an excess of heat or cold; the occasion of it surfeit or deficiency of nourishment; the location of it blood, marrow or the brain. Disease may come about from external causes, from the quality of water, local environment or toil or torture. Health, on the other hand, is a harmonious blending of the qualities.

The Hippocratic Corpus

This theory of health subsequently became influential in Hippocratic medicine.

III.3. [Hippocrates], *Ancient medicine* 14 (I.602,9-14L = *CMG* I.1,
pp. 45-6 Heib.)

It is is linked here with an indefinite number of opposites by the author of this Hippocratic treatise.

... there exists in man the salt, bitter, sweet, acid, astringent, insipid and countless other things, possessing powers of all kinds in number and in strength. These when mixed and blended are neither manifest nor cause man pain; but whenever one of them is separated off and becomes isolated, then it is both manifest and causes man pain.

III.4. [Hippocrates], *Nature of man* 4 (VI.38,19-40,9L = *CMG* I.1,3,
pp. 172-4 Jou.)

And here linked with the theory of the four humours.

The body of man has in itself blood, phlegm, yellow bile and black bile. These constitute the nature of his body, and through these he feels pain or enjoys health. Now he is particularly healthy when these constituents are in due proportion to one another with regard to blending, power and quantity, and when they are perfectly mixed. Pain is experienced whenever one of these constituents is deficient or in excess or is isolated in the body and is not blended with all the others. For, whenever any one of these is isolated and stands by itself, of necessity not only does the place which it left become diseased, but also the place where it stands and floods causes pain and distress through being over-full.

Philistion of Locri

For Philistion see **VI.14-17.**

III.5. *Anonymus Londinensis* 20.25-37 (Jones, 1947, p. 80)

This theory is also adopted by 'Sicilian' medicine and linked with the four element theory by Philistion.

Philistion of Locri thinks that we are composed of four 'forms', that is of four elements – fire, air, water, earth. Each of these, too, has its own power; of fire the power is the hot, of air it is the cold, of water the moist, and of earth the dry .... Diseases are caused by the elements when the hot and moist are in excess, or when the hot becomes less and weak.

For the full context see **VI.16.**

Plato

III.6. Plato, *Timaeus* 82A

From Philistion it is taken over by Plato in the *Timaeus*.

The body is composed of four elements – earth, fire, water and air; disorders and diseases are caused by an unnatural excess or deficiency of these elements ....

See **VI.18**.

Alcmaeon and empirical medicine

Although greatly influenced by the Natural Philosophers, Alcmaeon nevertheless rejects their a priori deductions from a single *archê* and advocates instead an empirical approach as more suitable for medicine.

III.7. Diogenes Laërtius VIII.83 (DK 24B1)

In the opening words of his book Alcmaeon displays a much more modest attitude when he contrasts the certainty attainable (only) by the gods with the inferential procedures mortals have to employ. His outlook here stands in marked contrast to the dogmatic certitude prevalent elsewhere among the Presocratic philosophers. He rejects their dogmatic belief in a single *archê* and their confident deductions from it.

Alcmaeon of Croton, son of Peirithous, spoke these words to Brotinus. *'Concerning things unseen the gods possess clear understanding, but in so far as men can proceed by inference [tekmairesthai] ... I say as follows.'*

This more sceptical and empirical approach can be traced back further to the philosopher/poet, Xenophanes of Colophon.

III.8. Xenophanes at Sextus Empiricus, *Against the mathematicians* VII.49ff. (DK 21B34)

Clear knowledge about divine matters and about natural science, according to Xenophanes, lies beyond human attainment.

Certain truth (*to saphes*) no man has seen, nor will anyone know about the gods and about everything about which I speak; for even if he should fully succeed in saying what is the case, nevertheless he himself does not know, but in all things there is opinion.

For the continuance of these more empirical attitudes in Hippocratic medicine see **V.1-5**.

III.9. Xenophanes at Stobaeus, *Physical extracts* 1.8.2 (DK 21B18)

Xenophanes's scepticism regarding the possibility of humans' attaining knowledge about such matters is also coupled with the belief expressed here that such knowledge that can be acquired by mortals can only be attained by a process of protracted research.

The gods did not reveal to men all things in the beginning, but in the course of time, by searching they find out better.

III.10. Theophrastus, *On the senses* 25 & 26 (DK 24A5)

Alcmaeon's researches into the nature of the sense organs (preserved here by Theophrastus), together with other physiological enquiries, exercised a strong influence upon later philosophical thought and contributed to the trend manifested by certain of the Presocratic philosophers in the second half of the fifth century to turn from macrocosm to microcosm.

[25] Among those who explain sensation by what is unlike, Alcmaeon begins by defining the difference between man and the lower animals. Man, he says, differs from other creatures because he alone has understanding, whereas they have sensation, but not understanding; thought and sensation are different, not, as Empedocles holds, the same. He next speaks of each sense separately. Hearing, he says, takes place through the ears because they contain empty space, which resounds. Sound is produced by the cavity and the air echoes it. Smelling is effected by means of the nostrils when air is drawn up into the brain. Tastes are distinguished by the tongue. Since it is warm and soft it dissolves substances by its heat and, owing to its porous and delicate structure, it receives and transmits the flavour.

[26] Eyes see through the water surrounding them. That the eye contains fire is evident, for the fire flashes forth when it is struck. Vision is due to the gleaming element and the transparent when it gives back a reflection; the purer this element is, the better the eye sees. All the senses are connected in some way to the brain. Consequently they are incapacitated if it is moved or shifts its position. For it obstructs the passages through which the sensations take place. Concerning touch he tells us neither the manner nor the means whereby it is effected. This, then, is the extent of his explanation.

THE PRESOCRATIC PHILOSOPHERS

The Presocratic philosophers, themselves influenced by medicine, turn from macrocosm to microcosm and seek to base medical and physiological theories upon a unifying hypothesis. Three philosophers especially, Empedocles, Diogenes and Democritus, reveal this tendency,

Empedocles

III.11. Diogenes Laërtius VIII.59 (DK 31B111)

In his poem, *Purifications*, Empedocles reveals his medical interests and confidently describes some benefits that will accrue from studying his work.

You shall learn all the drugs that are a defence against ills and old age ...
you will bring back from Hades the strength of a man who has died ....

III.12. Diogenes Laërtius VIII.62 (DK 31B112)

Here he describes his success as a healer.

When I come to flourishing towns I am honoured by men and women. They
follow me in their thousands, asking me where is the road to profit, some
desiring oracles, while others long pierced by grievous pains, ask to hear
the word of healing for all kinds of illness.

III.13. Simplicius, *Commentary on Aristotle's Physics*, 300.19 (DK 31B96)

Here in a fragment preserved from his work *On nature*, Empedocles bases his
views upon the composition of the human body upon his unifying hypothesis, the
four element theory.

The kindly earth received in her broad melting-pots two parts of gleaming
Nestis <i.e. water> out of the eight and four of Hephaistus <i.e. fire>; and
there came into being white bones divinely fitted together by the cement-
ing of Harmony.

III.14. Simplicius, *Commentary on Aristotle's Physics* 32.3 (DK 31B98)

Blood and flesh are held to be formed from mixtures of the four elements.

Earth, anchored in the perfect harbours of Cypris, chanced to meet in
almost equal quantities with Hephaistus <i.e. fire> and rain <i.e. water>
and all-shining aither <i.e. air>, either a little more, or less, where there
was more. From these there came into being blood and the various forms
of flesh.

III.15. Aëtius, *On the opinions of the philosophers* V.22.1 (DK 31A78)

According to this doxographical evidence sinews, sweat, and tears are similarly
formed.

Empedocles says that flesh originates from the four elements mixed in
equal proportions; sinews from fire and earth mixed with double the
amount of water; the claws of animals come into being from the sinews in
so far as they happen to be chilled by contact with the air; bones from two
parts of water and two of earth but four of fire, these parts being mixed
with the earth. Sweat and tears come from blood as it dissolves and melts
away according to its fluidity.

III.16. Aristotle, *On sensation* 437b23ff. (DK 31B84)

Here Empedocles employs a lantern-simile, rich in Homeric overtones and *double entendres,* to elucidate the predominant role played in the process of vision by two of his elements, fire and water. (See, too, Theophrastus, *On the senses* 8 (DK 31A86).)

Even as when a man, intending to make a journey through the wintry night, makes ready a light, a flame of blazing fire, fastens to it linen screens against all manner of winds and they scatter the blasts of the ever-blowing winds, but the light leaping out through them, shines across the threshold with unfailing beams, as much as it is finer; even so did she <i.e Love> give birth to the round-eyed pupil,[1] the primeval fire, enclosed in membranes and fine tissues.[2] These keep out the deep water that surrounds the pupil, but they let through the fire, as much as it is finer.

[1] Or 'round-eyed baby girl'.
[2] Or 'fine linen' (swaddling clothes).

Diogenes of Apollonia

III.17. Theophrastus, *On the senses* 43 (DK 64A19)

Diogenes similarly reveals medical interests and evidently regarded the state of the tongue as an important diagnostic aid.

Diogenes holds that the tongue is pre-eminently capable of discerning pleasure, for it is exceedingly soft and open in texture and all the vessels lead into it. Consequently the majority of the symptoms displayed by those who are ill are found in the tongue. In the case of other animals, too, the colour of the tongue reveals their symptoms. The intensity and nature of their symptoms are reflected in the tongue.

III.18. Ps.-Galen, *On the humours* (XIX.495K = DK 64A29a)

According to this pseudo-Galenic passage Diogenes also believed in diagnosis by colour.

And, indeed, just as the predominance of the humour is diagnosed from colour, so also from colour is disease diagnosed. This is nothing less than the most accurate of the greatest means of diagnosis. To Diogenes and the wise men of his time, it is considered to be a form of prophecy. For those men have made much debate about colour and distinguished diseases, too, by difference of colour calling the red-coloured, sanguineous; the yellow, those in whom the bitter humour is in excess; the black, those who have an excess of black bile and the white, phlegmatic ... to colours alone they attributed the whole differentiation of disease.

III.19. Simplicius, *Commentary on Aristotle's Physics* 152.18 (DK 64B4)

Diogenes here stresses the vital importance of his first principle, air, for human life.

Besides, in addition to these, these, too, are important indications <sc. that air is the first principle>. Man and other living creatures live by means of air, through breathing it. And this is for them both soul and intelligence ... if this is removed, they die and their intelligence fails.

III.20. Theophrastus, *On the senses* 43 (DK 64A19)

Health, too, is ultimately based upon his first principle.

Pleasure and pain come about in this way. Whenever a large amount of air mixes with the blood and lightens it, being in accordance with nature and permeating throughout the whole body, pleasure ensues; but whenever the air is present contrary to nature and does not mix, then the blood sinks down, becomes weaker and denser, and pain ensues. Similarly confidence, *health* and their opposites.

Democritus

III.21. Aristotle, *On respiration* 471b30ff. (DK 68A106)

In similar fashion the Atomist, Democritus, accounts for respiration and death upon the basis of his unifying hypothesis, the atomic theory.

<Democritus> states that respiration prevents the soul from being extruded from the body. ... He identifies the soul with the hot, as primary shapes of his spherical particles. When these particles are being compressed by the pressure of the environment, he says that respiration intervenes to help. For in the air there is a large number of these particles ... so that when the animal respires and the air enters, these enter along with it and, relieving the pressure, prevent the soul within the animal from passing out. For this reason life and death depend upon inspiration and expiration; for when the pressure of the environment prevails, and the air can no longer enter from outside and counteract it, since it is impossible to breathe in, then death supervenes. For he considers death to be the passing-out of such shapes from the body due to the pressure of the surrounding air.

According to Leucippus a milder and reversible preponderance of outflow over inflow of these atomic particles induces sleep. (See DK 67A34).

III.22. Theophrastus, *On the senses* 60 (DK 68A135)

Sense-perception, too, is based upon atomic theory.

Democritus does not put forward a unitary account of all <sensory objects>: some he distinguishes by the size <of their atoms>, others by their shape and some by their atomic order and position.

III. Alcmaeon and the Presocratic philosophers

III.23. Aëtius, *On the opinions of the philosophers* V.3.6 (DK 68A141)

Here the doxographer attributes pangenesis to Democritus.

Democritus holds that the seed is derived from the whole body and the most important parts such as the bones, flesh and sinews.

III.24. Aristotle, *Generation of animals* 764a6ff. (= DK 68A143)

Democritus employs this theory to explain sexual differentiation in animals.

Democritus, the Abderite, says that the differentiation of female and male occurs in the womb. It is not the case, however, that one creature becomes female and the other male through heat and cold, but from which of the two sexes the seed coming from the <sexual> part prevails. By this female and male differ from one another.

*

No Greek medical literature prior to the Hippocratic *Corpus* has survived. Alcmaeon of Croton is the only pre-Hippocratic Greek medical writer whose views have come down to us even in fragmentary form. That they survived at all may have been pure accident. Alcmaeon's interests seem to have been primarily medical and physiological (see Diogenes Laërtius VIII.83 DK 24A1), but, like those of so many of his Greek contemporaries, they were wide. Some of the problems that engaged his curiosity subsequently aroused the interest of the natural philosophers. Aristotle, therefore, took note of his opinions and he was later dutifully included by Theophrastus in his *Physical opinions*. Although we possess only fragmentary information regarding his medical beliefs, it is nevertheless sufficient to reveal that he displays the same outlook which characterises the Milesian Natural Philosophers before him and the Presocratic Philosophers after him. Just as Anaximander had viewed the cosmos in terms of a balance or even a legal contract between equal opposed forces [III.1], so, in the human body, health is held by Alcmaeon to be due to the equilibrium (*isonomia*) of the powers composing it [III.2], while the supremacy (*monarchia*) of any one of them causes disease. Here is revealed a totally different conception of disease from that encountered previously in Greek epic. In Homer the more dramatic diseases, at any rate, are represented as being outside nature and subject to the whim of the gods. Although Hesiod took a step away from this belief and held that diseases were not invariably subject to individual divine decision, but were capable of attacking people of their own accord [I.14], he nevertheless shares with Homer the belief that they possessed a separate existence of their own. Alcmaeon rejects this conception of disease and holds it to be due to disturbances of the body's natural equilibrium and, in consequence, subject to the same rules that operate in the world at large. This medical theory became very influential and was adopted within the Hippocratic *Corpus* [see, for example, III.3]. It was also linked in combination with Empedocles's four element theory with the humoral theory [III.4]. Its subsequent influence can be traced through Philistion of Locri [III.5] to Plato [III.6], who also uses it as the basis for his ethical theory of pleasure and pain.

Alcmaeon's physiological interests and particularly his researches into the nature of the sense-organs [III.10] also seem to have had an important influence

38

upon later philosophical thought. His preoccupation with these matters seems to have stimulated the interest of later philosophers. After him psycho-physiological investigations become almost standard topics of inquiry among later Presocratic philosophers (see Longrigg, 1993, p. 53ff.).

Although Alcmaeon displays the same rational attitudes as the Natural Philosophers, he nevertheless rejects the dogmatic certitude so prevalent among them and reveals a more modest attitude when he contrasts the certainty attainable (only) by the gods with the inferential procedures which mortals are forced to employ [**III.7**]. He thus renounces the dogmatic belief of his philosophical contemporaries in a single *archê* and their confident a priori deductions from it and advocates instead a more empirical approach, derived, perhaps, from Xenophanes of Colophon (see Sextus, *Against the mathematicians* VII.49ff. DK 21B34 [**III.8**]), which was more suitable for the development of medicine and adopted widely in Hippocratic medicine [see **V.1-6**].

As a result of the widening interest in medicine in the fifth century, the impulse to turn from macrocosm to microcosm quickened considerably. The philosophers began increasingly to apply their views about the world at large to man himself and base their medical and physiological theories upon their unifying philosophical hypotheses. The most influential philosophers in this respect are Empedocles of Acragas, Diogenes of Apollonia, and the Atomist, Democritus of Abdera. The two former had medical interests and may even have actually been doctors themselves [**III.11, 12, 17 & 18**]. Empedocles is keenly interested in the human body and seeks in his didactic hexametre poem, *On nature,* to explain its composition, its organs and their functions upon the basis of his highly influential four element theory, which dominated philosophy and science for over two millennia [**III.13-16**]. Diogenes, who had revived the monistic hypothesis of Anaximenes that air was the first principle [**III.19;** see **II.6 & 7**], in similar fashion, sought to account for health and disease upon this philosophical basis [**III.20**]. Evidence has survived (DK 68B234 & DK 68B159) attesting to Democritus's medical interests. His biological theories, in particular, seem to have been formulated in accordance with his general philosophical theory. The atomic theory clearly underlies his explanations of the mechanism of respiration [**III.21**], sense-perception [**III.22**], and, probably, reproduction and embryology [**III.23 & 24**].

Philosophy, then, came to exercise a powerful influence upon the development of medicine and from this connection medicine derived certain important benefits. It now became incorporated within self-consistent and tightly integrated systems. Rational modes of explanation, based upon formal, deductive reasoning and sustained by logical argument, were now adopted to account for health and sickness. Man himself was considered to be part and parcel of an ordered world whose laws were discoverable, a product of his environment, made of the same substances and subject to the same laws of cause and effect that operate within the cosmos at large. Furthermore, the diseases to which he is prone were themselves defined strictly in accordance with the same natural processes and ran their course within a set period of time totally independent of any arbitrary, supernatural interference. However, the disadvantageous effect of this influence was almost equally great, for along with the above benefits, medicine adopted, too, an undue tendency to deduce explanations from a preconceived position, which resulted in a propensity to accommodate observed facts to pre-established convictions. This had an adverse effect upon the development of a more empirical method more appropriate for the subsequent development of medicine, as the author of *Ancient medicine* is at pains to point out [**V.1**].

IV

The Hippocratic Corpus and the Hippocratic question

HIPPOCRATES

In the Western world Hippocrates was considered to be the ideal physician. Hippocratic medicine was held to embody the proper approach to problems of health, disease, and patient care, and after his death he came to be regarded as the 'Father of Medicine'. Despite his eminence comparatively little is known about him and it is not possible even to attribute a single treatise to him with any degree of confidence. Our earliest evidence concerning him is preserved in the works of Plato and Aristotle.

IV.1. Plato, *Protagoras* 311BC.

Socrates, addressing his young friend, Hippocrates, who has come to ask him to make arrangements for him to study with the sophist, Protagoras, draws a parallel with the young man's namesake.

Tell me, Hippocrates, I said, you are now endeavouring to resort to Protagoras and pay him money as a fee on your own behalf, what kind of a man do you think you are going to and what will he make of you? Suppose you had it in mind to go to your namesake, Hippocrates, the Coan, the member of the Asclepiadae, to pay him a fee on your own behalf and someone asked you to tell him to what sort of a man you are intending to pay a fee. What would you have answered? I would have said, he replied, that I am intending to pay a fee to a doctor. With the intention of becoming what? A doctor, he said.

Here, then, we learn that Hippocrates was an Asclepiad and charged a fee for tuition. Since Socrates goes on to ask the same questions with regard to the sculptors, Polycleitus and Pheidias, it may be inferred that Hippocrates was a well-known doctor at the time whose name would be as immediately recognised as those of these famous sculptors.

IV.2. Aristotle, *Politics* 1326a13-16

Aristotle, too, alludes to Hippocrates's eminence as a doctor.

A state, too, has a certain function so that the state that is most capable of fulfilling this function must be considered the greatest, just as one would say that Hippocrates was greater, not as a man, but as a doctor, than someone who surpassed him in bodily size.

The three surviving biographies of Hippocrates, like the Pseudo-Hippocratic *Letters*, are late and provide untrustworthy and, at times, even conflicting evidence. Three legends, in particular, seem to have been invented to illustrate particular virtues attributed to Hippocrates; his eradication of the Athenian plague was created to illustrate his brilliance as a doctor [see **X.10**]; his refusal to work for Artaxerxes, king of the Persians, to show his patriotism as a Greek [**IV.3**], and his cure of King Perdiccas's love-sickness to show his diagnostic skill [**IV.4**].

IV.3. Ps.-Soranus, *Life of Hippocrates according to Soranus* 8 (*CMG* IV IIb., p. 176)

In this biography, once supposed to have been written by Soranus of Ephesus, Hippocrates is portrayed as a patriot.

He was such a Philhellene that, when his fame became known as far as the Persians, and Artaxerxes for this reason begged him to come to him ... offering great gifts, Hippocrates refused because of his dignity, indifference to money, and his love of home.

IV.4. Ps.-Soranus, *Life of Hippocrates according to Soranus* 5 (*CMG* IV IIb., p. 176)

Here his diagnostic skill in determining Perdiccas's illness is described.

<Hippocrates> treated all Greece and was so admired that he was summoned by Perdiccas, King of the Macedonians, who was thought to be consumptive, to come to him at public expense ... Hippocrates diagnosed that the affliction was psychic in origin. For, after the death of his father, Alexander, Perdiccas fell in love with his concubine, Phila. Hippocrates revealed what had happened to her when he observed that the king completely changed colour when he looked at her. He cured the disease and restored him to health.

Erasistratus is credited with a similar diagnosis of the illness of Antiochus I, who had fallen in love with his stepmother, Stratonice.

IV.5. *Decree of the Athenians* (IX.400,15-402,12L)

The following decree contains these and other aspects of Hippocratic legend.

It has been decreed by the Council and by the people of Athens:
Whereas Hippocrates of Cos, a doctor and descendant of Asclepius, has shown a great and salutary goodwill towards the Greeks by sending his disciples to various places when a plague came upon Greece from the land of the barbarians and has prescribed the treatments to be applied to escape safely from the plague that was coming upon them, thus

demonstrating how the healing art of Apollo transmitted to the Greeks saves those among them who are sick:

Whereas he has bountifully produced books composed on the art of medicine in his desire that there should be many doctors to save lives:

Whereas, when the king of Persia summoned him and offered him honours equal to his own and all the gifts that he, Hippocrates, might ask for, he disdained the promises of the barbarian, because he was an enemy and common foe of the Greeks.

Therefore, so that the People of Athens might be manifest in their choosing continued benefits for the Greeks and in order to give a fitting reward to Hippocrates for his services, it has been decreed:

To initiate him at state expense into the Great Mysteries, like Herakles, son of Zeus:

To crown him with a wreath of gold to the value of one thousand gold coins:

To proclaim publicly the crowning at the time of the great Panathenaia, during the gymnastic contest:

To allow all the children of the Coans to have ephebes' training in Athens with the same rights as Athenian children, since their homeland produced such a man:

Finally, to give Hippocrates Athenian citizenship and grant him sustenance for life in the Prytaneum.

The 'achievements' of Hippocrates

IV.6. Pliny, *Natural history* 29.2

Pliny, citing Varro as his source, records the story that Hippocrates learned medicine from the 'cures' inscribed on the walls of the temple of Asclepius at Cos.

The subsequent history of medicine lay hidden in darkest night until the Peloponnesian War. Then Hippocrates, who was born on the island of Cos, among the foremost in fame and power and sacred to Aesculapius, restored it to the light. It had been customary for patients recovered from illness to inscribe in the temple of that god an account of the help that they had received, so that afterwards similar treatment might prove beneficial. Hippocrates is said to have written out these inscriptions, and, as Varro among us believes, after the temple had been burned, founded that branch of medicine called 'clinical'.

Archaeological evidence, however, seems to indicate that the Asclepieion was not built until relatively late in the fourth century BC.

IV.7. Cornelius Celsus, *On medicine*, Proem 8 (*CML* I, p. 18 Marx)

Hippocrates separated medicine from philosophy.

... Hippocrates of Cos, a man first among all men worthy of being remembered, outstanding for his skill and eloquence, separated this branch of learning from the study of philosophy.

It seems doubtful that we shall ever know for certain what prompted this assessment. Philosophical speculation is prominent in many of the treatises of the Hippocratic *Corpus*. While some scholars believe that Celsus had in mind the treatise *On ancient medicine* 20 here **[IV.11]**, Mudry makes the interesting suggestion (1982, p. 64) that Celsus's comment has a purely literary connotation and that he is claiming that Hippocrates was responsible for the introduction of a specific medical literature divorced from the writings of the philosophers.

EVIDENCE OF HIPPOCRATES'S METHODOLOGY AND THEORY OF DISEASE

IV.8. Plato, *Phaedrus* 270C-D

Plato in an ambiguous passage here alludes to Hippocrates's methodology.

Socrates: Do you think that it is possible to understand the nature of the soul intelligently apart from the nature of the whole?[1]

Phaedrus: If we are to put any trust in Hippocrates, the Asclepiad, we cannot even understand the nature of the body apart from this method.

Socrates: Yes, my friend, and he is correct. However, in addition to Hippocrates we must examine reason and see whether it is in agreement with him.

Phaedrus: I agree.

Socrates: Consider, then, what it is that Hippocrates and true reasoning mean by the examination of nature. Ought we not to reflect about the nature of anything whatsoever in the following manner: first, to consider whether that in regard to which we wish ourselves to be experts and able to make another so is simple or multiform; secondly, if it is simple, to consider what natural capacity it has of acting or being acted upon in relation to other things; but, if it is multiform, then having enumerated the forms, to see first in the case of one of them, and then in the case of each, what is that capacity to act or to be acted upon which makes it be what it is.

Phaedrus: Possibly, Socrates.

Socrates: At any rate the method which neglected these investigations would resemble the gropings of a blind man ....

[1] Unfortunately the expression 'the nature of the whole' is ambiguous and controversy has arisen as to whether it means the whole of nature, the whole of the body, or the whole body-soul complex.

IV.9. *Anonymus Londinensis* 5.35-7.40 (Jones, 1947, pp. 34-42)

The following extract from this second-century AD Egyptian medical papyrus now in the British Museum, which here attributes a specific theory of disease to

Hippocrates, is held to be derived ultimately from Meno's lost history of medicine, written as part of the systematisation of knowledge carried out within the Lyceum.

(5) Hippocrates has said that breaths (*physai*) are causes of disease, as Aristotle has said in his account of him. For Hippocrates says that diseases are brought about in the following manner. Either through the quantity of things taken, or through their diversity, or, because the things taken turn out to be strong and difficult to digest, residues are produced, and when the things that have been taken are too many, the heat (6) that produces digestion is overpowered by the multitude of the foodstuffs and does not effect digestion. From the hindrance of digestion residues ensue. When the things that have been taken are diverse, they fight against one another in the belly, and, because of the strife, there ensues a change into residues. However, when they are very coarse and hard to digest there thus arises a hindrance to digestion because of the difficulty of assimilation and so there ensues a change into residues. From the residues gases rise which, when carried upwards, bring on diseases. The man said these things stirred by the following conviction. For breath surpasses the most necessary and most powerful component within us, since health results from its free and disease from its impeded flow. He says that we are like plants. For, as they are rooted in the earth, so are we, too, rooted in the air by our nostrils and our whole body. At any rate we are like those plants called 'soldiers'. For, just as they, rooted in moisture, are carried now to this moisture now to that, so we, too, being plants, as it were, are rooted in air and are in motion, changing now to this position, now again to another. If this is so, it is clear that breath is the most important factor. On this explanation, when residues occur breaths arise from them which rise up as vapour and cause diseases. Diseases are caused in accordance with the variation of the breaths. If the breaths are rapid they cause disease; if they are infrequent they again bring on disease. The change of breaths also causes diseases. These changes take place in two directions, towards excessive heat or excessive cold. The nature of the change determines the character of the disease. This is what Aristotle thinks about Hippocrates. But, as Hippocrates himself says, diseases are caused by differences in the nature of the human constitution. (7) But still, Hippocrates says that diseases come into being either from the air or from regimen and he is pleased to outline these matters in the following way. For, he says, whenever many are seized contemporaneously by the same disease, the causes must be attributed to the air. For air produces the same disease. However, when many different forms of diseases occur, he says, employing unsound reasoning, that regimen must be held to be responsible. For sometimes many different diseases arise from the same cause. For, surely, surfeit is productive of fever, pleurisy and epilepsy and it brings forth diseases, too, in accordance with the constitution of the ingesting body. For it is not the case with all bodies that, when there is a single cause, there is also produced forthwith a single disease but, as we said, many diverse

forms of disease. Conversely, there are times when the same affections are caused by different causes. For diarrhoea is caused both by surfeit and also by acridness, if there is any untoward flow of bile. From this it is clear that the man is mistaken about these matters, as we shall show as our argument progresses. That, however, must be said, because Aristotle speaks otherwise about Hippocrates and he himself says diseases come about in a different way.

Attempts to identify a genuine Hippocratic work

IV.10. [Hippocrates], *Breaths* 3, 4, 5, 7 (VI.92,21-94,3L; VI.96,1-11L; VI.96,12-14L; VI.98,15-100,10L = *CMG* I.1, pp. 92-5 Heib.)

Diels identified the theory of disease expounded in this treatise with that attributed to Hippocrates in the *Anonymus Londinensis* **[IV.9]**; then simply refused to accept this evidence. The majority of scholars also deny the value of this evidence. (For a different view, however, see Langholf, 1986.)

[3] The bodies both of other animals and of man are nourished by three kinds of nutriment, solid food, drink and *pneuma*. In bodies *pneuma* is called breath, outside it is called air. This is the greatest power of all and is in all ....

[4] That air is strong in the case of whole <entities, such as the sea and the earth> has been said. For mortals, again, this is the cause of life and the cause of disease for the sick. It happens that so great is the need of *pneuma* for all bodies that a man, deprived of everything else, both food and drink, could live for two, three or more days, but, if the entrance of *pneuma* into his body were cut off, he would die in a brief part of a day revealing the body's greatest need for *pneuma*. Furthermore, all the rest of man's activities are intermittent. For life is full of changes. But respiration alone is continuous for all mortal creatures.

[5] ... Now, it has been said that all living things participate to a large extent in air. After this, it must be remarked that it is likely that diseases come about from no other source than this ....

[7] I shall go on to describe the fever caused by bad regimen. By bad regimen I mean, in the first place, when someone gives the body more wet or dry food than it can take and does not counter the excess of nutriment with exercise and, secondly, when one takes in foods that are varied and dissimilar. For dissimilar foods disagree and some are digested quickly and others more slowly. Along with much food much *pneuma* must also enter. For along with everything that is eaten or drunk *pneuma* enters the body to a greater or lesser extent. This is clear from the following: most people belch after food and drink. For the enclosed air rushes upwards when it has burst the bubbles in which it is hidden. When, then, the body is full of food, it becomes full of *pneuma*, too, when the foods remain a long time. They remain a long time because they cannot pass through owing to their bulk. When the lower belly is obstructed, the gases (*physai*) rush

through the whole body and, falling, upon the parts that are most full of blood, they chill them.

IV.11. [Hippocrates], *Ancient medicine* 20 (I.620,14-622,9L = *CMG* I.1, p. 51 Heib.)

Littré (Hippocrates, Vol. I. p. 301ff.), holding that the reference to 'the nature of the whole' at *Phaedrus* 270C-D **[IV.8]**, denotes the nature of the universe, seeks to identify this treatise as a genuine work of Hippocrates on the basis of the following passage. Jones is inclined to agree (1923, Loeb Vol. I p. 5) but believes that the resemblances show that the author of this work was Hippocratic (i.e. he held views similar to Hippocrates), not that he was the historical Hippocrates.

I consider that clear knowledge about nature can be acquired from no other source than medicine. One can attain this knowledge when medicine itself has been properly comprehended, but until then it seems to me to be far from possible. I mean knowledge of <the results> of this investigation, what man is, through what causes he comes into being, and the rest of it accurately. Since this at least, I think, it is necessary for a physician to know about nature, and be very eager to know, if he is going to perform any of his duties, what man is in relation to what he eats and drinks, and in relation to his habits generally, and what will be the effect of each upon each individual.

Festugière (1948, p. 62, n. 74) and other scholars, however, maintain that the position attributed on this interpretation to Hippocrates is closer to that attacked by this medical author; that, whereas the *Phaedrus* passage would imply that medicine depends on natural science, the converse is actually asserted in *Ancient medicine* – that the study of nature depends on medicine.

IV.12. [Hippocrates], *Regimen* I. 2 (VI.468,6-470,13L = *CMG* I.2,4, pp. 122-4 Jo.)

Smith (1979, p. 47) believes that *Regimen* I can be identified as a genuine work of Hippocrates and maintains that this passage reveals the methodology attributed by Plato to Hippocrates at *Phaedrus* 270C-D **[IV.8]**.

I declare that he who is intending to write correctly about human regimen must first acquire knowledge and discernment of the nature of man as a whole – knowledge of his original constituents and discernment of the components by which he is controlled. For, if he is ignorant of the original constitution, he will be unable to gain knowledge of their effects; if he is ignorant of that which is prevailing in the body, he will be incapable of administering suitable treatment to the patient. These things, therefore, the author must know, and, further, the power possessed severally by all the food and drink of our diet, both that derived from nature and that from human art. For it is necessary to know how one ought to take away the power of those that are naturally strong and how one ought to add strength

46

through art to those that are weak, whenever the opportunity for each might occur. But even when men understand what has been said, the treatment of a patient is not yet sufficient in itself because eating alone cannot keep a man healthy if he does not also take exercise. For food and exercise, while possessing opposite qualities, contribute mutually to produce health. For it is the nature of exercise to use up material, but of food and drink to make up deficiencies. And it is necessary ... to discern the power of the <various types> of exercise ... to know which of them tends to increase flesh and which lessen it ... to know also the correspondence between exercise and the bulk of the food, the constitution of the patient, the age of the individuals, the seasons of the year, the situations of the regions in which the patients live, the changes of the winds, and the state of the year. A man must observe the rising and settings of the stars, that he may know how to guard against changes and excesses of food, drink, winds, indeed the whole cosmos, from which arise diseases for men.

IV.13. [Hippocrates], *Regimen* III.74 (VI.614,21-616,4L = *CMG* I.2,4, p. 206 Jo.).

Here Smith (1979, p. 53) sees parallels with *Anonymus Londinensis* 6.11 **[IV.9]**, where a similar theory of causation of disease by gases produced from unassimilated food is attributed to Hippocrates.

The following symptoms also arise from surfeit. When the belly digests the food but the flesh rejects it, the nutriment, remaining inside, causes wind. After luncheon the flatulence subsides, for the lighter is expelled by the stronger and the afflictions seems to have been got rid of. But on the next day the affliction returns in a far greater degree. When, by daily increase, the surfeit becomes strong, what is already present overpowers what is further ingested, generates heat, disturbs the whole body and causes diarrhoea.

But the contention that gases cause disease is only an incidental point made in this treatise. If *Regimen* had really been the work of Hippocrates referred to here in the *Anonymus Londinensis*, then one might have expected the gases theory to be the dominant aetiology in this treatise.

*

Until not so very long ago, it was widely believed that the temple of Asclepius at Cos was the cradle of Greek rational medicine. It was argued that, just as Egypt and Mesopotamia had priest-physicians so, in similar fashion, the priests of Asclepius were physicians; that his temples were centres of medical research and training, where experience was accumulated and transmitted to later generations; that Hippocrates, the 'Father of Medicine', was himself an Asclepiad, a member of its hereditary priesthood **[IV.1 & 8]**; and, finally, that Hippocrates was said to have been the first to separate medicine from philosophy **[IV.7]**, thereby creating rational medicine at Cos. By the early Roman period the story that Hippocrates had learned medicine by studying the *iamata* on display on the walls of the Asclepieion at Cos had become widespread **[IV.6]**. Strabo further informs us (*Geography* XIV.2.19) that 'Hippocrates was trained in the knowledge of dietetics by the cures dedicated there'. Upon the basis of this evidence, then, the claim has frequently been made that Hippocratic medicine had its origin in temple practice. It should be noted, however, that the temple cures are in most instances immediate miracles whereas Hippocratic treatments present detailed observation of the course of diseases over a period of several days, even weeks, and in a high proportion of cases end fatally. Furthermore, the circumstantial details recorded by Pliny are highly dubious. Archaeological investigation seems to indicate that the Asclepieion was not built until relatively late in the fourth century BC by which time the island was already famous for its secular healers. Equally dubious is the argument that the Asclepiads were priest-physicians and, therefore, since Hippocrates himself is explicitly designated as an Asclepiad, Hippocratic medicine must have developed from temple practice. It is now generally held that the Asclepiads were not temple-physicians but rather doctors who were members of a *koinon* or guild [see **I.29**] which was initially a clan of hereditary physicians who worshipped Asclepius as the patron of their art and claimed descent from the god in much the same manner as the Homeridae traced their descent from Homer. This medical clan, it has been suggested, developed into something like a guild by the further admission or adoption of new members from outside the clan, and ultimately the term Asclepiad acquired the connotation of medical practitioner. In any case, the impression of medical practice presented by the Hippocratic treatises themselves is that of a wide and open calling without restrictions as to who might or might not set himself up as a practitioner. To practise medicine at Cos it was not necessary either to be a priest or a member of an exclusive guild. It is true, however, that there exist some striking affinities between Hippocratic medicine and the healing practised within the temples of Asclepius. But it seems far more likely that religious medicine is itself here influenced by its secular counterpart than *vice versa*. Thus the view that Hippocratic medicine had its origin in temple practice is untenable.

Both Plato and Aristotle attest to Hippocrates's eminence as a doctor and between them contribute a small amount of information **[IV.1, 2 & 8]**. Unfortunately, the *Letters* and the three surviving biographies of Hippocrates are late and provide untrustworthy and, at times, even conflicting evidence. Three legends, in particular, seem to have been invented to illustrate particular virtues attributed to Hippocrates: his eradication of the Athenian plague [see **X.10**] his refusal to work for Artaxerxes **[IV.3]**; and his cure of King Perdiccas **[IV.4]**. Some further evidence is afforded by the *Anonymus Londinensis* **[IV.9]**, a medical papyrus in the British Museum dating from the first century AD, which contains some material thought to have been ultimately derived from the history of medicine written by Aristotle's pupil, Meno, as part of the systematisation of knowledge carried out within the Lyceum. From the sum of this information it may be accepted with reasonable certainty that Hippocrates came from the island of Cos and was a contemporary of Socrates; that he was an Asclepiad, a member of a guild of physicians which claimed descent from Asclepius, the god of healing; that he became the most famous physician and teacher of medicine of his time and taught for a fee.

It is unfortunate, however, that this evidence does not provide sufficient definite information either of his methodology or of his doctrines to enable any one of the more than sixty treatises comprising the *Corpus* to be positively identified as having been written by Hippocrates himself. The heterogeneous nature of this collection, the variations in style and, at times, the conflicting and even contradictory standpoints manifested in the individual treatises make it evident that Hippocrates could not himself have been the author of all of them. The works, too, are clearly of varying dates. Whereas some seem to have been written in the fifth century, others are later. *On the heart,* for example, judging from its sophisticated account of the anatomy of the heart, should be dated close to or even within the third century BC [see **XIV.14**].

The Hippocratic *Corpus,* then, is a medley of treatises that vary widely in subject-matter, style and chronology. There is no inner unity except that all these works are written in the Ionic dialect; they are all connected more or less closely with medicine or one of the allied sciences, and the *Corpus* as a whole is marked by a virtual complete absence of magic and superstition. It has been suggested that the works composing it all arrived anonymously at the library at Alexandria and remained there until the third century BC, when the schools of Herophilus and Erasistratus developed the techniques of historical interpretation and set up Hippocrates as the 'Father of Medicine' by attributing to him an increasing number of these anonymous manuscripts. Other scholars, however, believe that the Hippocratic *Corpus* is the remains of the library of the medical school at Cos which was at some subsequent date incorporated within the Great Library at Alexandria, where it was re-copied and, perhaps, increased by the addition of volumes which had not belonged to the original collection. Certainly, the latter hypothesis well accords with the nature of the *Corpus,* since such a library would have been likely to have contained works of various dates and derived from different schools together with some of no great interest or medical value which had been presented by the library or acquired by chance.

Notwithstanding the scant, controversial, and ambiguous nature of our evidence, scholars have long sought to identify genuine works of Hippocrates himself. Their conclusions have been heavily influenced by ancient tradition and subjective value-judgements. In his *editio princeps* of the *Anonymus Londinensis* (1893a) Diels identified the medical theory attributed to Hippocrates in this papyrus [**IV.9**] as that expounded in the treatise *Breaths* [**IV.10**], but simply refused to accept this evidence, maintaining that no knowledgeable student of the subject could take this sophistic work to be a genuine work of Hippocrates. In 1901 Wilamowitz took a very sceptical view of the matter and described Hippocrates as *'ein berühmter Name ohne den Hintergrund irgend einer Schrift'* (a famous name without the background of a single treatise). This radical assessment was subsequently repeated by Edelstein in the 1930s and has recently been endorsed by Lloyd. However, as Pohlenz (1938, p. 3) has pointed out, it would be something of a paradox if, when so many treatises are attributed to Hippocrates, nothing of his genuine writings has survived. Accordingly, despite the forceful arguments of the sceptics, attempts to identify a genuine work continue to be made. The line of approach is generally the same: once the authenticity of one or a few treatises has been established – to the author's satisfaction – upon the basis of the external evidence listed below, then the range of works that may be considered to be by Hippocrates is widened by using arguments based upon internal evidence, i.e. based upon connections existing between different treatises within the *Corpus.* But no consensus has been attained amongst modern scholars. Controversy still rages and disagreements remain as wide as ever.

Recently an interesting attempt to identify a work as genuinely Hippocratic has been made by W.D. Smith, who sees affinities between the methodology attributed to Hippocrates by Plato in the *Phaedrus* and *Regimen* I.2 [**IV.12**] and argues that this treatise seems to have been the source of Meno's report. But, in spite of the parallels Smith draws between *Regimen* and the *Anonymus Londinensis* and, in particular, that between *Regimen* III.74 [**IV.13**] and *Anonymus* 6.11 [**IV.9**], where, as Smith points out, an identical theory of the causation of disease by gases produced from unassimilated food is put forward and attributed to Hippocrates, it remains doubtful that a genuine work has been identified. An obvious drawback, of course, is that the passage in *Regimen* attributing the cause of disease to gases is, in fact, only an incidental part of the treatise; if *Regimen* had really been the work Meno had in mind, one would expect the gases theory to be the dominant aetiology of this treatise. But it is not.

See, especially, Edelstein, 1939; Lloyd, 1975c; Smith, 1979.

V

Philosophy and medicine in the fifth century II: Presocratic philosophy and the Hippocratic Corpus

Although medicine was initially indebted to philosophy, its continued subordination to it proved a serious handicap to its subsequent development. The danger to medicine inherent in the attempts made by the natural philosophers to account for the composition of the human body and explain its physiology upon the basis of their unifying hypotheses was recognised and vigorously attacked by certain of the Hippocratic authors.

ATTACKS ON PHILOSOPHICAL INTRUSION
INTO MEDICINE

V.1. [Hippocrates], *Ancient medicine* 1 & 2 (I.570-572,15L = *CMG* I.1, pp. 36-7 Heib.)

Here our Hippocratic author rejects attempts to base medicine upon philosophical postulates which he regards should be more fittingly applied to the 'mysteries of heaven and the regions below the earth'.

All those who have attempted to speak or write about medicine have assumed for themselves a hypothesis as the basis for their discussion – heat, cold, moisture, dryness, or anything else they wish, narrowing down the causal principle of diseases and death for men and making it the same in all cases. They are manifestly in error in many of their novelties. They are especially blameworthy because they are dealing with an art that really exists, one employed upon the weightiest of considerations by all men, who hold in especial honour its good practitioners and craftsmen. This would not be so if there were no medical art at all, or no research were carried out in it and no discovery made; but all would be equally inexperienced and unlearned in it and the treatment of the sick would be managed entirely by chance. As it is, however, this is not so; but, just as in the case of all the other arts, their practitioners differ greatly from one another in respect of their manual skill and intellect, so, too, is it the case in medicine. Consequently I considered that it had no need of a new-fangled hypothesis, as do obscure problems which necessarily require the use of a hypothesis if one attempts to discuss them, for example those of the heavens and the regions below the earth. If anyone were to express a judgement about these matters, it would not be clear either to the speaker himself or to his

51

audience whether his statements were true or not. For there is no test whose application brings certain knowledge. [2] But medicine has long had everything to hand, with a principle and method already discovered by which many good discoveries have been made over a long period; while what remains will be discovered, if the enquirer is competent and is familiar with discoveries already made and conducts his enquiry with these as his starting-point. But whoever rejects and spurns all these and attempts to carry out his enquiry by a different method and by a different fashion and then declares that he has made some discovery, deceives and is deceived. For it is impossible.

V.2. [Hippocrates], *Ancient medicine* 12 (I.596,8-598,2L = *CMG* I.1, p. 44 Heib.)

He stresses that medicine is a long-established art with its own methodology.

I say that we must not for this reason reject the ancient art of medicine as being non-existent or as ill-founded in its research if it does not attain exactitude in every respect: but we ought far rather, since (I believe) it has the power to have risen by reasoning from great ignorance to approximate exactness, to admire its discoveries as being the result of good and correct research, not of chance.

V.3. [Hippocrates], *Ancient medicine* 20 (I.620,7-12L = *CMG* I.1, p. 51 Heib.)

Empedocles is expressly cited as representative of this 'new-fangled' philosophical approach to medicine ...

Certain physicians and sophists assert that it is impossible for anyone to know medicine who does not know what man is and that to treat patients correctly it is necessary to learn this. Their doctrine, however, tends towards philosophy in the manner of Empedocles and others who have written about nature, what man is originally, how he first came into being and from what elements.

V.4. [Hippocrates], *Ancient medicine* 20 (I.620,12-14L = *CMG* I.1, p. 51 Heib.)

... whose application is scornfully dismissed.

All that has been said or written by sophist or physician about nature I consider is of less concern to the art of medicine than to painting.

V.5. [Hippocrates], *Ancient medicine* 9 (I.588,11-590,4L = *CMG* I.1, p. 41 Heib.)

It is stressed that medicine is not an exact science.

Many other ills, different from those of repletion, but no less grievous, result also from depletion. Because they are far more varied they also require a greater accuracy of method. For it is necessary to aim at some measure. But there is no measure you could find, either number or weight, by reference to which you would gain accurate knowledge, other than the sensation of the body.

Consequently it is our task to acquire knowledge so accurate that our margins of error are small. I strongly commend the physician whose errors are small; but exactness is seldom to be seen.

This more sceptical and empirical approach advocated by the author of *Ancient medicine* can be traced back to Alcmaeon [see **III.7**] and further still to Xenophanes of Colophon [see **III.8 & 9**].

V.6. [Hippocrates], *Epidemics* III, Case 16 (III.146,7-148,5L)

It is exemplified most strikingly in the *Epidemics*, which have come to be regarded as the very model of clinical observation. The following case study is not untypical.

In Meliboea a youth who had been feverish for a long time as a result of drunkenness and much sexual indulgence took to his bed. His symptoms were shivering, nausea, insomnia, and lack of thirst.

On the first day, there passed from his bowels a large quantity of solid stools with much fluid. During the following days he passed a large quantity of watery, greenish excrement. His urine was thin, sparse, and of bad colour. His respiration was at long intervals and deep after a time. There was a rather flabby tension of the upper part of the abdomen extending laterally to both sides. Cardiac palpitation was continuous throughout. The urine was oily.

Tenth day: he was delirious, but calm, well-behaved, and silent. Skin dry and taut; stools either copious and thin or bilious and greasy.

Fourteenth day: all symptoms exacerbated. Delirious with much rambling speech.

Twentieth day: out of his mind; much tossing about. No urine passed: small amounts of fluid retained.

Twenty-fourth day: died.

V.7. [Hippocrates], *Nature of man* 2 (VI.34,8-16L = *CMG* I.1,3, pp. 166-8 Jou.)

This treatise, unlike *Ancient medicine*, does not attack the intrusion of philosophy in general, but restricts its attack to those who attempt to base medicine upon a unitarian hypothesis.

Turning to the physicians, some assert that man is composed of blood, others of bile, and some of phlegm. These, too, come to the same conclusion as the philosophers that there is a basic unity of substance (although each has his own chosen name for it), that this entity changes its appearance and properties under constraint of heat or cold to become sweet or bitter, white or black and so forth. But to me these views do not seem to be correct ....

V.8. [Hippocrates], *Nature of man* 2 (VI.36,12-16L = *CMG* I.1,3, p. 170 Jou.)

The author's own theory, that the body is composed of the four humours [**III.4**], is believed to be empirically justified. This theory, however, itself reveals philosophical influence and is the counterpart of the four element theory.

I, for my part, shall prove that what I shall declare to be the constituents of man are, according to both convention and nature, always the same and unchanging, whether the man is young or old or whether the season is cold or hot. I shall also furnish proofs and set forth the necessary causes whereby each constituent increases or declines in the body.

CONTINUING PHILOSOPHICAL INFLUENCE ON MEDICINE

These attempts to withstand philosophical intrusion proved unavailing, and many treatises reveal diverse philosophical influences.

V.9. [Hippocrates], *Breaths* 4, 5 (VI.96,1-14L = *CMG* I.1, pp. 93-4 Heib.)

Despite the antagonism displayed by the author of *Nature of man* towards attempts to base medicine upon a monistic hypothesis and his hostility towards Diogenes of Apollonia in particular, the latter's influence is clearly apparent in *Breaths*.

For mortals, too, this <aêr> is the cause both of life and of diseases in the sick. So great happens to be the need all bodies have for breath that while a man can abstain from everything else, both food and drink, for two, three, or more days, and live, yet, if the breathing-passages into the body should be cut off, he would die in a brief portion of a day, showing that the body has the greatest need of breath. Furthermore, all other activities of mankind are intermittent, for life is full of changes; but breathing alone is continuous for all mortal creatures as they exhale and inhale. [5] So then, it has been said that every living creature is associated with air to a great extent. After this it must be stated that it is likely that maladies occur from no other source than this ....

V.10. [Hippocrates], *Sacred disease* 14 (VI.386,15-388,4L)

This treatise, too, reveals the influence of Diogenes in its elaboration of a theory of disease based upon the belief that the brain is the seat of the intelligence –

Men ought to know that the source of our pleasures, merriment, laughter

and amusements as well as our grief, pains, anxiety and tears is none
other than the brain. It is by this organ especially that we think, see, hear
and distinguish between the ugly and the beautiful, the bad and the good,
the pleasant and unpleasant. Somethings we differentiate by convention,
others by our perception of expediency. By this same organ, too, we become
mad or delirious, and are assailed by fears and panics, sometimes by night,
sometimes even in the daytime, by insomnia, sleepwalking, thoughts
that do not come, ignorance of established usage and actions out of
character. These things we suffer all come from the brain whenever it
is unhealthy ....

V.11. [Hippocrates], *Sacred disease* 16 (VI.390,10-20L)

– and again in its adoption of the theory that air is the source and principle of
intelligence.

For these reasons I consider the brain to be the most potent organ in the
body. So long as it is healthy, this is our interpreter of the phenomena
caused by air. It is the air that supplies intelligence. Eyes, ears, tongue,
hands and feet carry out the actions determined by the brain. For the
whole body participates in intelligence in proportion to its participation in
air. The brain serves as messenger to comprehension. For when a man
draws in breath, the air first reaches the brain, and so is dispersed into
the rest of the body, having left in the brain its essence and whatever of
intelligence it possesses.

V.12. [Hippocrates], *Nutriment* 18, 19, 21, 22, 23 & 24 (IX.104-106L =
  CMG I.1, pp. 80-1 Heib.)

The author of this treatise, adopting Heraclitus's aphoristic style, applies his
theory of change to the assimilation of food.

[18] Purging upward or downward, neither upward nor downward.

[19] In nutriment purging excellent, in nutriment purging bad; bad or
excellent are relative.

[21] Nutriment not nutriment if it has no power. Not nutriment nutriment if it can nourish. Nutriment in name but not in deed; nutriment in
deed but not in name.

[22] From within it reaches the hair, nails and the extreme surface;
from without nutriment reaches the innermost parts from the extreme
surface.

[23] Confluence is one, conspiration one, all things in sympathy. All the
parts forming one whole and severally the parts in each part with reference to the work.

[24] The great beginning arrives at the furthermost part. From the
furthermost part it arrives at the great beginning. One nature to be and
not to be.

V.13. [Hippocrates], *Regimen* I.4-5 (VI.474,8-476,13L = *CMG* I.2,4, pp. 126-8 Jo.)

This treatise, also written in Heraclitean style, displays reminiscences of Anaxagoras and, possibly, Empedocles and Archelaus as well.

Each of these elements has the following attributes. Fire is hot and dry, water cold and wet. By mutual exchange fire has moisture from water. (For in fire there is moisture.) Water has dryness from fire. (For there is dryness in water.) This being the case, there separate off from one another many forms of every kind, both of seeds and of living creatures, which are not at all like one another either in appearance or power. For, seeing that they never stay in the same condition, but are always changing to this or that, from these elements, too, are separated off things which are necessarily unlike. So of all things nothing perishes nor does there come into being anything that did not exist before. Things change by mingling and separating. It is generally believed that one thing increases and comes into being from Hades, while another diminishes and perishes from the light into Hades. For they trust their eyes rather than their intelligence though they are not adequate even to judge what they have seen. But I use my intelligence to explain these things. For both the things of the nether world and of this world are alive. And if there is life there cannot be death, unless all things die with it. For whither will death take place? Nor can what is not come into being. For whence will it come? For all things increase and decrease to the greatest possible maximum or minimum extent. Whenever I speak of anything 'coming into being' or 'passing away', I am merely using popular expressions. By these terms I really mean 'mingling' and 'separating'. The situation is as follows: 'becoming' and 'perishing' are the same thing; 'mingling' and 'separating' are the same thing; 'increasing' and 'diminishing' are the same thing; 'becoming' and 'mingling' are the same thing; 'passing away', 'diminishing' and 'separating' are the same thing and so is the relation of each to all and all to each. Yet nothing of all things is the same. For concerning these things custom is opposed to nature.

[5] But all things, both human and divine, are in a state of flux upwards and downwards by exchanges.

V.14. [Hippocrates], *Sevens* 5 (VIII.636L)

The influence of Pythagorean numerology has been discerned in this treatise –

Thus in the nature of man there are seven seasons, called ages: childhood, boyhood, adolescence, young manhood, mature manhood, late maturity, old age; these are as follows: childhood up to seven years (to the change of teeth); boyhood to the emission of semen (to fourteen years: twice seven); adolescence up to <the growth of> the beard (to twenty-one years: thrice seven); young manhood up to full bodily growth but completed in thirty-five years (five times seven); maturity up to forty-nine years (seven times seven); later maturity up to sixty-three years (nine times seven). From then onwards old age (fourteen times seven).

V.15. [Hippocrates], *On fleshes* 19 (VIII.608,22-614,13L)

– and again here.

The age of man is seven days <i.e. it runs in sevens>. First proof: when the seed enters the womb, in seven days it has all the necessary parts of the body .... Second proof: many of those wishing to abstain from food and drink for seven days die within this period .... Third proof: the infant born at seven months has come into being by reason and lives. Such is the rapport and precise number it bears regarding the hebdomads .... Fourth proof: children acquire their full complement of teeth when seven years have passed ....

V.16. [Hippocrates], *On generation* 8 (VII.480,7-482,2L)

The theory of pangenesis held by the atomist, Democritus **[III.23 & 24]**, may have influenced this author's theory of reproduction (see Lonie, 1981, pp. 124-39)

Seed is a product that comes from the entire body of both the female and the male; weak seed comes from the weak parts, and strong seed from the strong parts. The child must necessarily correspond. Whenever a greater quantity of seed is derived from any part of the father's body than from the corresponding part of the mother's body, the child will, in that part, bear a closer resemblance to its father; and *vice versa*. It is not possible, however, for the child to resemble its mother in all respects, and its father in none; or the converse of this; nor for the child to resemble neither parent in any respect. But it must necessarily resemble each parent in some respect, seeing that the seed comes from both parents to form the child. Whichever parent contributes more to the likeness and from more parts of the body, the child resembles that parent in more respects. And it sometimes happens that a daughter bears a closer resemblance in more respects to her father than to her mother, whereas a boy more closely resembles his mother than his father. These facts are great illustrations in proof of my earlier argument that there is in both the female and in the male both male-procreation and female-procreation.

V.17. [Hippocrates], *Nature of the child* 31 (VII.540,1-542,1L)

Democritean influence, it has also been maintained, underlies the explanation of the conception of twins outlined here.

Twins are born from a single act of intercourse in the following way: wombs have multiple cavities, curved in shape, at varying distances from the *pudenda*. Animals which produce large numbers of offspring have more of these cavities than those which produce fewer. This is true of domestic and wild animals and of birds. Whenever the semen happens to be divided into two cavities on its arrival in the womb, and neither of the cavities releases it into the other, then each of these separate portions in each cavity envelopes itself within a membrane and becomes alive in the same way as I have said the single embryo does. That twins are born from a single act of intercourse is illustrated by the bitch, sow and those other animals which produce two or even more young from one copulation; each of the embryos in their wombs occupies its own cavity and membrane. We ourselves see these things happening and these animals for the most part produce all their offspring on the same day. In the same way, twins are born to the woman, too, as a result of a single copulation, each in its own cavity and membrane. She bears both of them on the same day, one emerging first with its membrane, then the other. Because twins are born with one of either sex, I maintain with man and woman – indeed, in every animal – there exist both weaker and stronger varieties of sperm. The sperm does not come out all at once, but spurts out in two or three spasms. It is not possible that all the sperm, both the first and the last to be ejaculated, should always be of equal strength. The cavity, then, which happens to be entered by the thicker and stronger sperm develops a male. Conversely, a female develops in that entered by the moister and weaker sperm. If strong sperm enters both cavities, both offspring become male; if the sperm that enters both is weak, both offspring become female.

Wellmann originally claimed (1929a, pp. 306-9) that Democritean influence underlies the explanation of twins outlined here. The atomist's theory of multiple birth in animals (see Aelian *Nature of animals* XII.16 DK 68A151) seems to have been adapted in order to account for the birth of human twins. As Lonie has pointed out (1981, p. 253), the above account reads oddly unless one supposes that the medical author is referring in his opening sentence to animals, not humans. This view has recently been attacked by Jouanna (1992a, p. 102ff.). Certainly there are differences in detail, most notably in the number of incidences of copulation in each case, but the close similarities that remain nevertheless suggest that the medical author has comprehensively modified the original theory of pangenesis.

*

The rejection of belief in the supernatural causation of disease and in the efficacy of incantations and purifications marks medicine's greatest and most enduring debt to philosophy. However, the developing science had a heavy price to pay since the continued subordination of medicine to philosophy proved a serious handicap to the former's development because the procedure of the natural philosophers was predominantly *a priori* and deductive. The attempt to apply philosophical postulates to medicine in the manner seen above is vigorously attacked by the author of the Hippocratic treatise, *Ancient medicine.* In this remarkable treatise we find for the first time a distinction drawn between medical 'science' and philosophy. The author is clearly conscious of the opposition between the dogmatic *a priori* methodology of the natural philosopher and the more empirical procedure of the physician [V.1]. In Chapter 20 he expressly singles out Empedocles as representative of the objectionable influence of this 'new-fangled' philosophical approach to medicine **[V.3]**.

In *Ancient medicine*, then, any attempt to resort to unverifiable generalisations to account for the causation of disease is fiercely rejected **[V.4]**. In stressing the importance of empirical observation in medicine, its author reveals an awareness of methodological issues and the distinctions that should be drawn between different intellectual disciplines. Yet, notwithstanding his denunciation of attempts to base medical theory upon a 'new-fangled' philosophical hypothesis, he is himself vulnerable to the very criticisms he levels at his opponents in that he himself subscribes to a postulate which is hardly less speculative when he adopts a theory of health **[III.3]** which, as has been shown, can be traced back to Alcmaeon and ultimately to Anaximander [see **III.2 & 1**]. This discrepancy between his declared policy and actual practice, however, does not invalidate his important recommendation that unverifiable *a priori* postulates should be excluded from an empirical science like medicine. Although, admittedly, his medical theory is not without certain similarities to that which he singles out especially for attack, it is necessary to realise that he is firmly convinced that the theory that he adopts has been confirmed by long experience and has led to many excellent discoveries over a long period of time **[V.1 & 2]**. This sceptical, empirical and more realistic attitude adopted by the author of *Ancient medicine* **[V.3 & V.5]** can also be traced back to Alcmaeon who, in the opening words of his treatise, draws a sharp distinction between human inference and divine certainty **[III.7]**. It has been claimed that this less confident attitude towards knowledge was 'inculcated by the nascent science of medicine with its detailed observation of particular cases and its awareness of fallibility in diagnosis'. But protagonists of this view have overlooked the fact that this same outlook is unequivocally put forward by the philosopher/poet Xenophanes of Colophon **[III.8 & 9]**. Thus the more empirical outlook which confronts the dogmatic approach of the natural philosophers and which is exemplified most strikingly in the *Epidemics* I & III **[V.6]**, is itself nevertheless a direct outcome of earlier Presocratic philosophical debate.

The same hostility towards the encroachment of philosophy into the sphere of medicine is displayed by the author of *Nature of man*. The target, however, is more restricted and the attack is specifically directed against the attempt to base medicine upon the unitarian hypothesis that man is composed of a single substance **[V.7]**. His own theory, which he believes to be empirically justified **[V.8]**, that the human body is composed of four humours **[III.4]** itself reveals philosophical influence and is, in fact, the medical counterpart of the Empedoclean theory of the four elements. It is highly ironical that a treatise so concerned to attack the intrusion of philosophy into medicine should itself not only reveal strong philosophical influence in this way but also, as a result of this influence, should formulate a theory which, more than any other, was to contribute to the dominance of philosophy over medicine for the next two millennia and beyond.

In spite of these vigorous – though not entirely self-consistent – attacks upon the intrusion of philosophy into medicine, the temptation to formulate axiomatic systems based upon first principles from which explanations of particular phenomena could be deduced proved no less strong in medicine than in Greek science generally and several treatises in the Hippocratic *Corpus* manifest this tendency to a marked degree. Nothwithstanding the specific attack in *Nature of man* upon any attempt to base medicine upon a monistic hypothesis in general and the hostility displayed there towards Diogenes of Apollonia in particular, two works, *Breaths* and *Sacred disease*, are patently influenced by this philosopher. While the former work follows Diogenes in his belief that air is of fundamental importance in the world generally and is instrumental in causing disease **[V.9, cf. III.19 & 20]**, the latter elaborates a comprehensive explanation of disease upon the basis of two theories held by Diogenes – the belief that the brain is the seat of the intelligence and that air is the source and principle of intelligence in the living organism [III.19, V.10 & 11].

The influence of Heraclitus is also marked in the *Corpus*. In *Nutriment*, for example, a later Heraclitean, skilfully reproducing his master's aphoristic style, applies his theory of perpetual change to the assimilation of food by a living organism [V.12]. *Regimen* I is also written in Heraclitean style, and reminiscences of Anaxagoras and, possibly, Empedocles and Archelaus can also be found in this treatise [V.13]. The influence of Pythagorean numerology may also be present in *Sevens* [V.14] and *On fleshes* [V.15], and, perhaps, in the importance assigned to 'critical days' generally, since Celsus actually refers to them as 'Pythagorici numeri' (*On medicine* III.4.15). Influence of the atomic theory may also be detected within the treatises *Nature of the child*, *Diseases* IV and *On generation*, though nowhere is this influence explicit. The theory of pangenesis, subscribed to by Democritus, may have been the source of the doctrine expounded at *On generation* 6-8 [V.16]; the description of the growth of hair at *Nature of the child* 20 closely parallels the growth of horn attributed to Democritus by Aelian (*Nature of animals* XII.18-20 DK 68A153-5) and Democritean influence is held by some scholars to underlie the explanation of twins described at *Nature of the child* 31 [V.17].

Philosophical influence, however, was not limited to the adoption by medical writers of unifying philosophical postulates. Many of the Presocratic philosophers had themselves developed a keen interest in medicine and biology and certain of the particular theories which they had put forward in these fields, whether derived directly from their general hypotheses, or, at least, formulated in accordance with them, exercised a very considerable influence upon contemporary and subsequent medical theory. The two most influential philosophers in this respect were Empedocles and Diogenes of Apollonia, as has been seen, and certain of the physiological doctrines initially propounded, or at least developed in part by them exercised a lasting influence – particularly through the 'Sicilian' tradition. Among these doctrines might be mentioned the theory of *pneuma*; the concept of innate heat as the prime agent of embryological, digestive and other physiological processes; the idea that blood was manufactured in the liver and served as the agent of nutrition, and the notion that the semen, like milk, was a form of surplus nutriment [see VI.7-13 and the references cited there.]

The Hippocratic *Corpus*, then, reveals abundant evidence of the influence of philosophy. Without its philosophical background Hippocratic medicine is inconceivable. Although the continued subordination of medical theory to philosophical postulate proved harmful in that the logical satisfaction of an axiomatic system was frequently purchased at the cost of a diminution of empirical observation, nevertheless, on balance, philosophy did more good than harm. For from its philosophical background, medicine derived its rational attitudes and modes of explanation, its belief that human beings were a product of and influenced by their environment, made of the same substances and subject to the same physical laws as the world at large, together with the view that diseases were the result of strictly natural causes and ran their individual courses within a set period of time, totally independent of any arbitrary, supernatural interference.

See, especially, Longrigg, 1989.

VI

Philosophy and medicine until the fourth century: 'Sicilian' medicine and its influence

'Sicilian' medicine exercised a dominant influence in Greek medicine from its inception in the fifth century, throughout the fourth, and up to the Hellenistic era and beyond.

MEDICINE IN MAGNA GRAECIA

VI.1. Herodotus, *Histories* 3.131

Some early evidence of medical activity in Magna Graecia in the sixth century is recorded by Herodotus, who considers that the best physicians in Greece at the time were those of Croton. The reputation of Crotoniate doctors was subsequently further enhanced by Alcmaeon [see **Chapter III**]. Here Herodotus describes some of the adventures of Democedes, 'the most skilful physician of his time' (*Histories* 3.125).

Democedes, unable to bear his harsh-tempered father, left him and went to Aegina. In his first year there he excelled the other physicians despite being without all the instruments of his calling. In his second year the Aeginetans paid him a talent to be their public physician. In the third year the Athenians hired him for a hundred minae, and Polycrates <the tyrant of Samos> in the next for two talents. Thus he came to Samos and it was not least due to him that the Crotoniate doctors were held in high esteem. (For at this time the best physicians throughout Greece were those of Croton, those of Cyrene were second.)

Democedes remained in the service of Polycrates until the latter was put to death by the Persian satrap, Oroites, in 522 BC. For further adventures of Democedes see **XV.7 & 8**.

'SICILIAN' MEDICINE

VI.2. Galen, *On the method of medicine* 1.1 (X.5-6K = (in part) DK 31A3)

'Sicilian' medicine is ranked by Galen next to that of Cos and Cnidus.

In former times there was great rivalry between the doctors in Cos and at Cnidus as they strained to prevail in the number of their discoveries. For these were the two surviving branches of the Asclepiads in Asia, after the decline of the Rhodian branch. They were joined in that 'noble strife', which Hesiod praised, by the doctors from Italy, Philistion, Empedocles, Pausanias and their disciples. There were these three wonderful bands of doctors competing with each other. The Coan group was fortunate in having the most and the best performers, but the Cnidian ran it close. The *Italian*, too, was of no small merit.

VI.3. Pliny, *Natural history* 29.4-5 (DK 31A3)

Pliny records here the name of another famous Sicilian doctor (in a passage which also reveals the manner in which the later Empiricist sect sought to prove that their persuasion was older than that of their rivals, the Dogmatists).

Another group <of doctors>, which men called 'empirical' from their reliance on experience, began in Sicily, with Acron of Acragas, who was recommended by the authority of the physicist, Empedocles.

EMPEDOCLES

The most influential ideas in Western Greek medicine, however, were formulated at Acragas in Sicily by Empedocles. Many influential theories characteristic of 'Sicilian' medicine can be traced back to Empedocles, notably the beliefs that the human body is composed of the four elements and that the predominance of any one of them causes disease; that the heart is the seat of the intelligence; that innate heat is the underlying agent of physiological processes; that respiration serves to cool the innate heat; that blood acts as the agent of nutrition and is manufactured in the liver; and that the semen is a form of surplus nutriment (i.e. blood).

Composition of the body and theory of health

VI.4. Theophrastus, *On the senses* 10 (DK 31A86)

The role of the four elements in the composition of living creatures.

Empedocles ... adds:
'For from these <i.e. the four elements> all creatures have been made and fitted together and by them they think and feel pleasure and suffer distress.'

See also **III.13-16**.

Seat of the intellect

VI.5. Porphyry, *On the Styx* (Stobaeus, *Selections* I.49.53 = DK 31B105)

Empedocles places the seat of the intellect in the 'blood round the heart'.

Empedocles thus appears to say that the blood is the organ of intelligence. <He says that the heart is> 'nurtured in the sea of pulsing blood, where especially is what men call thought: for the blood around the heart is thought.'

See, too, Censorinus 6.1 (DK 31A84) and Theophrastus, *On the senses* 10 (DK 31A86).

Respiration

VI.6. Aristotle, *On respiration* 473a15ff. (DK 31B100)

Despite Aristotle's comment here it seems likely that Empedocles did subscribe to the belief that respiration serves to cool the innate heat.

Empedocles also discusses respiration, but not its purpose,[1] nor does he make it clear at all whether all animals respire or not. And in speaking of respiration through the nostrils he thinks he is speaking of respiration in its primary sense .... (473b1) Empedocles says that inhalation and exhalation take place because there are certain veins, which contain some blood but are not full of blood. They have passages to the external air, smaller than solid particles, but larger than those of air. In consequence, since the blood naturally moves up and down, when it is moved down, the air flows in and inhalation takes place; but when it goes up, it drives the air out and exhalation occurs. He likens this process to what happens with clepsydras:[2] 'This is the way all things breathe in and out: they all have channels of flesh that the blood leaves, stretched out over the innermost surface of the body and at the mouths of these the innermost surfaces of the nostrils are pierced right through with close-set pores so that the blood is kept in, but an easy path is cut for the air to pass through. Then, when the fine blood rushes away from the pores, the blustering air rushes in with furious surge; and when the blood leaps up, the air breathes out again. Just as when a girl plays with a clepsydra of gleaming bronze – when she puts the mouth of the pipe against her shapely hand and dips it into the smooth body of shining water, no liquid still enters the vessel, but the bulk of the air within, pressing upon the frequent perforations, holds it back, until she uncovers the dense stream. But then, as the air gives way, an equal amount of water enters. In just the same way, when water occupies the depths of the bronze vessel and the neck and the passage are closed by human flesh, the air outside, striving inwards, holds the water back, holding its surface firm at the gates of the ill-sounding strainer, until she lets go with her hand and then again (the reverse of what happened before) as the air rushes in, an equal amount of water rushes out before it. And in just the same way, when the fine blood surging through the limbs rushes backwards and inwards, straightaway a stream of air with swift surge comes pouring in, but, when <the blood> leaps up, an equal amount of air in turn breathes back out again.'[3]

[1] This criticism is of doubtful validity. For it seems that Philistion [see **VI.14ff.**]

derived from Empedocles not only the four element theory and the doctrine of innate heat [see **VI.16**], but also his view of the purpose of respiration. Several Presocratic philosophers immediately subsequent to Empedocles, who have clearly taken into account certain of his biological theories, also subscribe to the belief that the purpose of respiration is to moderate the innate heat.

[2] The clepsydra is a domestic utensil with perforations at the bottom and a vent at the top. By blocking and unblocking this vent liquids can be transferred from one container to another.

[3] According to Aristotle Empedocles here adopts the normal belief that we breathe in and out through the mouth and/or nostrils only. Many scholars have argued, however, that Aristotle has here mistakenly translated the Greek as 'nostrils' instead of 'skin' and they maintain that the simile entails cutaneous respiration as well as respiration through the mouth and nostrils. Such a belief in cutaneous respiration is held by Philistion [see **VI.16**] and Plato [**VI.22**], both of whom, as shall be seen, are much influenced by Empedocles's biology.

Blood the vehicle of nutrition; digestion as putrefaction

VI.7. Aristotle, *Generation of animals* 777a7ff. (DK 31B68)

Aristotle here criticises Empedocles's belief that mother's milk is corrupted blood.

Milk is concocted, not corrupted blood. Empedocles was either wrong in his assumption or made a bad metaphor when he said:

On the tenth day of the eighth month <the blood> became a white putrefaction.[1]

[1] Here Empedocles resorts to word-play and exploits the similarity between *puon* (pus) and *puos* ('beestings', colostrum or the first milk secreted towards the end of pregnancy). See further Plutarch, *Natural questions* 2.912C (DK 31B81) and Ps.-Galen, *Medical definitions* 99 (XIX.372K & DK 31A77).

Empedocles believes that blood is the vehicle of nutrition and that milk is a surplus residue of blood.

VI.8. Simplicius, *Commentary on Aristotle's Physics* 371.33 (DK 31B61)

Simplicius records Empedocles's belief in the haematopoeic function of the liver.

... and all the parts that came together in such a manner as to be able to secure preservation, became living creatures and survived through fulfilling for one another a basic need, the teeth cutting and grinding up the food, the belly digesting it and the *liver turning it into blood*.

VI.9. Plutarch, *Table talk* V.8.2, p. 683E (DK 31B150)

Plutarch's brief quotation seems to carry an allusion to the same belief.

The liver ... rich in blood.

The blood, a compound of all the elements in (more or less) equal proportions

(Simplicius, *Commentary on Aristotle's Physics* 32.3 = DK 31B98) is then distributed through the blood vessels (Soranus, *Gynaec.* I.57.42.12 Ilb. DK 31A79) and assimilated by the body by a process of 'like to like' (Aëtius V.27.1 DK 31A77). Empedocles apparently considered flesh to be a thickening and secondary formation of the blood since both are composed essentially according to the same formula (cf. B98 last line and Aëtius V.22.1 DK 31A78) – although, presumably, blood would contain a somewhat larger proportion of water than flesh. This theory that the blood served as the agent of nutrition has been well described as 'one of the fundamental discoveries of ancient physiology' and the general theory of digestion/nutrition which assigned a haematopoeic function to the liver subsequently became the most widely accepted theory of digestion in European medicine until the seventeenth century AD.

Seminal theory

Unfortunately no direct evidence of Empedocles's views on the nature of the semen has survived; but there can be no doubt that he, no less than other contemporary Presocratic thinkers, was deeply interested in this matter (see Aristotle, *Generation of animals* 747a34 DK 31B92).

VI.10. Aristotle, *On the soul* 405b1ff. (DK 31A4)

In the following passage Aristotle represents Hippon delivering a polemic against the view that the soul is blood and seeking to refute this view by pointing out that the soul or life principle is transmitted with the semen.

Some of the commoner intellects like Hippon have declared the soul to be water. They seem to have been persuaded by the fact that the seed of all animals is moist. For he seeks to confute those who say that the soul is blood on the ground that the seed is not blood.

The theory under attack here is almost certainly that of Empedocles (see Longrigg, 1993, p. 76). Since Empedocles believed that mother's milk [see **VI.7**] as well as tears and sweat were similarly formed (Aëtius V.22.1 and Plutarch *Natural questions* 20.2 p. 917A DK 31A78), it seems likely that he held a similar view regarding the nature and formation of semen and considered it a form of blood.

VI.11. Aristotle, *History of animals* 512b1ff. (DK 64B6)

The above seminal theory, when further elaborated by Diogenes of Apollonia, became the dominant view in later Greek biology. At the end of a long fragment preserved here by Aristotle, Diogenes describes the spermatic veins and then, after declaring that the thickest blood is consumed by the fleshy parts, maintains that the surplus blood passes into these veins and then becomes fine and warm and foamlike.

<Diogenes holds that> there is also another pair of veins, delicate ones, running from each of these <i.e. the splenetic vein and the hepatic vein> through the spinal marrow to the testicles. Another pair, running beneath the skin through the flesh to the kidneys, terminate with men at the testicles and with women at the womb .... These are called the spermatic

veins. The thickest blood is imbibed by the fleshy parts; when it passes beyond into these regions it becomes thin, warm and foamlike.

VI.12. Clement, *The teacher* I.6.48 (DK 64A24)

The role of the innate heat in the production of semen.

Certain thinkers also suggest that the seed of living creatures is essentially foam of the blood, which, on being agitated and stirred up during intercourse by the innate heat of the male, is turned into foam and deposited in the spermatic veins. Thence Diogenes of Apollonia wished sexual intercourse to be called 'aphrodisial'.

VI.13. [Vindicianus], *On the seed* 3 (DK 64B6 = Wellmann, 1901, p. 210)

The role played by the *pneuma*.

Diogenes the Apolloniate said in his book on physics that the essence of the semen is like the foam of the blood; for the breath drawn in by respiration keeps the blood in suspense (?), one part of which is imbibed by the flesh, another overflows into the seminal vessels and produces semen which is nothing other than the foam of the blood agitated by the breath.

From the above evidence it can be seen that Diogenes not only shares with Empedocles the theory of the innate heat but also, like him, believes that blood is the vehicle of nutrition and that the semen is surplus nutriment, i.e. blood – but blood which has become 'like foam' through an admixture of air. It seems that Diogenes here has modified the Empedoclean theory that the soul is blood in order to meet Hippon's criticism that the soul cannot be blood because the semen, which transmits the soul or life-principle, is not blood. This view that the semen was a modification of surplus nutriment, i.e. blood that, when 'concocted' by the superior heat of the male and mixed with *pneuma*, took on its characteristic white, foam-like appearance, was to prove highly influential in the history of biology. It was adopted by Aristotle [see **VI.32-4**], who even made the same appeal to etymology as Diogenes. It was subsequently adopted by the Alexandrians [see **VI.45**]. It was taken over by the Stoics (*SVF* 128) and Galen later subscribed to it (*On the seed* 1 & 2 *passim* (IV.512-651K) [see **VI.34**]).

PHILISTION OF LOCRI

Although a native of Locri in southern Italy, Philistion was called 'the Sicilian' because of the medical views he adopts. Empedoclean influence is plainly apparent in his adoption of the four elements as the basis for his own medical theory [**VI.16**].

Date of Philistion's medical activity

VI.14. Diogenes Laërtius VIII.86 (= *Philistion* Fr. 3 Wellmann, 1901)

Diogenes records here the tradition that he was a teacher of Eudoxus.

Eudoxus of Cnidus ... learned geometry from Archytas and medicine from Philistion, the Sicilian, as Callimachus says in his *Catalogues* ....

VI.15. Ps.-Plato, *Second Letter* 314D (*Philistion* Fr. 2 Wellmann, 1901)

Although this letter is of doubtful authenticity, the implication that Philistion served as medical adviser to Dionysius might nevertheless be correct.

Do you <i.e. Dionysius II> still need Philistion? If so, by all means keep him; but if not, send him here and let Speusippus have his services. Speusippus joins me in this request; and Philistion also promised me that if you release him he would be eager to come to Athens.

The comic poet Epicrates, while poking fun at the Platonic method of diairesis, mentions 'a certain doctor from the land of Sicily' taking part in the process (Athenaeus 2, 59ff.) – which makes one wonder whether Philistion fulfilled the desire ascribed to him in the Second Letter and visited Athens.

Composition of the body and theory of health and respiration

VI.16. *Anonymus Londinensis* 20.25-50 (Jones, 1947, p. 80)

Philistion adopts the four element theory as the basis of his medical theory but identifies each element with one of the four opposites, hot, cold, wet or dry. Like Empedocles he believes that diseases are caused whenever one or other of these elements becomes predominant.

Philistion of Locri thinks that we are composed of four 'forms', that is of four elements – fire, air, water, earth. Each of these, too, has its own power; of fire the power is the hot, of air it is the cold, of water the moist, and of earth the dry. According to him diseases come into being in many ways, but speaking more generally and in outline it is possible to speak of a threefold causation: (1) because of the elements; (2) because of the condition of our bodies; (3) because of external causes. Diseases are caused by the elements when the hot and moist are in excess, or when the hot becomes less and weak. They arise through three types of external causes: (1) by wounds and sores; (2) by excess of heat, cold and the like, or change from heat to cold or cold to heat; (3) by change of nutriment to what is unsuitable or destructive. Diseases are caused by the condition of the body in the following way. 'When', he says, 'the whole body breathes well and the breath passes through without hindrance, health ensues. For breathing takes place not only through the mouth and nostrils, but also throughout the whole body.[1] When the body does not breathe well, diseases ensue, and in different ways. For, when breathing is checked throughout the whole body, a disease ....'

---

[1] This theory that breathing takes place not only by way of the mouth and

nostrils, but also over all the body, has been widely believed to be a direct borrowing from Empedocles. Recently, however, this traditional interpretation of Empedocles's famous fragment (Fr. 100, see **VI.6**) has been challenged and the belief that Empedocles is here committed to a theory of respiration through pores in the skin has been rejected. Both Philistion and Plato, who are in other respects demonstrably influenced by Empedocles, believe that respiration took place through the skin and thus offer some support to the traditional interpretation. Yet it is hard to accept that Aristotle, who otherwise makes no mention of skin-breathing in his discussion of Empedocles's theory, could have been mistaken in translating the ambiguous *rhinôn* as 'nostrils' rather than 'skin' and that Empedocles could have failed to mention the nostrils in an account of mammalian respiration (see, especially, O'Brien, 1970, pp. 140-79).

VI.17. Galen, *On the use of respiration* 1 (IV.471K = *Philistion* Fr. 6 and *Diokles* Fr. 15 Wellmann, 1901)

Like Empedocles, Philistion seems to have held that the purpose of respiration is to cool the innate heat.

What is the important benefit provided for us by respiration? Is it generation of the soul itself, as Asclepiades says? Or, not generation, but a sort of strengthening of the soul, as Praxagoras ... says? Or is it a sort of cooling of the innate heat, as Philistion and Diocles held?

PLATO

It seems likely that it was through Philistion that Plato became so deeply influenced by 'Sicilian' medicine.

Composition of the body: theory of health

VI.18. Plato, *Timaeus* 81E-82A

Plato, too, adopts the four element theory and, like Empedocles, accounts for disease upon the basis of the excess or deficiency of the elements.

The origin of diseases is, I suppose, plain to all. There are four forms from which the body is composed, earth, fire, water, air, and disorders and diseases arise from the unnatural excess or deficiency of these, or from their displacement from their proper place to an alien one; and, furthermore, since there happen to be more than one variety of fire and the other elements, the reception by the body of an inappropriate variety of one of them and all similar irregularities produces disorders and diseases.

VI.19. Plato, *Timaeus* 82B-E

Composition of the bodily parts and the causes of disease. A second and more serious category of disease is caused when the formation of secondary substances is reversed. The brief allusion to the basic triangles reveals that Plato's account of the diseases of the tissues is based upon his geometrical atomism.

Again, as there are secondary formations in nature, there is a second category of diseases to be noted by one who is minded to understand them. Since marrow, bone, flesh, and sinew are composed of the elements – and blood also is formed of these bodies, though in a different way – most of the other diseases arise in the same manner as those previously described; but the most severe of them have dangerous results in this way: whenever the process of formation of these secondary substances is reversed, then they are corrupted. In the natural course of events, flesh and sinews arise from blood – sinew from the fibrin to which it is akin, flesh from the coagulation of what is left when the fibrin is removed. Furthermore, the viscous, oily substance that comes from the sinews and the flesh, not only glues the flesh to the structure of the bones, but also nourishes the growth of the bone itself around the marrow; while at the same time the purest part, consisting of triangles of the smoothest and oiliest sort, filtering through the close texture of the bones, from which it distils in drops, waters the marrow. When the process takes place in this order, the normal result is health.

Seat of the intellect

Plato, however, departs from the 'Sicilian' tradition and follows Alcmaeon in making the brain, rather than the heart, the seat of intellect.

VI.20. Plato, *Timaeus* 73C-D

Here Plato locates the highest and intellectual part of the soul in the head.

And that portion of the marrow that was destined to receive into itself, as if into plough-land, the divine seed, he <i.e. the Demiourgos> moulded into a perfect sphere and named it 'brain' (*enkephalos*)[1] with the intention that, when each living creature had been completed, the vessel containing it would become the head (*kephalos*).

[1] Plato here calls the brain *enkephalos* to signify that it would be contained in the head (*en kephalô*). Given the scale of the influence of 'Sicilian' medicine upon the *Timaeus,* Plato must have had very compelling reasons for departing from the belief in the primacy of the heart. In this passage the immortal part of the soul is located in the brain-marrow in the head, which is then, to avoid pollution, physically separated from the mortal parts of the soul by the neck, deliberately interposed to keep them apart. Having thus provided for the physical separation of the highest and intellectual part of the soul, Plato evidently felt under no less an obligation to separate it from the lower functions physiologically as well. Empedocles believed that the soul was blood, and in his system blood also serves as the seat and agent of thought. But, in addition to believing the soul to be blood and blood around the heart to be the seat of intellectual activity, Empedocles also believed that the blood served as the agent of nutrition. This latter belief was subsequently adopted by Plato. Having done so, he evidently could not then accept that the one substance (blood) could serve as the agent for two very diverse functions – that of transmitting (via the semen – itself a residue of the blood) the

immortal element of the soul, and, at the same time, of catering to the appetites by serving as the agent of nutrition. Accordingly, he distanced himself from the view that the semen is blood, and adopted instead the theory of Alcmaeon and others that the semen is brain-substance and, like Alcmaeon, located the seat of the intellect in the head.

Respiration

VI.21. Plato, *Timaeus* 70C-D

Plato, too, believes that respiration is for cooling purposes.

<The younger gods[1]>, then, forseeing that all such passion would come about by means of fire, devised support for the heart in the structure of the lung, making it soft and bloodless, perforated by cavities like a sponge, so that by absorbing breath and drink,[2] and cooling by respiration, it might also provide relief in the heat of passion. For this reason they cut air-channels to the lung and set it around the heart as a cushion, so that when passion was at its height, the heart might beat against a yielding body, be cooled down and, being less distressed, might be able to aid the spirited element in the service of reason.

[1] i.e. the offspring of the Demiurge who are entrusted with this task.
[2] This view that some part of what is drunk goes to the lungs was widely held in antiquity.

VI.22. Plato, *Timaeus* 79A-E

The rhythmical movement of respiration is maintained mechanically by the principle of 'circular thrust' (later called *periôsis* or *antiperistasis* by Aristotle and others). Since there is no empty space, on exhalation the expelled breath dislodges the neighbouring air, which successively displaces its own neighbours and, under this transmitted compulsion, a current of air is driven round and enters the body through the pores of the flesh. The initial cause of this impulse is the internal fire which has its own tendency to move upwards to its like.

Let us consider again the process of respiration and the causes by which it has come to be such as it is now. It is as follows. Since there is no void into which any of the moving particles could enter, and the breath moves outward from us, what follows is plain to everyone: the breath does not enter a void, but pushes the neighbouring air from its place. The air displaced keeps on successively displacing its neighbour and everything by this law of necessity comes round to the place from whence the breath came forth, and enters in there, and following the breath, fills up the vacant place. All this happens simultaneously like a rotating wheel because no void exists. Consequently the chest and lung, when they let out the breath are filled again by the air surrounding the body, which filters in through the pores of the flesh and is driven around again, the air which is driven away and passes out through the body pushes the breath around inwards through the passages of the mouth and nostrils. We must suppose the reason for the commencement of this process to be as follows. In every living creature the inner parts about the blood and veins are the hottest .... We must agree that heat naturally moves outwards towards to its own place and to its kindred element and, as there are two outlets, the one through the body, and the other through the mouth and the nostrils, when it moves towards the one, it drives round the air at the other, and the air that is driven around falls into the fire and becomes warm, whereas the air that passes out is cooled. But when the heat changes and the air particles at the other exit grow warmer, the hotter air inclining in that direction and carried towards its native element, fire, pushes around the air at the other. The air being affected and reacting constantly in the same way, thus sets up by both impulses a circular motion oscillating now this way now that and brings about inhalation and exhalation.

Plato's account is somewhat obscure because it is not explicitly stated that the air must go out by the same way that it entered.

VI.23. Aristotle, *On respiration* 472b13ff.

The process is more clearly described by Aristotle:

<Plato> says that when the heat passes out through the mouth, it pushes the surrounding air which is carried around and enters through the porous parts of the flesh into the same place whence the internal heat passed out, making reciprocal replacement because no void can exist. When the air has become hot it passes out again *by the same route* and pushes back inwards through the mouth the expelled hot air. We continue to do this unceasingly, inhaling and exhaling.

Thus the process, as Galen remarks in *On the doctrines of Plato and Hippocrates* 8. 8 (V.711K), comprises a series of half-turns in contrary directions, corresponding to the rhythmical reversal of the currents of air.

Digestion

VI.24. Plato, *Timaeus* 80D-E

Plato adopts the theory that the blood is the agent of nutrition.

The fire cuts up the food and rises inside the body following the breath. As it rises with the breath, it fills the veins from the belly by pumping into them from thence the cut-up particles of food. And because of this in all living creatures the streams of nutriment have come into being flowing throughout the whole body. These nutritive particles, being freshly cut and coming from kindred substances – some from fruits, some from cereals, which the god planted for us for this very purpose, to serve as food – have all sorts of colours because of their mixture; but red is the predominant hue that pervades them, a natural consequence wrought by the cutting of the fire and its imprint upon the liquid. Hence the colour of the stream throughout the body has the appearance we have described; this we call 'blood', which is the nutriment of the flesh and the whole body, whence each part draws water for itself and replenishes the base of the depleted part.

<h2 style="text-align:center">ARISTOTLE</h2>

Aristotle, in his turn, adopts the four element theory, but rejects Plato's geometrical construction of the 'elements'.

The four element theory and the composition of the body

VI.25. Aristotle, *On coming-to-be and passing-away* 330a30-b6.

Aristotle here couples each 'element' with binary combinations of four primary opposites.

The elements <i.e. the elementary opposites> are four in number and of the four there are six pairings.[1] It is not in the nature of contraries to be paired with one another. (It is impossible for one and the same thing to be both hot and cold, or, again, wet and dry.) Obviously the pairings of the elements will be four in number: hot and dry, hot and moist, and, again, cold and dry and cold and moist. They are attached correspondingly to the so-called simple bodies, fire, air, water, and earth. For fire is hot and dry, air hot and moist (for air is something like steam), water cold and moist, and earth cold and dry. Thus the *differentiae* are distributed among the primary bodies in a rational way ....

[1] i.e. from these four basic opposites six couples are mathematically possible.

VI.26. Aristotle, *Parts of animals* 646a8-24

The role of the opposites in the formation of the bodily parts:

The nature and number of the parts of which animals are severally composed are matters which have already been set forth in detail in the *History of animals*. We must now enquire what are the causes that in each case have determined this composition .... There are three degrees of composition; of these the first ... is composition out of the so-called elements, such as earth, air, water and fire. Perhaps, however, it would be more accurate to say composition out of the elementary powers <*dynameis*, i.e. the opposites>; not, indeed, out of all of these, but out of a limited number as defined in previous treatises <e.g. **VI.25**>. For moist and dry, hot and cold form the material of all compound bodies; and all other differences are secondary to these, viz. heaviness or lightness, density or rarity, roughness or smoothness .... The second degree of composition is that by which the homogeneous parts of animals, such as bone, flesh, and the like, are constituted out of the primary substances. The third and final stage is the composition which forms the hetero-geneous parts, such as a face, a hand, etc.

Although Aristotle brought elements and opposites into harmony and developed an ingenious scheme for the mutual interchange of the elements (see *On coming-to-be and passing-away* 331a25ff.), surprisingly he does not employ this new system in his biological works but uses instead a correlation of elements and opposites identical to that expounded by Philistion **[VI.16]** and subsequently adapted by Diocles **[VI.35]**. Fire is hot, water wet, earth dry and, most remarkably, air is cold (not hot and moist). Not even the schematic requirements of his physics are allowed by Aristotle to supersede this fundamental tenet of 'Sicilian' medicine that air is cold.

The seat of the intellect

VI.27. Aristotle, *Motion of animals* 703a13ff.

Aristotle subscribes to the view that the heart is the seat of the intellect.

Since the origin of motion is in some animals situated in the heart, ... it is clear for this reason that the innate *pneuma* also is situated there.

Respiration

VI.28. Aristotle, *On respiration* 475b16ff.

Aristotle holds that respiration serves to cool the innate heat.

As for those animals with blood and a heart, all that have a lung admit the air and effect cooling through breathing in and out.

VI.29. Aristotle, *Parts of animals* 668b33ff.

The lungs perform this cooling function. Aristotle here rejects Plato's suggestion that one of their functions is to cushion the throbbing heart.

The reason why any group of living-creatures possesses a lung is because they are land-animals. It is necessary for there to be a means of cooling the heat of the body; sanguineous animals need cooling from outside because they are very hot. ... The organ of respiration is the lung. It has its source of motion from the heart and it offers wide space for the entrance of the breath because it is large and spongy. When the lung rises up, the breath rushes in, and when it contracts, the breath goes out again. (The theory that the lung cushions the throbbing of the heart is not correct.)

VI. 'Sicilian' medicine and its influence

Digestion and nutrition

VI.30. Aristotle, *Parts of animals* 650a3ff.

Digestion is effected through the agency of the innate heat.

Everything that grows must of necessity take food. For all of them their nourishment comes from the wet and the dry <i.e. from solids and liquids> and the digestion and transformation of these is effected by the agency of heat. Therefore, if for no other reason, all animals and plants must possess in themselves a natural source of heat ....

VI.31. Aristotle, *Generation of animals* 743a4ff.

The blood is the vehicle of nutrition.

The formation of the uniform parts takes place through cooling and heating for some things are compounded and solidified by cold and some by heat .... The nourishment oozes through the veins and channels in the various parts, just as water does in unfired earthenware, and there comes into being flesh or its counterpart, compounded by the cold and consequently dissolved by fire. The excessively earthy parts of the nourishment as it rises up, having little moisture and heat, become cooled and, as the fluid evaporates along with the heat, become hard and earthy in appearance, for example, nails, horns, hooves, and beaks .... Sinews and bones are formed by the internal heat as the moisture dries up.

Seminal theory

VI.32. Aristotle, *Generation of animals* 726b1-12

The semen is a residue of blood.

It has been said previously that the final form of nutriment for sanguineous animals is the blood, or its analogy for the non-sanguineous. Since the semen is both a residue of nutriment and of nutriment in its final form, it must be either blood, or an analogue of blood, or something compounded of these two. And since it is from concocted blood divided in a certain manner that each of the parts comes into being, the concocted semen is distinguished to a higher degree from the blood, whereas that which is not concocted has come forth bloody before now in the case of those who strain themselves by indulging too frequently in sexual intercourse, it is clear that the semen must be a residue of sanguineous nutriment, which in its final form is distributed among the parts of the body. And on account of this it possesses great power. For the evacuation of pure healthy blood is enfeebling.

VI.33. Aristotle, *Generation of animals* 735b32ff.

The role of the innate heat in seminal production.

... the semen comes out of the body thick and white; it contains much warm air because of the internal heat of the animal; but once it has come out, when the warmth has dissipated and the air is cooled, it becomes moist and dark.

VI.34. Aristotle, *Generation of animals* 736a13ff.

The effect of the *pneuma*. Here Aristotle makes an identical appeal to etymology to that previously employed by Diogenes [see **VI.11-13**].

The reason for the semen's whiteness is that the semen is foam, and foam is white ... it seems that the foamy nature of the semen did not escape the notice of thinkers of old. At any rate, it is from this characteristic of the semen that they have derived the name of the goddess <i.e. Aphrodite> who presides over the union of the sexes.[1]

[1] See, too, Galen, *On the seed* 1 & 2 *passim* (IV.512-651K) and especially IV.531K: 'You <Aristotle> are one of those who have well drawn an analogy between semen and foam, declaring that the latter produces many bubbles, invisible because of their smallness, that coalesce into one. And you do not find fault with the story that Aphrodite was born from foam.'

DIOCLES OF CARYSTUS

It is clear from the surviving fragments that Diocles was greatly influenced by 'Sicilian' medicine.

The four element theory and the composition of the body

VI.35. Galen, *On the method of medicine* 7.3 (X.462K = *Diokles* Fr. 7 Wellmann, 1901, p. 119)

Like Philistion Diocles based his medical theory upon the four element theory and characterised each element with one of the four primary opposites, hot, cold, moist or dry.

Diocles ... and almost all the most famous doctors ... share the same opinion regarding the nature of the body and believe that all other bodies and not least those of animals are a mixture of the hot, the cold, the dry, and the moist.

The seat of the intellect

VI.36. Theodoret V.22.6 (= Aëtius, *On the opinions of the philosophers*, IV.5.6-8. Diels, 1879, p. 391 = *Diokles* Fr. 14 Wellmann, 1901)

The heart is the seat of the intellect.

Empedocles and Aristotle, Diocles[1] and the company of the Stoics chose the heart for the seat of the intellect. Some of these placed it in the ventricle of the heart, others in the blood ....

[1] Reading with Diels (op. cit., p. 204, n. 1): ʽΑριστο<τέλης, Διο>κλῆς' to replace the otherwise unknown ʽΑριστοκλῆς'.

VI.37. [Vindicianus], *On the seed* 41 (= *Diokles* Fr. 14 Wellmann, 1901, who accepts Diels's emendation above)

The theory of *pneuma* is linked with the view that the heart is the seat of the intellect.

The controlling principle of the soul is located in the heart, which through the fineness of the breath is disseminated throughout the whole body.

VI.38. [Vindicianus], *On the seed* 44 (= Wellmann, 1901, p. 234)

Diocles's (?) view on the relation of heart and brain.

Phrenetic passion, he <Diocles?> said, comes about because of the formation of a tumour in the heart which cuts off the blood-supply and normal heat by which the brain supplies perception and intelligence. There are two sides to the brain; one provides intelligence, the other sensation – the one on the right provides sensation, the one on the left, intelligence. Lying beneath the brain is the heart, which is always vigilant, listening and understanding ....

If this information reproduces a genuine belief of Diocles, it would appear from the curious doctrine described above that he was suggesting a compromise theory which, while maintaining the primacy of the heart, also recognised the physiological importance of the brain. The brain supplies the contents of both sensation and intelligence, but it is the heart which hears and understands.

Respiration

For Diocles's belief that respiration serves to cool the innate heat, see Galen, *On the use of respiration* 1 (IV.471K = *Diokles* Fr. 15 = *Philistion* Fr. 6 Wellmann) quoted above **VI.17.**

Digestion

VI.39. Ps.-Soranus, *Medical questions* 61 (= *Diokles* Fr. 22 Wellmann, 1901)

Digestion is a product of putrefaction.

How did Hippocrates and Erasistratus and Diocles ... account for the digestion of food and drink? Hippocrates said that digestion was brought about by the innate heat within us, Erasistratus said that the food was ground down and dissolved, but Diocles held that it became putrefied.

Seminal theory

VI.40. [Vindicianus], *On the seed* 2 (= *Diokles* Fr. 9 Wellmann, 1901)

Semen is a product of nutriment.

But Diocles, the disciple of Hippocrates, in response to all these declarations regarding the nature of the semen said to counter the first of them: since one and the same stuff that descends through certain courses of veins will become in one place phlegm, in another bile (i.e. *cholera rubea*), in another black bile, and in another blood, the semen, too, comes to be from nourishment, i.e. from food and drink, from which the four humours themselves are nourished ....

Although Diocles evidently believed that the semen was a product of nourishment he seems to have rejected the belief that it was the 'foam of the blood' see [Vindicianus], *On the seed* 7 (= *Diokles* Fr. 11 Wellmann, 1901).

PRAXAGORAS OF COS

Praxagoras, too, like Aristotle and Diocles, reveals the continued influence of 'Sicilian' medicine. Elsewhere, however, he reveals independence of thought and rejects some 'Sicilian' theories.

The seat of the intellect

VI.41. Galen, *On the doctrines of Hippocrates and Plato* 1.6 (V.187K = *CMG* V.4, 1,2 p. 80 De Lacy = *Praxagoras* Fr. 11 Steckerl)

According to Galen's (anachronistic) assessment here Praxagoras is linked with Aristotle in holding the heart to be the seat of the intellect.

... one might justly censure Aristotle and Praxagoras, who declare, contrary to the evidence, that the heart is the source of the nerves.[1]

[1] The nerves were later discovered by Herophilus.

Tertullian, *On the soul* 15.5 (p. 20 Waszink = *Praxagoras* Fr. 29 Steckerl)

Tertullian links Praxagoras with Empedocles in subscribing to this belief as to the seat of the intellect.

That verse of Orpheus or Empedocles: 'Man's sensation is the blood around the heart' – Praxagoras likewise understands these things ....

VI.43. Athenaeus, *Scholars' banquet* 15.687e (= *Praxagoras* Fr. 30 Steckerl)

Athenaeus links him here with Phylotimus.

... but also because they believed that the soul is situated in the heart, as the doctors Praxagoras and Phylotimus have handed down to us.

The Stoics cite Praxagoras as an authority in support of their belief that the heart is the seat of the intellect (Galen, *On the doctrines of Plato and Aristotle* 1.7 = V.189K = *CMG* V.4,1,2, p. 82 De Lacy = *SVF* II.897).

Respiration

Praxagoras, however, rejects the 'Sicilian' belief that the purpose of respiration is to cool the innate heat and believes that its function is to 'strengthen the soul'. See Galen, *On the use of respiration* 1 (IV.471K = *Diokles* Fr. 15 = *Philistion* Fr. 6 Wellmann = *Praxagoras* Fr. 32 Steckerl) quoted above **VI.17.**

Digestion and nutrition

VI.44. Galen, *On natural faculties* 2.8 (II.117K = *Scripta minora* III, p. 186 Helmreich = *Praxagoras* Fr. 18 Steckerl)

But he does accept the 'Sicilian' belief that digestion is effected by the innate heat and that the nutriment is blood.

These men <i.e. Hippocrates, Aristotle, Praxagoras, Phylotimus and many others> have pointed out that, when the nutriment is altered in the veins by the innate heat, blood is produced when the heat is in moderation, but the other humours when it is disproportionate.

The continued influence of 'Sicilian' medicine can be traced to Hellenistic times and beyond.

THE ALEXANDRIANS: HEROPHILUS AND ERASISTRATUS

The most striking evidence of the influence of 'Sicilian' medicine upon the Alexandrians may be seen in the seminal theory adopted by them.

Seminal theory

VI.45. [Vindicianus], *On the seed* 1 (Wellmann, 1901, p. 208 = (in part)
Herophilus Fr. 104 von Staden)

The Alexandrians, too, subscribe to the belief that the semen, like mother's milk, is a form of blood.

Alexander Philalethes, a pupil of Asclepiades, says in the first book of his treatise, *On the seed*, that the essence of semen is the foam of the blood in agreement with the opinion of Diogenes. Erasistratus and Herophilus likewise say that the essence of semen is blood. The Stoic philosophers were of the same opinion ... First, then, as Herophilus says the severance of bodies, which the Greeks call 'dissection' (*anatomê*) testifies to this. For, whereas the interior parts of the seminal vessels more remote from the genitals are seen to be blood-red ... those lower down and nearest to the genitals have the colour of semen. This proves that the blood enters into the seminal vessels but, by virtue of these vessels, becomes white and, having been changed, is transformed into the quality of semen. Just as in the case of females, too, after childbirth, if any blood has not yet been consumed in nourishing the uterus, it flows by a natural course into the breasts and, by virtue of these organs, it turns white and acquires the quality of milk.

*

Herodotus preserves our earliest evidence of medical activity in Magna Graecia, the Greek city states of Southern Italy and Sicily. In his tale of the adventures of Democedes and the latter's successful treatment of the Persian king, Darius and his queen, Atossa [see **XV.7 & 8**], he informs us that the physicians of Croton were at this time considered to be the best in Greece **[VI.1]**. According to Herodotus, Democedes's success enhanced the reputation of the Crotoniate doctors. This reputation was later further enhanced by the work of another citizen of this town, Alcmaeon, one of the great pioneers of rational medicine, whose theories and influence are described above **[Chapter III]**. However, it was at Acragas in Sicily that the most influential ideas in Western Greek medicine were formulated – by Empedocles, whose claims to fame as a doctor **[III.11 & 12]** are supported by references to him in later medical works. Although Empedocles has been described as the 'founder of the Sicilian school of medicine' and it has even been claimed that Galen actually made Empedocles the founder of the 'Italian school of medicine', neither Galen **[VI.2]** nor any other ancient authority expressly states this. While certain of his medical and physiological theories were clearly influential in Magna Graecia, it must remain extremely doubtful that he founded a school in the strict sense. Accordingly, it seems preferable to speak of 'Sicilian medicine' rather than of a 'Sicilian school of medicine'.

Certain of the theories characteristic of 'Sicilian' medicine were to prove highly influential in the history of medicine and can be traced from Empedocles to the fourth century BC when they were adopted by such important thinkers as Philistion of Locri, Plato, Aristotle, Diocles of Carystus, and Praxagoras. Subsequently some of them were adopted by the Alexandrians and by Galen and their influence can be traced until as late as the seventeenth century AD. Among these doctrines might be mentioned the theory that the human body is composed of the four elements earth, air, fire, and water and that the predominance of any one of them results in deviations from health, sanity and wisdom;[1] that the heart is the central organ of sensation and seat of the intelligence; the concept of innate heat as the prime agent of embryological, digestive and other physiological processes; the belief in the cooling function of respiration; the idea that blood serves as the vehicle of nutrition and is manufactured in the liver and the notion that the semen, like milk, is a form of surplus nutriment. (Not all of these theories, of course, were adopted, each and every one, by those named above.)

Although Philistion was a native of Locri in southern Italy, he was called 'the Sicilian' because of the medical views he adopts. Empedoclean influence is plainly apparent in his adoption of the four elements as the basis for his own medical theory [VI.16]. However, in identifying each element with one of the four opposites, hot, cold, wet, or dry, he evolves a more effective correlation of elements and opposites and parts company in this respect, at any rate, with the element theory as it is revealed in the surviving fragments of Empedocles's poem *On nature*. In other respects he reveals a closer allegiance to Empedocles; for example, in his belief that diseases are caused whenever one or other of the elements becomes predominant; in his belief in the concept of innate heat and his view that the purpose of respiration is to cool the innate heat [VI.17]. His theory that breathing 'takes place not only by way of the mouth and nostrils, but also over all the body' [VI.16] has also been widely believed to be a borrowing from Empedocles. But, as was seen above, this traditional interpretation of Empedocles's famous fragment (B100) [VI.6] has been challenged and the belief that the latter subscribed to a theory involving breathing through pores in the skin has been rejected.

It is unfortunate that no unimpeachable testimony as to the time of Philistion's medical activity has survived. However, we learn from Diogenes Laërtius [VI.14], on the authority of Callimachus, that Eudoxus learned medicine from him and in the Second Letter, purportedly written by Plato to Dionysius II, tyrant of Syracuse, the former requests that Philistion should be allowed to come to Athens [VI.15]. This letter is of dubious authenticity, yet its implication that Philistion served as a medical adviser to Dionysius might be true notwithstanding and would thereby establish Plato's acquaintance with him. At the very least, it entails that its author thought that Philistion was alive at this time.

Plato first visited Magna Graecia when he was almost forty (i.e. *c.* 387 BC). He subsequently visited Sicily on two further occasions, in 367 and again in 362, in the hope of converting the younger Dionysius to philosophical principles of government. It seems likely that it was through Philistion that he became so deeply influenced by 'Sicilian' medicine. This influence is most clearly apparent in his cosmological dialogue, the *Timaeus* which includes a description of the structure and functions of the human body together with an account of the diseases to which it is prone. Although Plato adopts the four element theory as the basis of this structure, he contends that far from being original principles, elements (*stoicheia*, i.e. 'letters', as it were, of the universe), they should not be ranked even as low as syllables (48B). Since he conceives the world to be the result of a divine plan, the 'elements', too, he argues must have a rational structure, which he finds in two basic geometrical shapes, the right-angled isosceles and the right-angled scalene triangles.

Aristotle's father, Nicomachus, was a member of the guild of the Asclepiadae and traced his descent from his namesake, the son of Machaon and grandson of Asclepius. He became court physician and friend to Amyntas III, King of Macedon, the grandfather of Alexander the Great. His mother was also a member of an Asclepiad family. However, Aristotle did not follow the hereditary calling of his family, but instead entered the Academy in his eighteenth year. There is no doubt, however, that he retained his family's interest in anatomy and medicine. Diogenes Laërtius (5.25) lists two separate works by him on anatomy, and Aristotle himself refers on about twenty occasions to a work entitled *Anatomai*, 'Dissections', in seven books, which was apparently an illustrated handbook with a zoological commentary. Diogenes also mentions a treatise on medicine in two books and in addition it has been claimed that the few lines at the end of the *Parva naturalia* (*On respiration* 480b22-30) which preserve Aristotle's attitude towards medicine are survivors from a separate, but no longer extant, treatise entitled *On health and disease*. Although Aristotle chose not to follow in his father's footsteps, medicine was accorded an important place among the subjects studied within the Lyceum. A history of medicine was compiled by the Peripatetic, Meno, as a counterpart to the histories of philosophy, geometry, astronomy, and theology written as part of the systematisation of knowledge undertaken by the Lyceum. As a result of this activity, medicine, like other emergent sciences, became increasingly less an integral part of natural philosophy, although philosophical influences continued to play a powerful role in its development.

Aristotle's biological and zoological works reveal a keen interest in empirical phenomena and are impressive for their close and detailed observations. Although his attitude in this particular respect is vastly different from that of Plato, he is nevertheless fundamentally in agreement with him in his general attitude towards medicine. For, like Plato, he is firmly committed to the belief that the first principles of medicine should be derived from general philosophical principles (*On sensation* 436a19ff. See, too, *On respiration*, loc. cit. above). Again like Plato, Aristotle adopts the four element theory as the basis of his physics. He rejects totally, however, the latter's geometrical construction of the elements and instead correlates them with binary combinations of the four traditional opposites, the hot, cold, wet, and dry **[VI.25]**, in a manner which displays close affinities with the roles assigned to these opposites in certain Hippocratic treatises and which prompts the reflection that one may not be unjustified in seeing here an important influence, in its turn, of medicine upon philosophy.[2]

Diocles of Carystus was clearly held in the highest regard as a doctor. Pliny, for example, describes him as 'second in time and fame to Hippocrates' (*NH* 26.10 = *Diokles* Fr. 5 Wellmann) and [Vindicianus] tells us that the Athenians called him a 'younger Hippocrates' (Ch. 2 = *Diokles* Fr. 2 Wellmann). There has been, and continues to be, considerable debate concerning the date of Diocles's medical activity. It is clear from the surviving fragments that he was greatly influenced by 'Sicilian' medicine. For example, like Philistion, he based his medical theory upon the four element theory and characterised each element with one of the four traditional opposites, hot, cold, moist or dry **[VI.35]**; he believed that respiration took place not only through the nose and mouth, but also through the pores of the skin, and that its purpose was to cool the innate heat **[VI.17]**; he held that the heart was the seat of the intellect **[VI.36-38]**; he believed that digestion was effected by a process akin to putrefaction **[VI.39]**; and other parallels can be drawn between these two thinkers' views on embryology and menstruation. In other respects, however, Diocles reveals the influence of Hippocratic medicine.

VI. 'Sicilian' medicine and its influence

Because of these 'Sicilian' influences it was originally assumed that Diocles was a contemporary of Philistion and that both were contemporaries of Plato's earlier years and active in the first third of the fourth century BC. Jaeger, however, persuaded by coincidences of thought and language he detected between the fragments of Diocles and Aristotle's own philosophical theories and formulations, challenged this hitherto widely accepted view. Maintaining that Diocles's style reflected the philosophical terminology of Aristotle, he concluded that Diocles must have flourished when the Peripatetic school was at its height, i.e. about the end of the fourth century BC.[3] While not all scholars are prepared to accept this assessment, the general consensus among scholars is that Diocles was a contemporary of Aristotle and was associated with the Lyceum.

Galen informs us that Diocles was the first, to his knowledge, to write a special treatise on (animal) anatomy (*On anatomical procedures* 2.1 (II.282K = *Diokles* Fr. 23 Wellmann). Thus Diocles may well have played an influential role in the development of anatomy in the Lyceum. It is unfortunately impossible to reconstruct Diocles's views on the anatomy of the heart with any certainty since our evidence is meagre, controversial and has patently been subjected to doxographical distortion, However, if we accept Diels's emendation of a passage on Theodoret **[VI.36]** and make allowance for Stoic contamination, then Diocles would appear to have assigned the seat of intellectual activity to the heart like 'Empedocles, Aristotle and the Stoic sect'. (In similar manner, Diels emended a second reading in Aëtius and substituted 'Diocles' for 'Diogenes' in a passage where the subject is said to have located the 'governing principle' (*hêgemonikon*) in the 'arterial' i.e. pneumatic cavity of the heart (the left ventricle) **[XIV.12]**.

In physiology, too, Diocles, influenced by 'Sicilian' medicine, seems to have played a leading role in the important and influential developments that took place in the Lyceum. While his indebtedness to Philistion and 'Sicilian' medicine is pronounced, it is clear that he has developed his physiological theories beyond what he adopted from Philistion and has integrated Hippocratic elements into his 'Sicilian' legacy to form a more comprehensive and integrated synthesis than that achieved by Aristotle. He based his physiology upon the same four opposites that Philistion had previously linked with the four elements. Like Empedocles, he is said to have held that the digestive process was a form of corruption (*sêpsis*) brought about by the action of the innate heat contained within the stomach **[VI.39]**. Blood, he believed, was the normal result of this process. However, when the heat was excessive, bile was produced; when deficient, phlegm was the result. In this way the four element theory was brought into conformity with the theory of the four humours. Like Philistion and Plato, Diocles held that diseases were caused by an imbalance of the elements **[IX.13]**. He also shared with them the belief that some diseases occur whenever the passage of the *pneuma* through the pores in the skin is impeded due to the influence of bile and phlegm upon the blood in the veins [see **Chapter IX**]. His belief that the semen is derived from nutriment **[VI.40]** also reveals 'Sicilian' influence.

Praxagoras, too, like Aristotle and Diocles, reveals the continued influence of 'Sicilian' medicine. He held, for example, that the heart was the seat of the intellect **[VI.41-43]** and believed that digestion was effected by the transformation of nutriment into blood by a process brought about by the action of the innate heat **[VI.44]**. The immediate influence of Diocles may be seen here since other views are held in common. Elsewhere, however, Praxagoras reveals independence of thought and rejects 'Sicilian' influence. Compare, for example, his belief that the purpose of respiration is not to cool the innate heat, but rather to provide nourishment for the psychic *pneuma* **[VI.17]**. The most striking influence of 'Sicilian' theory upon the two great Alexandrians may be seen in their view of the nature of the semen **[VI.45]**.

[1] This belief can be traced back ultimately to Alcmaeon of Croton: see **III.2**.

[2] See Longrigg, 1993, Appendix, pp. 220ff.

[3] Jaeger's findings have recently been submitted to detailed critical examination by von Staden, 1992a, pp. 227-65.

VII

Early Alexandrian medical science

In the third century BC Greek Rational Medicine was transported to Egypt and levels of sophistication in the knowledge of human anatomy were attained at Alexandria that remained unsurpassed until the Renaissance. Some scholars have seen this advance as directly due to knowledge derived from native Egyptian burial rites.

DISSECTION AND VIVISECTION

Egyptian mummification

VII.1. Herodotus, *Histories* 2.86-7

As can be seen from this passage, the practice of the Egyptian mummifiers can hardly have contributed directly to the sophisticated anatomical descriptions of the Alexandrians. Even the most expensive method of embalming involved dragging the brain out through the nostrils with an iron hook, while less costly techniques used cedar oil in order to dissolve the stomach and intestines.

First the embalmers draw out parts of the brain through the nostrils with an iron hook and inject drugs into the rest .... Those wishing to avoid expense by choosing the second process are prepared in the following way. The embalmers charge their syringes with cedar oil and fill the belly of the corpse with it, without any incision or disembowelling, but injecting the drench and stopping its return. Then they embalm the body for the prescribed number of days. On the last day they let out from the belly the oil which they had injected previously. So great is its power that it brings out with it the stomach and the intestines in a state of dissolution. The natrum meanwhile has dissolved the flesh and nothing is left of the corpse save skin and bones.

It seems more likely, then, that the influence of embalming contributed more indirectly to the development of anatomical research at Alexandria in that it helped medical researchers working there to rid themselves of the inhibitions investing the dissection of the human body that were still in vogue at the time in mainland Greece.

Human dissection and vivisection at Alexandria

The charge of vivisection has aroused considerable controversy, but positive statements of the Roman encyclopaedist, Cornelius Celsus **[VII.2 & 4]**, and the

Christian writer, Tertullian **[VII.5]**, attesting to this practice cannot lightly be disregarded.

VII.2. Cornelius Celsus, *On medicine* Proem 23-4 (= *CML* I, p. 21 Marx)

Celsus records that Herophilus and Erasistratus vivisected criminals from the royal gaols.

Moreover, since pains and various kinds of diseases arise in the interior parts, the Dogmatists think that no one can apply remedies for them who is ignorant of the parts themselves. Therefore it is necessary to cut into the bodies of the dead and examine their viscera and intestines. They hold that Herophilus and Erasistratus did this in by far the best way when they cut open live criminals they received out of prison from the kings and, while breath still remained in these bodies, they inspected those parts which nature had previously kept enclosed ....

Vivisection defended

VII.3. Cornelius Celsus, *On medicine* Proem 26 (= *CML* I, p. 21 Marx)

Celsus adds that the Dogmatists defended their standpoint against charges of inhumanity by claiming that the good outweighed the evil:

... nor is it cruel, as most people state, that remedies should be sought for innocent people of all future ages in the execution of criminals, and only a few of them.

Celsus's own view

VII.4. Cornelius Celsus, *On medicine* Proem 74-5 (= *CML* I, p. 29 Marx)

Whereas Celsus approves of dissection, he is hostile to vivisection. His account is restrained and he evidently does not doubt the tradition.

But to cut open the bodies of men while still alive is both cruel and superfluous: to cut open the bodies of the dead is necessary for medical students. For they ought to know the position and arrangement of its parts – which the dead body exhibits better than a wounded living subject. As for the rest, experience will demonstrate it rather more slowly, but much more mildly, in the course of treating the wounded.

Vivisection attacked

VII.5. Tertullian, *On the soul* 10 (Waszink)

Tertullian's evidence is much less restrained and some scholars believe that his total opposition to pagan researchers diminishes the value of his evidence. But it should not be overlooked that Christian polemic is here based upon Methodist doctrine, since Tertullian is reproducing the views of the Methodist doctor, Soranus of Ephesus.

<Herophilus> that doctor, or rather, butcher, who cut up innumerable human beings so that he could investigate nature and who hated mankind for the sake of knowledge. I do not know whether he investigated clearly all the interior parts of the body, since what was formerly alive is altered by death, not a natural death, but one which itself changes during the performance of the dissection.

THE ALEXANDRIANS

Herophilus

The brain and nervous system

Herophilus follows Aristotle (see *History of animals* 495a10ff.) in distinguishing between the cerebrum and the cerebellum and seems to have been the first to distinguish and describe the main ventricles of the brain, assigning great significance in particular to the fourth ventricle. He specified the fourth ventricle of the cerebellum as the seat of the intellect [**VII.6-7**] and aptly compared the cavity in the rear portion of the floor of the fourth ventricle to the cavity in the pens in use at that time in Alexandria [**VII.7** *anaglyphê kalamou*]; the Latin translation of this term, *calamus scriptorius* or *calamus Herophili*, remains in current medical use. The three membranes of the brain were also recognised by Herophilus and described by him as 'chorioid' [**VII.8 & 9**] because he thought that they resembled the chorionic envelope surrounding the foetus. He observed, too, the depression of the occipital bone where the sinuses of the *dura mater* meet and likened it to the trough or reservoir (*lenos*) of a wine-press [**VII.10**]. (The Latin translation, *torcular Herophili*, is also still in contemporary medical use.) His most impressive contribution to anatomy, however, is his discovery of the nervous system. Having discovered the nerves and demonstrated that they originated from the brain, he then distinguished between the sensory and motor nerves [**VII.9**] and traced the optic nerves from brain to eye.

VII.6. Galen, *On the use of the parts* 8.11 (III.665-7K = I, pp. 482-4 Helmreich = *Herophilus* Frs 77a & 78 von Staden)

Galen records some of Herophilus's views on the anatomy of the brain.

Now since all the nerves throughout the body below the head grow either from the cerebellum (*parenkephalis*) or from the spinal marrow, it was necessary for the ventricle of the cerebellum to be of quite a considerable size and get a share of the psychic pneuma which had previously been prepared in the front ventricles. In consequence there had to be some passage from them into it. This ventricle also seems large, but the passage entering into it from the anterior ventricles is also very large indeed. It is through this passage alone that the cerebellum (*parenkephalis*) is connected to the cerebrum (*enkephalos*). For thus Herophilus and his followers are accustomed to call each part of it. The anterior part, on the one hand, was called by this name of the whole (i.e. *enkephalos*) on account of its size. For, being of double form, as has been said, each of its parts is far larger than the whole *parenkephalis*. The posterior part, however, got its name because the anterior part had been the first to appropriate for itself the name of the whole (i.e. *enkephalos*) and it was no longer possible to find a different, more fitting, name for the cerebellum (*parenkephalis*) than the one it now bears. ... Since the cerebrum is separated from the cerebellum, as has also been stated previously, by the fold of the thick membrane (*dura mater*) but needs to be attached – even if only at a single part – for the sake of the formation of the above-mentioned passage – the cerebrum has brought both its ventricles to a termination in one place, which some anatomists count as a fourth ventricle of the entire brain ....

Those who have considered this cavity <i.e. the part of the brain beyond the common cavity or 'chamber'> to be a sort of fourth ventricle, say that it is the most important of all of the ventricles throughout the whole of the brain. But Herophilus seems to suppose that not this ventricle but the one in the cerebellum is the more important.

VII.7. Galen, *On anatomical procedures* 9.5 (II.731K = in part *Herophilus* Fr. 4 von Staden)

Herophilus specifies the fourth ventricle of the cerebellum as the seat of the intellect and compares the cavity in the rear portion of its floor to that in the pens in use at the time in Alexandria.

Next pay attention how, when the vermiform process is bent forwards, the result is that the posterior ventricle of the brain, the fourth, is exposed, and when it is moved the opposite way the greatest portion of the ventricle is covered and only that part is visible which Herophilus likened to the cavity in the pen (*kalamos*) with which we write. It is really so: it has a kind of hollow in the middle like an incision and on either side of it each of the two lateral parts stretches upwards to as great a height as it rises in pens from the middle line. They carve out the pens we write with in this fashion especially at Alexandria. Herophilus lived there so it is likely, I suppose, that when he was dissecting he invented this name influenced by the similarity of the image.

VII.8. Galen, *On anatomical procedures* 9.3 (II.719-20K = *Herophilus* Fr. 124 von Staden)

The chorioid membranes of the brain.

You will also see in the ventricles of the brain what are called the 'chorioid plexuses'. Herophilus and his followers call them 'chorioid coils', clearly calling them with a slight change of name after the membranes (*choria*) which are wrapped round in a circle outside foetuses and are plexuses of veins and arteries held together by thin membranes.

VII.9. Rufus, *On the naming of the parts of man* 149-50 (p. 153
Daremberg/Ruelle = *Herophilus* Fr. 125 von Staden)

Herophilus discovers the nervous system and distinguishes between sensory and motor nerves.

The tunic covering the ventricles of the brain on the inside is chorioid. Herophilus also calls it 'chorioid membrane'. The excrescences from the brain he calls sensory and purposive (i.e. motor) nerves, through which sensory and purposive motion and all bodily action are accomplished.

VII.10. Galen, *On the use of the parts* 9.6 (*CMG* II.19 Helmreich =
Herophilus Fr. 123 von Staden)

The *torcular Herophili.*

At the top of the head the folds of the membrane that conduct the blood unite in a certain common place like a cistern, which for this very reason, it was Herophilus' custom to call a 'wine-vat' (*lênos*). From thence, as from some acropolis, the <sinuses> send forth channels to all the parts lying beneath them.

The vascular system

Although it was the traditional view that the liver was the starting point of the veins, Herophilus cautiously confessed his uncertainty upon this matter **[VII.11]**. He described the 'great vein' (i.e. the portal vein) which grows downwards near the middle of the *dôdekadaktylos ekphysis* (the 'growth of twelve fingers' breadth' i.e. the duodenal process) (Galen, *On anatomical procedures* 6.9, II.572K). Nothing else has survived of his views on the hepatic vascular system. The scattered references in secondary sources are insufficient to enable us to reconstruct all of his views on the structure of the heart, although he had evidently dissected it and seems to have had some knowledge of its valves since Galen regards his description of them to be inadequate compared with the accuracy attained by Erasistratus **[see VII.17]**. His interest in the vascular system, however, was not confined to the heart and his descriptions of the subclavian vein and the carotid arteries as well as other vessels of the head, abdominal cavity, and reproductive organs have survived. Praxagoras had previously differentiated between veins and arteries (see Galen, *On fullness* 11, VII.573K). Taking up this interest of his master, Herophilus drew more precise anatomical distinctions between these vessels and was the first to point out that the coats of the arteries were six times thicker than those of the veins **[VII.12]** and also noted that in dead bodies veins, emptied of blood, collapse, whereas arteries do not.

VII.11. Galen, *On the doctrines of Hippocrates and Plato* 6.5 (= V.543K
= *CMG* V.4,1,2, p. 392 De Lacy = *Herophilus* Fr. 115 von Staden)

Herophilus confesses himself at a loss as to whether the liver is the starting-point of the veins or not.

None of the anatomists, on coming to describe the anatomy of the veins, was able to pass over the liver and postulate a different but appropriate starting-point for his elucidation; but, whether he said he was at a loss regarding a starting-point, as Herophilus did, or that he had clear knowledge on this matter, as many others did, including my master Pelops, nevertheless practically all of them made their elucidation, at least, starting from the liver.

VII.12. Galen, *On the use of the parts* 6.10 (III.445K = I, p. 325 Helmreich = *Herophilus* Fr. 116 von Staden)

Herophilus differentiates between veins and arteries.

Herophilus seems to have estimated correctly when he stated that the artery is six times thicker than the vein.

The liver

Aristotle had recognised the vital significance of the liver (*Parts of animals* 670a23ff.). His description of its anatomy, however, is limited and is based primarily upon comparative anatomy.

VII.13. Oribasius, *Medical collections* 24.25.1-6 (*CMG* VI.2,1 = Vol. III, pp. 36-7 Raeder. Excerpted from Galen, *On anatomical procedures* 6.8 (II.570K = *Herophilus* Fr. 60b von Staden)

Herophilus provides the first accurate and detailed description of the human liver. It is apparent from the passage below that he has dissected a good many livers, both human and animal.

The liver is not the same in all men both with respect to its size and the number of its lobes. At any rate, Herophilus, writing about it most accurately, reports as follows in these very terms: 'The human liver is of good size and larger than that in certain other creatures comparable in size to man. At the point at which it touches the diaphragm, it is convex and smooth. But, where it touches the stomach and the convexity of the stomach, it is concave and irregular. It resembles here a kind of fissure <i.e. the portal fissure> at which point even in embryos the vessel from the navel is rooted in it. The liver is not alike in all creatures, but differs in different animals both in breadth, length, thickness, height, number of lobes and in the irregularity of the frontal part, where it is thickest, and in the relative thinness of its surrounding extremities. In some creatures the liver has no lobes at all, but is entirely round and not differentiated. But in some it has two lobes, in others more and in many even as many as four.' Herophilus, therefore, was right in his account and, besides, he wrote truly in this same second book of his work *On anatomy* that in the case of a few men and not few other creatures the liver occupies a part of the left side. He himself mentioned only the hare, leaving it to us to investigate the other animals also ....

The eye

VII.14A. Rufus, *On the naming of the parts of man* 153 (p. 154 Daremberg/ Ruelle = (in part) *Herophilus* Fr. 89 von Staden)

His careful anatomical researches also enabled Herophilus to make some striking advances in knowledge of the anatomy of the eye. We learn here from Rufus of Ephesus that he recognised that it had four tunics rather than just the three previously recognised [see also **XIV.4**].

Of the tunics of the eye, the first which is visible has been named the 'horn-like' <i.e. the cornea>; of the others, the second is called the 'grape-like' and 'chorioid'; the part lying beneath the 'horn-like' is called the 'grape-like' because it resembles a grape in its external smoothness and internal roughness; the part beneath the white is called 'chorioid' because, being full of veins, it resembles the chorioid <membrane> that encloses the foetus. The third tunic surrounds the 'glass-like' humour <i.e. the vitreous humour>: on account of its fineness its ancient name is 'arachnoid' <i.e. like a spider's web>. But, since Herophilus likens it to a drawn-up casting-net, some also call it 'net-like' <i.e. retiform, hence 'retina' derived from the Latin for 'net'>. Others also call it 'glass-like' from its humour. The fourth tunic encloses the crystalline humour; originally it was without a name, but later it was called 'lentiform' <i.e. like a lentil, hence 'lens' from the Latin> on account of its shape and 'crystalline' because of the humour it contains.

The above passage is frequently cited in histories of science, histories of medicine and histories of ophthalmology as evidence of the high levels attained in knowledge of the anatomy of the eye in the latter part of the first century AD. However, comparison with the following passage reveals that they each preserve independently quite a detailed account of Herophilus's ophthalmology going back ultimately to his treatise *On the eyes*.

VII.14B. Ps.-Rufus, *On the anatomy of the parts of man* 9 (Daremberg/ Ruelle pp. 170ff. = (in part) *Herophilus* Fr. 87 von Staden)

Further information is provided in this work, which was originally believed to have been written by Rufus, but subsequently discovered not to be genuine. The two accounts are essentially in harmony but clearly independent of each other.

There the web of the tunics which compose the eye is as follows: the one positioned in front of all the others is called 'first' by virtue of its position and 'white' because of its colour. The first tunic is called the 'white'. This same tunic is called the 'horn-like' <cornea> whether because of its elasticity or because the adjacent humour within shines through it as though through horn or because, like horn, it is divided into individual layers. The second tunic closely adheres to the first as far as the so-called 'corona' <i.e.

the rim of the cornea where it joins the sclerotic>. It preserves its distance relative to its own middle and has a circular perforation. The perforated body is smooth externally where it joins the cornea, but is rough by reason of the parts on the interior surface, being formed of a tissue of vessels, 'like the skin of a grape', as Herophilus says. It is called the 'second' tunic because of its position, 'perforated' by reason of its constitution, 'grape-like' from its resemblance and 'chorioid' because it is furnished with blood vessels like the chorion. The third tunic arising from the same passage <i.e. the optic nerve> encloses a humour similar to the white of an egg, the so-called 'glass-like' humour <i.e. the vitreous humour>. This tunic is exceedingly fine. It is called 'glass-like' from the coagulation of the humour, 'web-like' from its fineness and 'net-like' <i.e. retiform> on account of the interweaving of the vessels and its shape. For from a narrow beginning it widens and becomes hollow towards the point where it receives the fourth tunic, which surrounds the humour resembling crystal <i.e. the aqueous humour>. One half of this tunic peeps out unbroken at the aperture of the second; the other half is joined to the arachnoid. This tunic, then, is called 'disk-like' and 'lentiform' from its shape, but 'crystalline' from the congelation of the humour. Some anatomists do not think it right to call this a tunic, but say that it is a kind of integument-like coagulation.

The reproductive organs

Herophilus's investigation of the reproductive organs resulted in discoveries which were a considerable advance upon the rather primitive beliefs previously held. (See, for example, **VII.15A** below where Galen records that Aristotle believed that the testicles performed a function similar to that of loom-weights.) It is clear that Herophilus's dissections included human subjects, both male and female. He denied that special pathological conditions appertained to women (except for conception, gestation, parturition and lactation and their opposites) [**XVI.3 & 4**]. He did not, however, completely emancipate himself from the traditional outlook which sought to explain the structure and function of female genitalia by analogy with the male. He believed that both the testes (which he called *didymoi*, 'twins') and the spermatic vessels were responsible for the formation of the semen, which he regarded as a product of the blood [see **VI.45**]. He also distinguished between the various parts of the spermatic duct system. It seems likely that he also identified (and named) the epididymis, the dilations (*ampullae*) of the two *vasa deferentia*, which he called 'varicose assistants' (*parastatai kirsoeideis*), and the two seminal vesicles, which he named 'glandular assistants' (*parastatai adenoeideis*). Rejecting the belief in a two-chambered uterus, he described accurately the uterus [**VII.15B-C**], ovaries and the Fallopian tubes. He also called the ovaries *didymoi* and held that they 'differed only slightly from the testicles of the male'. He likened the 'seminal ducts' (i.e. the Fallopian tubes) to the seminal vessels of the male.

VII.15A. Galen, *On the semen* I.16 (IV.582-3K = *CMG* V.3,1, p. 134
De Lacy = *Herophilus* Fr. 189 von Staden)

The male organs of reproduction.

<The seminal> fluid contained in the epididymis is transferred from the
<testicle> to the epididymis, just as it is transferred from here into the
spermatic vessel. The part of this vessel hard by the stem <of the penis>
Herophilus named 'varicose assistant'. Even Herophilus is mistaken in
that he assigns a greater role in the generation of semen to the seminal
vessel than to the testicles. However, he was not as mistaken as Aristotle
who likened the testicles to loom-weights.

VII.15B. Galen, *On the use of the parts* 14.11 (IV.193K = II, p. 323
Helmreich = *Herophilus* Fr. 109 von Staden)

The female reproductive organs.

The 'horns' <i.e. the Fallopian tubes> go to the vessels from the female's
own 'testicles' <i.e. ovaries> and for this reason they tilt upwards as
though towards the flanks and gradually becoming narrower they termi-
nate in extremely narrow ends, each of which is attached to the 'twin' on
its own side. For such is the name Herophilus gives to the 'testicle'.

VII.15C. Galen, *On dissection of the uterus* 9 (II.900-901K = *CMG*
V.2,1, pp. 48-50 Nickel = *Herophilus* Fr. 107 von Staden)

Besides, the seminal vessels which issue from the <female> 'testicles' <i.e.
the ovaries> manifestly contain semen – again in similar manner as in the
case of the males. Close to the testicles themselves these vessels are wide
and have a perceptible hollowness, but a little further away they become
narrower and, as it were, 'unhollow'; then they become wide again at the
'horns' <i.e. the Fallopian tubes>, where they also grow into the uterus.
Neither Aristotle, nor Herophilus ... knows of these insertions. I have
mentioned these authorities not only because they are ignorant of them
but because they dissected excellently .... For neither do I dare to condemn
them because of their accuracy in other respects, nor are these vessels so
small that they would escape anyone's notice. But, on the one hand,
regarding the vessels that grow into the neck of the bladder they accurately said both that they enter into the same place as is also the case with
males, and that these vessels are glandular and extend from the 'testicles',
growing alongside the uterus. But concerning the vessels at the 'horns'
they said nothing.

For Herophilus's pulse theory see **XI.10-17**.

Erasistratus

The brain and nervous system

Although Herophilus was the actual discoverer of both sensory and motor nerves, Erasistratus carried the inquiry into the brain and nervous system considerably further and his discoveries here put the work of his predecessor in the shade. His description of the structure of the brain, as can be seen from Galen's verbatim account below, reveals greater accuracy than that attained by Herophilus.

VII.16. Galen, *On the doctrines of Hippocrates and Plato* 7.3 (V.602-4K = *CMG* V.4,1,2 p. 440 De Lacy = *Erasistratus* Fr. 289 Garofalo)

Galen preserves verbatim Erasistratus's description of the anatomy of the brain.

His account is as follows: 'I examined also the structure of the brain. It was divided into two parts, like that of other animals, and has ventricles lying there, elongated in shape. These two ventricles were connected by a passage where the two parts are joined. From here the passage led into the so-called *epenkranis* <i.e. the cerebellum>, where there was another small ventricle. Each of the parts was divided off by itself – as was also the cerebrum, which was similar to the jejunum and had many folds. The *epenkranis* was to a still greater extent than the cerebrum furnished with many varied convolutions. So the observer learns from these that, just as in the case of the other animals, the deer, the hare, or any other that far excels the others in running, is well provided with muscles and sinews useful for this function, so in man, too, since he is far superior to other animals in intellect, this organ is large and very convoluted. All the nerves grow out of the brain, and, speaking generally, the brain seems to be the source of bodily activity. For the sensory channels from the nostrils opened onto it as did those from the ears. And from the brain nerves led to the tongue and the eyes.

The above description seems to have been based upon human as well as upon animal brains. Like Herophilus **[VII.6]** Erasistratus distinguished the *cerebrum* (*enkephalos*) from the *cerebellum* (which he called *epenkranis* not *parenkephalis*, as the former had done). He also described in some detail the cerebral ventricles or cavities within the brain. It seems likely that he agreed with Herophilus that the fourth ventricle of the *cerebellum* was the seat of intellectual activity since his observations that the *cerebellum* of the human brain has more convolutions than that of other animals had led him to the conclusion that the number of convolutions varied according to the degree of intellectual development. He was also in agreement with Herophilus that the brain was the starting point of all the nerves **[VII.9]** and, like him, differentiated between the sensory and motor nerves.

The heart and vascular system

In several respects Erasistratus's work displays marked advances upon that of his predecessors. Galen was prompted to remark that his accurate account of the valves of the heart made it superfluous to describe them himself.

VII.17. Galen, *On the doctrines of Hippocrates and Plato* 6.6 (548-50K = *CMG* V.4,1,2 p. 396 De Lacy = *Erasistratus* Fr. 201 Garofalo)

Galen provides the following verbatim account of the anatomy of the heart taken from Erasistratus's treatise *On fevers*.

The phenomenon how membranes adhere to the mouths of the vessels which the heart employs in the service of introducing and expelling its material is examined by Erasistratus in his work *On fevers*. Some have had the effrontery to deny the existence of these membranes and claim that they were invented by a follower of Erasistratus to establish his doctrine. But knowledge of them is so widespread among doctors that anyone who was not aware of them would seem to be utterly out of date. There are at the mouth of the *vena cava* three membranes which, in their arrangement, are very like the barbs of arrows – whence, I imagine, some of the Erasistrateans called them 'tricuspid'. At the mouth of the 'vein-like' artery (which is what I call the divided vessel leading from the left ventricle of the heart into the lungs) the membranes, though very similar in shape, are unequal in number. For to this mouth alone, only two membranes adhere. Each of the other two mouths has three membranes. As Erasistratus says in his explanation of the phenomenon, each of the two mouths evacuates material, the one evacuates blood to the lung, and the other *pneuma* into the whole living-creature. These membranes, in his opinion, perform a reciprocal service for the heart, by alternating at the appropriate times – those which adhere to the vessels which lead matter into the heart from the outside, are tripped by the entrance of the material and, falling back into the cavities of the heart, by opening their mouths, give an unimpeded passage to what is being drawn into that cavity. For, he says, material does not rush in spontaneously, as into some inanimate vessel; but the heart itself, dilating like a coppersmith's bellows, draws the material in, filling itself in diastole. Membranes, which, he said, lie on the vessels which lead material out of the heart, are considered by Erasistratus to behave in the opposite way. For they incline outwards from within and, being tripped by the material passing out, open their mouths for as long as the heart is supplying material. But for all the rest of the time they firmly close their mouths and do not allow any of the material which has been emitted to return. So, too, the membranes upon the vessels which lead material into the heart close their mouths whenever the heart contracts and do not permit any of the material drawn in by it to flow back again to the outside.

Erasistratus was probably the first to discover the co-ordinated function of all four main valves of the heart. As is evident from the above account, he had a clear knowledge both of their form and function and regarded them correctly as mechanisms for maintaining the flow in a single direction. Consequent upon his discovery of these valves he considered the heart to be a kind of double pump, 'a two-stroke (i.e. combined suction and force) pump with double action (since it is designed to move two different fluids, blood and *pneuma*, simultaneously)' (Lonie). Some scholars, impressed by Erasistratus's account of the structure and operation of the heart, have claimed that he came near to or even anticipated Harvey's discovery of the circulation of the blood. But such claims are clearly untenable. Like Praxagoras, Erasistratus believed that the arteries contained *pneuma* – not blood **[VII.18]**. Furthermore, like other ancient physiologists, he believed that the blood was entirely consumed in the replacement of wasted tissue. The supply of blood was conceived as analogous to that of water in an irrigation system where the dry earth consumes the water in its runnels. Blood as pure nutriment is similarly consumed by the tissues and organs. This widespread belief in the total consumption of the blood precluded any suggestion of its being recycled.

Erasistratus, however, had not failed to observe that the arteries of living creatures spurt blood when cut and to account for this he invoked the principle of *pros to kenoumenon akolouthia* (lit. 'the following towards what is being emptied'), which he employs elsewhere to explain other physiological processes such as appetite, digestion, and the assimilation of nutriment **[VII.21]**. He maintained that when an artery was severed, the *pneuma* it contained escaped unperceived and created a vacuum whose pull drew blood from the adjacent veins (*paremptôsis*) through fine capillaries (*sunanastomôses*) which were normally closed. This blood then spurted out of the artery after the escaping *pneuma* **[VII.19 & 20]**.

VII.18. Galen, *On venesection against Erasistratus* 3 (XI.153K = *Erasistratus* Fr. 198 Garofalo)

Like Praxagoras, Erasistratus holds that the arteries contain *pneuma*.

<Erasistratus> believes that the artery is the vessel of the *pneuma*, the vein that of the blood. The larger vessels are continually divided into smaller but more numerous vessels and are carried all over the body; for there is no place where there does not exist a termination of a vessel. They finally come to an end in such minute terminations that by the closure of their extreme orifices the blood is held constrained within them. In consequence, although the orifices[1] of both veins and arteries lie alongside one another, the blood remains in its own boundaries <i.e. in the veins> and nowhere encroaches on the vessels of the *pneuma* <i.e. the arteries>. While this state of affairs continues, the living creature is under the control of a natural process.

[1] These terminal orifices are the *sunanastomôses* through which blood might pass but does not do so under normal circumstances.

VII.19. Galen, *On venesection against Erasistratus* 3 (XI.154K = *Erasistratus* Fr. 198 Garofalo)

Under abnormal conditions a transfusion of blood takes place from veins to arteries.

In wounds he blames inflammation <as a cause of disease> and then the transfusion <*paremptôsis*> of blood from the veins into the arteries. He says the reason for the transfusion is the blood following to fill up the space being emptied. For when at the wounded part of the damaged arteries all the *pneuma* is poured out in the region of the wound, and there is a danger of an empty space occurring, the blood follows through the *sunanastomôses* and fills up the place of the *pneuma* being evacuated. So when the <vessel> of the *pneuma* <i.e. the artery> is open <the blood> streams out, but when it is closed and shut, the blood is compressed within by the *pneuma* emitted from the heart and is crowded all together again in the vicinity of the wound and in this way causes inflammation.

VII.20. Galen, *Whether blood is contained naturally in the arteries* 2 (IV.708-9K = Furley & Wilkie, 1984, pp. 150-1)

Galen attacks Erasistratus's theory of *pros to kenoumenon akolouthia*.

For, if <as Erasistratus maintains> the *pneuma* in the arteries is entirely continuous and so mobile and subtle that it can easily be emptied out in a moment, it is not the case that only the *pneuma* in the pierced arteries will be evacuated, while that in all the others will remain. For it is clear that all the rest of the *pneuma* will readily follow its predecessor – the *pneuma* that was in the cut artery – and the evacuation will first become apparent in the last arteries <to be affected> which no longer have others from whence further *pneuma* might be drawn. It is in them first that the danger of the occurrence of empty space arises, unless some substance should fill the place of the *pneuma* that is being transferred. On account of this, as he himself says, the blood necessarily follows through the *sunanastomôses* by <the principle of> *pros to kenoumenon akolouthia* <lit. 'the following towards what is being emptied', i.e. *horror vacui*>; and this blood, as though attached to the *pneuma* at the extremities of the last arteries, will be evacuated before all the rest of the blood, but after all the *pneuma* in the arteries. Thus two very great absurdities will ensue according to this account: first, all the *pneuma* in the arteries is evacuated through the perforation made by the needle so swiftly that it is imperceptible and, secondly, that the animal is still alive when the whole of the vital *pneuma* is being evacuated.

Physiology

Erasistratus, it seems, had a greater interest in physiology than Herophilus and was more innovative. He seems to have adopted a corpuscular theory from the Peripatetic philosopher, Strato of Lampsacus, who had worked in Alexandria until his recall to Athens to take up the headship of the Lyceum upon the death of Theophrastus. Physiological processes, such as digestion, are explained by Erasistratus upon the basis of this theory. He believed that the supply of nutriment to each particular bodily part was effected by a process of absorption (*diadosis*) through extremely fine pores (*kenômata*) in the walls of the capillary veins contained within it. The particles of nourishment were able to pass through these very fine and ultimate branches of the venous system to fill, in accordance with the principle of *horror vacui* [**VII.21**] those spaces left empty by the evacuations and emanations described in **VII.22** below. Erasistratus also used this theory of nutrition to account for disease, whose main cause he held to be *plêthôra*, i.e. the flooding of the veins with a superfluity of blood engendered by an excessive intake of nourishment **[IX.21A & B]** (See, too, Galen, *On the use of the parts* 7.8, III.537-9K).

VII.21. Galen, *On the natural faculties* 2.6 (II.105K = *Scripta minora* III, pp. 177-8 Helmreich)

Although Galen here accepts Erasistratus's account of nutrition as broadly accurate and agrees that nutritive material is attracted sideways through the walls of the capillary vessels, he disagrees with the latter's view of the mechanism whereby it is effected (i. e. the *horror vacui*).

It is worth while giving heed to what Erasistratus says ... in the second book of his *General Principles*. 'In the ultimate simple <vessels> which are thin and narrow, nourishment comes about from the adjacent vessels when nutriment is drawn through the sides of the vessels and is deposited in the empty spaces left by the material which has been carried away.' In this statement, firstly, I admit and accept the phrase 'through the sides'. For, on the one hand, if the simple nerve received nutriment through its mouth, it would not be able thus to distribute it to its whole self; for the mouth is dedicated to the <reception of> the psychic pneuma. But it can take it in through the side from the adjacent simple vein. Secondly, I accept in Erasistratus's statement the expression which immediately precedes 'through the sides'. What does he say? 'The nutriment is drawn through the sides of the vessels.' I, too, agree that it is indeed drawn, but it has previously been shown that it is not drawn by 'following towards what is being evacuated'.

VII.22. *Anonymus Londinensis*, 33.43-51 (Jones, 1947, p. 126 = *Erasistratus* Fr. 76 Garofalo)

Erasistratus's attempt to prove that living creatures give off certain invisible emanations.

Erasistratus also attempts to establish the proposition <viz. that irrational animals give off emanations> in this way. If one were to take a creature, a bird for example or something of the sort, and place it in a vessel for some time without giving it any food, and then weigh it together with the excrement that had visibly been passed, one will find that there has been a great loss of weight, clearly because a considerable emanation, perceptible only by reason, has taken place.

Erasistratus may also have derived this experimental method from Strato. The above experiment anticipates that performed in the early seventeenth century by the Paduan professor, Santorio of Capo d'Istria, which is generally considered to mark the beginning of modern metabolic theory.

HUMAN ANATOMY AT ALEXANDRIA

The practice of human anatomy did not continue as a permanent feature of Alexandrian medical science. It is hard to account for the puzzling abandonment of a practice whose introduction had resulted in such striking successes.

VII.23. Rufus, *On the naming of the parts of man* 10 (p. 134 Daremberg/ Ruelle)

It is clear from this remark of Rufus, who himself considered human dissection to be the ideal, that by the first century AD this practice was already a thing of the past.

We shall try to teach you how to name the internal parts by dissecting an animal that closely resembles man .... In the past they used to teach this, more correctly, upon man.

VII.24. Galen, *On anatomical procedures* 1.2 (II.220K)

This passage has been cited in support of the view that in Galen's own day (second century AD) human dissection continued to be practised at Alexandria. But the importance of the study of the human skeleton is stressed here by Galen because knowledge of human anatomy was no longer based upon the dissection of human corpses, but upon creatures like the Barbary ape which resembled humans. Thus it was only through an accurate knowledge of the human skeleton that proper morphological analogies could be drawn.

Let it be your serious concern not only to learn accurately from books the shape of each bone, but also to carry out a keen visual examination of the human bones. This is very easy at Alexandria inasmuch as the physicians there employ visual demonstration in teaching osteology to their pupils. For this reason – even if for no other – try to visit Alexandria.

*

In the third century BC knowledge of human anatomy was greatly advanced in the Greek city of Alexandria. Levels of sophistication were attained which remained unsurpassed until the Renaissance. The immediate cause of these great scientific advances is not difficult to discern. For here certain medical researchers first began systematically to dissect the human body which in Ancient Greece had previously been protected from violation by powerful taboos. At Alexandria, however, an authoritarian state had come into being, whose founders, the first Ptolemies, sought to enhance their regime's prestige by fostering not only the arts but also the sciences. To further anatomical research, it is alleged, they even supplied criminals for dissection from the royal gaols **[VII.2-5]**.

Various suggestions have been made to explain this radical change and to account for human dissection in a Greek city. Edelstein, for example (1932, p. 67), thinks that this change was due to philosophical teachings, which took practical effect soon after Aristotle's death and which, in accentuating the significance of the soul, had, correspondingly, diminished the importance of the body. But he fails to explain why it was at Alexandria alone among Greek cities that human anatomy was practised. Other scholars have argued that the Alexandrians derived their impressive knowledge of human anatomy from a study of those abdominal organs that would be available from a corpse about to be mummified. But in Egypt, too, religious taboos surrounding the dead and the disposal of the body were so strong that it is most unlikely that corpses or human organs would have been available to Greek doctors from this source. Nor, indeed, is there any evidence to suggest that the latter derived any particular anatomical knowledge from Egyptian embalmers, whose own knowledge of anatomy was, in any case, rudimentary **[VII.1]**. A more plausible explanation is that embalming contributed indirectly to the creation of this new outlook at Alexandria, and that the transplantation of Greek medicine, as a result of the attraction of the excellent facilities for advanced research afforded in the Museum, into what was essentially a foreign environment where the dissection of the human body was not invested with the same inhibitions as in mainland Greece, resulted in a situation highly beneficial to the development of anatomical research.

Among the doctors attracted to work at Alexandria two were outstanding – Herophilus of Chalcedon and Erasistratus of Ceos. Herophilus, the elder, moved to Alexandria after initial training under Praxagoras. His greatest contributions to medical research were largely in anatomy and he conducted important investigations, based at times on human dissection, into the brain and nervous system, **[VII.6-10]**, the vascular system **[VII.11 & 12]**, the liver **[VII.13]**, the eye **[VII.14 A&B]**, and the reproductive organs **[VII.15A-C.]**. He was also keenly interested in sphygmology and further developed the pioneering investigations of his teacher, who had assigned to the pulse an important role in diagnosis and therapeutics **[XI.9-11]**. Herophilus also put forward a systematic (but largely fanciful) classification of different types of pulse **[XI.12-16]** and he is also credited with the first known attempt to measure and evaluate the pulse-rate as a diagnostic aid **[XI.17]**. His younger contemporary, Erasistratus, was the son of a doctor and first studied medicine in Athens as a pupil of Metrodorus, the third husband of Aristotle's daughter, Pytheas. According to one tradition, he associated with Theophrastus and other members of the Lyceum (Diogenes Laërtius V.57). About 280 BC he went to Cos, where the medical school of Praxagoras still flourished. Cos had strong cultural and political ties with Alexandria. Here he came under the influence of Chrysippus the Younger, the palace doctor of Ptolemy Philadelphus, and it may have been this personal connection which brought him to Alexandria. Like Herophilus, Erasistratus made important contributions to the development of anatomy, especially to cardiac anatomy **[VII.17]**. He also put forward a comprehensive and sophisticated system of physiology **[VII.21]**, seemingly derived from the Peripatetic, Strato of Lampsacus, to whom he also appears to owe his experimental methodology **[VII.22]** .

Although many works were attributed to Erasistratus in antiquity, notably upon anatomy, pathology, hemoptysis, fevers, gout, dropsy and hygiene, unfortunately none of them has survived. Galen is particularly hostile towards Erasistratus because he had rejected such traditional 'Hippocratic' beliefs and practices as the theory of the four humours and phlebotomy. As a consequence of Galen's frequent attacks, more evidence of Erasistratus's beliefs has survived than of those of Herophilus.

These two Alexandrians themselves represent the culmination of Alexandrian medical science. They are followed by an almost immediate decline. Each of them founded a medical school and the names of some of their followers have survived. None of these, however, seems to have made any really significant mark in the history of medicine. The two rival schools seem to have largely dissipated their energies in sophistry and unproductive sectarian strife. Nor, apparently, did the practice of human anatomy continue as a permanent feature of Alexandrian medical science. By the first century AD it was already, apparently, a thing of the past [VII.23 & 24]. It is difficult to explain the abandonment of a procedure whose introduction had achieved such dazzling successes. Faced with a lack of firm evidence one can only guess. Human dissection had never been widely accepted as a necessary part of medical science in Greece and there existed deep and abiding prejudices against it. These prejudices, however, had been temporarily overcome at Alexandria by the protection and provision of the first Ptolemies, keen to foster their regime's prestige by encouraging medical research as well as the other arts and sciences. However, if human dissection and vivisection aroused at an earlier date the sort of hostility which is recorded later, then it may well have been the case that subsequent Ptolemies, sensitive to charges of barbarism, simply withdrew their patronage from a practice which, instead of winning renown, was now bringing their regime into disrepute.

See, generally, von Staden, 1989; Longrigg, 1993, Ch. 7.

VIII

Hippocratic deontology

Our earliest evidence of debate in Ancient Greece concerning medical ethics and etiquette is preserved in the Hippocratic writings.

VIII.1. [Hippocrates], *Oath* (IV.628-32L = *CMG* I.1, pp. 4-5 Heib.)

The *Oath* is the most influential of all these treatises. It has for centuries served as an exemplar of medical etiquette and has influenced the attitudes of generations of doctors. The biographies of Hippocrates tell us that he accepted students on payment of a fee [see **IV.1**] and after they had sworn an oath. It has consequently been assumed that they swore by this oath preserved in the Hippocratic *Corpus*. This seems unlikely: the document is of uncertain date and also poses multiple problems of interpretation.

I swear by Apollo the healer, by Asclepius, by Health, by Panacea and by all the gods and goddesses, making them my witnesses that I will carry out to the best of my ability and judgement this oath and this covenant.

I will hold my teacher in this art equal to my parents. I will share my life with him and, if he needs money, I will give him a share of my own. I will regard his sons as my brothers and teach them this art, if they desire to learn it, without fee or covenant. I will impart precepts, lectures and all other learning to my own sons, to the sons of my teacher and to indentured pupils who have sworn the physician's oath, but to no one else.

I will use treatments for the benefit of the sick to the best of my ability and judgement; I will abstain from doing harm or wronging any man by it.

I will not give poison to anyone when asked to do so,[1] nor will I suggest such a course. Similarly, I will not give to a woman a pessary to procure an abortion. But I will keep pure and holy both my life and my art.

I will not use the knife, not even on sufferers from the stone,[2] but I will give way to men who are skilled in this craft. Into whatsoever house I enter, I will enter for the benefit of the sick. I will abstain from all voluntary wrong-doing and harm, and especially from sexual contacts with the bodies of women or of men, whether free or slaves.

Whatsoever I might see or hear, in the course of my treatment or even in private relations, which ought never to be divulged, I will keep silent, holding such things to be holy secrets. If, therefore, I fulfil this oath and do not break it, may I prosper in my life and my art, enjoying a good reputation amongst all men for all time. But if I transgress and forswear this oath, may my lot be the opposite.

101

¹ The Greek is ambiguous. It is generally assumed that the doctor is here required to swear that he will not give assistance to a patient contemplating suicide, but the text could equally well entail an interdiction against being involved in euthanasia or, more sinisterly, becoming an accessory to murder.

² The Greek is again ambiguous and it is uncertain whether the doctor is required here to renounce this particular operation or operative surgery altogether.

VIII.2. [Hippocrates], *Aphorisms* I.1 (IV.458L)

Decision and co-operation are both required in the exercise of a difficult art.

Life is short, art is long, opportunity fleeting, experiment dangerous, judgement difficult. Not only must the physician show himself prepared to do what is necessary; he must also secure the co-operation of the patient, the attendants, and of external circumstances.

VIII.3. [Hippocrates], *Epidemics* I.5 (II.634,8-636,4L)

The doctor is enjoined to ensure that his services are beneficial to his patient. The tripartite nature of the art of medicine.

Regarding diseases, make a practice of two things – to help, or, at least, to do no harm. The art has three factors, the disease, the patient, and the doctor. The doctor is the servant of the art. The patient must co-operate with the doctor in combating the disease.

VIII.4. [Hippocrates], *Aphorisms* VI.38 (IV.572L)

The dangers of doing harm to one's patient was recognised by the Hippocratic doctor. Here, for example, it is advised that treatment should be withheld in the case of certain cancers [see **XI.8**].

It is better not to treat those suffering from hidden cancers. For, under treatment, they swiftly die; but, if not treated, their lives are prolonged.

VIII.5. [Hippocrates], *Law* 2 (IV.638-640L = *CMG* I.1, p. 7 Heib.)

A doctor must be industrious, well-taught, and possess natural ability.

Whoever is going to acquire truly an understanding of medicine must possess the following advantages: natural ability, instruction, a suitable place for study, tuition from childhood, industry, and time. First of all, natural ability is required, for, if nature is in opposition, all is in vain. But when nature leads the way to what is best, the instruction of the art comes about. This must be acquired intelligently by one who from childhood has been taught in a place naturally suited for learning. Moreover, he must apply his industry so that learning, having become instilled, may bring forth a felicitous and abundant harvest.

VIII.6. [Hippocrates], *Physician* 1 (IX.204-206L = *CMG* I.1, p. 20 Heib.)

Qualities required in order to be a successful doctor.

The authority of a physician requires that he is of healthy complexion and plump as nature intended; for those who are not of this good physical condition are considered by the common people not likely to take good care of others. Next, he must be clean in person, well-dressed, and anointed with fragrant perfumes that do not in any way cause suspicion. This, in fact, is pleasing to the sick. Psychologically, the prudent doctor must bear these things in mind – not only to keep his silence but also to maintain a very well disciplined life-style. For his reputation will be greatly enhanced. He must be of good and honourable character and being such he will be grave and kind to all. For the forward and hasty character is despised, even though it may be very useful. He must also have regard to his freedom of action .... In appearance he must have a thoughtful but not harsh countenance; for harshness seems to suggest stubbornness and misanthropy. But, on the other hand, the man of uncontrolled laughter and excessive cheerfulness is considered vulgar. Such a disposition must especially be avoided. He must be fair in every social relationship, for fairness is a great help. Intimacy between the sick and their doctor is close. For patients put themselves in the hands of their doctors, who are constantly meeting women, maidens, and the most valuable possessions. So towards all these the doctor must exercise self-control. Such, then, should be the disposition of the doctor both psychologically and physically.

VIII.7. [Hippocrates], *Decorum* 7, 11-14, 16, 18 (IX.236-244L = *CMG* I.1, pp. 27-9 Heib.)

Recommended bed-side manner.

[7] The doctor must have a certain urbanity at his disposal, for the austere doctor is unapproachable to both the healthy and the sick. He must watch especially that he does not reveal much of his person, nor gossips to laymen, but says only what is necessary ... He must do none of these things superfluously or ostentatiously. Let all these things be considered beforehand so that they may be ready in advance for use as required. Otherwise, there must always be a lack when need arises.

[11] When you enter a sick man's room, after making these arrangements so that you may not be at a loss and having everything well-arranged for what is to be done, know what you must do before going in. For many cases need, not reasoning, but practical help. It is necessary from your experience to forecast what the issue will be. For it brings high esteem and is easily learned.

[12] On entering be mindful of your manner of sitting, and your reserve, your decorum, authoritative demeanour, brevity of speech, your composure, bedside manner, care, your response to objections, your

self-possession in the face of troublesome occurrences, your censure of disturbances, your readiness to fulfil your medical duties ....

[13] Make frequent visits. Be very careful in your examinations, redressing the things where you were deceived at the changes. For you will know the case more easily, and at the same time you will be more in touch. For instability is characteristic of the humours. Consequently they are easily altered both by nature and by chance. For disregard of them at the crucial time for help gives the disease a start and kills the patient.

[14] It is necessary also to keep an eye on the patients' faults. They often lie about taking the things prescribed. For they die through not taking disagreeable potions, whether purgative or therapeutic. What was done does not result in an admission, but the blame is laid upon the doctor.

[16] Do everything in a calm and orderly manner, concealing most things from the patient while treating him. Give what encouragement is required cheerfully and calmly, diverting his attention from his own circumstances; on one occasion rebuke him harshly and strictly, on another console him with solicitude and attention, revealing nothing of his future or present condition. For many patients through this cause have been pushed the other way ....

[18] Since these are the things that contribute to a good reputation and decorum in wisdom, in medicine and in the arts generally, the doctor must, after having distinguished the parts about which I have spoken, swathe himself always in his own art and maintain it and guard it, practise it and hand it on. For things that are glorious are carefully guarded amongst all men. And those who have journeyed through them are held in honour by their parents and children; and if any of them does not know many things, they are brought to understanding by the facts themselves.

VIII.8. [Hippocrates], *Precepts* 4, 6, 8, 10, 12 (IX.254-268L = *CMG* I.1, pp. 31-4 Heib.)

On the doctor/patient relationship.

[4] This piece of advice should also require our consideration, as it contributes something to the whole. For if you should begin with a discussion of petty fees, you will give the patient the impression that you are going to go away and leave him, if no agreement is reached, or that you will neglect him and will not make any prescriptions for the present time. One ought not, then, to be concerned about fixing a fee. For I consider an anxiety of this sort harmful to a troubled patient, much more so in the case of an acute disease. For the quickness of the disease, offering no opportunity for reprise, urges the good doctor not to seek gain, but rather to maintain his reputation. It is better, therefore, to reproach patients whom you have saved than to extort money from those who are in a critical condition.

[6] ... I recommend that you do not display overmuch incivility, but have

regard to your patient's means or wealth. On occasion give your services free, recalling the memory of an earlier debt of gratitude or making reference to your present good reputation. If an opportunity of serving a stranger in need should arise, you should especially render assistance to people like this. For where there is love of man, there is also love of the art. For some sick people, though aware that their condition is dangerous, simply by being well-pleased with the goodness of their doctor, take a turn for the better. It is well to be in charge of the sick for their health's sake, and to take thought for the healthy for the sake of their freedom from disease; but also to have regard for oneself for the sake of decorum.

[8] ... It is not shameful, if a doctor, being in difficulties in the present circumstances over some patient and in the dark through inexperience, should urge that other doctors be called in to inquire into the sick man's condition by consultation and that there might be fellow-workers to provide abundant help. In the case of a persistent disease, when the condition intensifies, because of their perplexity doctors for the most part turn aside under the circumstances. One must, therefore, at so critical a time, be bold. For never will I lay down such a thing in principle, that the art is condemned in this respect. Doctors when they meet must never be contentious and mock one another. For I will proclaim on oath that the reasoning of one doctor should never be jealous of another's. For it would appear as a show of weakness. Those who lightly do these things are rather 'kinsmen of the market-place'. Yet it is not a mistaken idea to call in a consultant. For in all abundance there is lack.

[10] ... You must also shun luxurious headgear with a view to procuring patients and elaborate perfume too. For a certain degree of inexperience in this respect will be sufficient to earn you slander, but a little eccentricity will be considered good taste ....

[12] The wish to give a lecture for love of a crowded audience is not a laudable desire; at least avoid citations from the poets, for laborious citation reveals a lack of ability.

*

The Hippocratic writings provide our initial evidence of Ancient Greek debate concerning medical ethics and etiquette. In Classical Greece there was no established medical profession; but, rather, a wide variety of often peripatetic healers competing for patients. There were few mandatory constraints upon medical practice and no fixed rules of ethical behaviour. The authors of the so-called deontological works of the *Corpus* – the *Oath*, the *Physician, Law, Precepts* and *Decorum*, however, recognised that a reputation for good conduct would be advantageous in the competition for patients and, each in its own way, laid down codes of behaviour defining the role and duties of the doctor with regard to his patients and society in general. The doctor is enjoined to ensure both that his medical knowledge is employed for good, not ill, and that his privileged relationship with his patients is not exploited in any way. The Hippocratic doctor, it is urged, should conduct himself in the manner of a man dedicated to his art and to the healing of his patients. He should be willing to learn from others and ready to consult other doctors whenever necessary. While concerned to foster his personal reputation, he should always do so within the strict bounds of decorum. Although constrained to make his living by charging a fee for his services, he should recognise that humanity demands that his patient's welfare must be paramount and that, under certain economic circumstances, he should be prepared to reduce or even waive his fee altogether to avoid worrying his patient. On such occasions, he should seek to avoid hurting his patient's feelings by tactfully suggesting some reason why the fee is not levied, perhaps by recalling some past service performed for him by that patient or by pointing out how his own reputation is enhanced by this action. He should be prepared to help in this way not only impoverished fellow-citizens but also destitute aliens.

Within the field of medical ethics modern Western medicine still owes an abiding debt to these Hippocratic writings, not only for the ideal of the dedicated, discreet, compassionate and, at times, selfless, doctor presented here, but also for the explicit rules and implicit assumptions that still govern the doctor/patient relationship today.

The most influential of these treatises is the *Oath*, which has for centuries served as an exemplar of Western medical etiquette and has determined the attitudes of generations of doctors. It is still commonly regarded as prescribing the proper standards for medical behaviour. Its pre-eminence over the centuries, however, has given it an authority in assessments of the medical ethics of the ancient world that it did not actually acquire until some centuries after its composition and, in consequence, perceptions of medical ethics have at times been distorted.[1] The *Oath* was, in fact, neither unique nor widely acknowledged as the universal model of ethical behaviour in ancient Greece and, in spite of its brevity, poses a multiplicity of problems for which no universally accepted solutions have yet been propounded. Edelstein has sought to solve several of these puzzles at a single stroke by maintaining that the *Oath* was formulated within the Pythagorean Brotherhood – a religious society with a high regard for the sanctity of life. But objections can be raised against this ingenious and economical hypothesis; for example, if the *Oath* was administered exclusively within the secret Pythagorean society, it is difficult to understand why it should have been written in Ionic rather than in Doric; again, since the *Oath* is clearly a most important document dealing with a highly serious subject-matter, should we not, on Edelstein's hypothesis, expect the neophyte doctor to have been constrained to swear by the 'tetractys of the decad', which was not only the 'mightiest oath' of the Pythagoreans but was also regarded by the Brotherhood as the 'source of health'?

See, especially, Edelstein, 1943; Temkin, 1991, Ch. 3; Nutton, 1993.

[1] See Nutton, 1993, p. 10ff.

IX

Disease and human physiology

In the Heroic age of Greece diseases were attributed to the wrath of the gods **[I.8-15]**. The influence of Ionian Rationalism, however, brought about a new outlook whereby diseases were defined in accordance with natural processes [see **Chapter III**]. A surviving fragment of Alcmaeon's work first reveals this philosophical influence upon medicine. Here disease is held to be a disturbance of the body's natural equilibrium and is thus considered to be a part of nature and subject to the laws that operate in the cosmos at large. The causation of disease is divided into two categories, internal and external, and among the external, environmental causes are explicitly mentioned [see **III.2**].

HIPPOCRATIC ATTITUDES TOWARDS DISEASE

The Hippocratics hold that diseases are definable strictly in accordance with natural processes and run their courses within set periods of time totally independent of any arbitrary supernatural interference.

IX.1. [Hippocrates], *Diseases* I.2 (VI.142,13-16L)

In this treatise striking affinities with Alcmaeon's views are found when the author couples a similar rational outlook towards disease with the same binary classification.

Now all our diseases arise from things *within the body*, bile and phlegm, or *from things external to it,* from toil and wounds, and from heat that makes it too hot, and cold that makes it too cold ....

Neither Alcmaeon nor our Hippocratic author defines the origin of the heat and cold which they both cite as activating disease. It is not inconceivable that they regarded these qualities as due to seasonal factors [see **IX.2**].

IX.2. [Hippocrates], *Aphorisms* III.1, 19-23 (IV.486 & 494-496L)

In this treatise an elaborate correlation is drawn between diseases and the seasons.

[1] The changes of the seasons are especially productive of disease, as are great fluctuations either of heat or cold within the seasons ....

[19] All diseases occur at all seasons, but some occur more frequently and with greater severity at certain seasons.

[20] For example, in spring, madness, melancholia, epilepsy, haemo-

rrhages, sore throats, nasal catarrhs, hoarseness, coughs, psoriasis, mentagra, whites, ulcerous eruptions – these are very frequent – abscesses, and arthritis.

[21] In summer, some of the foregoing occur together with continuous fevers, causus,[1] frequent tertian fevers, vomiting, diarrhoea, ophthalmia, earache, mouth-ulcers, gangrene of the genitals, and heat-spots.

[22] In autumn, many of the summer ailments occur as well as quartan fevers, irregular fevers, affections of the spleen, dropsy, consumption, strangury, leientery, dysentery, hip-disease, sore throats, asthma, intestinal obstruction, epilepsy, madness, and melancholia.

[23] In winter, pleurisy, pneumonia, nasal catarrh, hoarseness, coughs, pains in the chest, pains in the sides and loins, headaches, vertigo, and apoplexy.

[1] A bilious remittent fever.

IX.3. [Hippocrates], *Nature of man* 7-8 (VI.50,5-52,3L = *CMG* I.1,3, pp. 186-8 Jou.)

Diseases are here described as coming into being and passing away in accordance with the cyclical change of the seasons and linked with the theory of the four humours.

Just as in the year, at one time winter is especially powerful, at another time, spring, at another, summer, and autumn at another, so, too, in man at one time phlegm is predominant, at another, blood, at another bile, first yellow bile and then the so-called black bile .... In these circumstances those diseases that increase in the winter should decrease in summer and *vice versa* .... you should expect that those diseases that occur in the spring will depart in the autumn; likewise autumnal diseases must take their departure in the spring .... The physician, too, must treat diseases on the assumption that each of them is predominant in the body according to the season that is most in conformity with its nature.

In addition to this belief that seasonal factors were influential in the causation of disease, the role of environmental factors, adumbrated earlier by Alcmaeon, is extensively developed within the *Corpus*.

IX.4. [Hippocrates], *Airs, Waters, Places* 1, 3, 4, 5, 6 (II.12-24L = *CMG* I.1,2, pp. 24-34 Di.)

After stressing the importance of seasonal factors, this author turns to environmental factors, such as prevailing winds and the properties of water, and puts forward a classification of disease based upon a city's orientation.

[1] Whoever wishes to pursue properly the art of medicine must proceed as follows. First he must consider what effects each season of the year can produce; for they are not at all like one another but differ greatly both in

themselves and in their changes. Secondly, he must take into account the warm and the cold winds, especially those which are common to all mankind, but also those peculiar to a particular region. He must also consider the properties of the waters. For, as these differ in taste and weight, so the property of each greatly differs. Consequently, when a physician arrives at an unfamiliar city, he should consider its situations relative to the winds and the risings of the sun. For a northern, a southern, an eastern and a western orientation has a different effect <upon the health of its inhabitants> .... He must consider as thoroughly as possible also the nature of the waters, whether the inhabitants drink water that is marshy and soft or hard from high and rocky ground or brackish and costive ....

[3] ... a city facing the warm winds (these are the prevailing winds, i.e. those between the winter rising of the sun and its winter setting), but sheltered from the north winds: the waters are plentiful but brackish and necessarily near the surface, warm in summer, cold in winter. The heads of the inhabitants are moist and full of phlegm; their bellies are frequently disturbed by the phlegm flowing down from the head. Their constitutions are for the most part rather flabby. They are poor eaters and drinkers .... The endemic diseases are as follows: in the first place the women are sickly and subject to fluxes, next many are barren through disease and not naturally so. Miscarriages are frequent. Children are liable to convulsions and asthma and to what is thought to cause the disease of childhood and to be a sacred disease <i.e. epilepsy>. The men, on the other hand, suffer from dysentery, diarrhoea, ague, chronic fevers in winter, frequent pustules, and piles ....

[4] Cities with the opposite situation, facing the cold winds that blow from between the summer setting and the summer rising of the sun ... the water is generally hard and cold. The inhabitants are necessarily vigorous and lean; their bellies for the most part are costive and hard, but their chests are less constricted. They are bilious rather than phlegmatic. Their heads are healthy and hard but they are generally liable to ruptures. These are the endemic diseases. Pleurisy is frequent, as are those diseases considered to be acute. This must necessarily be the case, whenever the intestines are hard. And many suffer abscesses from the slightest cause ... inflammations of the eyes eventually occur ... men under thirty suffer violent epistaxis during the summer .... For the men these diseases are endemic ... for the women, on the other hand, in the first place many become barren on account of the water being hard, costive, and cold. Their menstrual discharges are not regular but are few and painful. Next childbirth is difficult, but miscarriage is rare. When they bear children, they cannot rear them, for their milk is dried up from the hardness and costive nature of the water. There are frequent cases of phthisis after parturition .... The children suffer from dropsy in the testicles when they are little ....

[5] The effect of the warm and the cold winds upon these cities is such

as has been described above. For those cities that are exposed to the winds between the summer and winter risings of the sun and to the opposite of these, the effects are as follows. Those that lie towards the risings of the sun are likely to be healthier than those turned towards the north and those exposed to the warm winds .... In the first place the heat and the cold are more moderate. Next, the waters ... must necessarily be clear, sweet-smelling, soft and pleasant in such a city .... The complexions of the inhabitants are healthier and fresher than elsewhere unless some disease prevents this ... they have a better temperament and a higher intelligence than those who are exposed to the north .... Their diseases are fewer and less severe and resemble those in cities turned towards the warm winds. The women there conceive very readily and have easy deliveries.

[6] Such are the conditions in these cities. Those that lie towards the settings of the sun and are sheltered from the east winds, while the warm winds and the cold winds from the north pass them by, necessarily have the unhealthiest situation ... the water is not clear ... in summer cold breezes blow from morning and there are heavy dews. For the rest of the day the westering sun thoroughly scorches the inhabitants. Consequently they are likely to be pallid and sickly and subject to all the diseases mentioned above ....

IX.5. [Hippocrates], *Airs, Waters, Places*, 5, 6 (II.24,4-8 & 26,5-6L = *CMG* I.1,2, pp. 32-4 Di.)

The classification of diseases upon environmental factors is carefully integrated with that based upon seasonal effects.

[5] A city so oriented <i.e. facing east> seems especially in its climate to resemble spring, because of the moderate degree of heat and cold; the diseases there, while resembling those that occur in cities facing the warm winds, are fewer and less severe.

[6] The orientation of the city <facing west> is such that it especially resembles autumn ....

IX.6. [Hippocrates], *Aphorisms* III.24-31 (IV.496-502L)

Here our author presents a classification of disease based upon the age of the patients that is quite as detailed as his earlier classification upon a seasonal basis.

[24] At different ages the following complaints occur: to little children and the new-born, thrush, vomiting, coughs, sleeplessness, terrors, inflammations of the navel, discharges from the ears.

[25] At the approach of teething, irritation of the gums, fevers, convulsions, diarrhoea, especially when cutting the canine teeth, both in the case of very fat children and those whose bowels are hard.

[26] To those who are older: tonsillitis, internal displacement of the

cervical vertebra at the occiput, asthma, stone-disease, round worms, intestinal worms, pedunculated warts, swellings of the glands at the ears, scrofulous swellings of the cervical glands, and all kinds of abscesses.

[27] Older children and those approaching puberty suffer many of these diseases and fevers of the more chronic type, and from bleeding from the nose.

[28] Most childhood conditions reach a crisis, some in forty days, some in seven months, some in seven years at the approach of puberty. But those that persist among boys and do not cease around puberty, or, in the case of girls, at the onset of menstruation, are likely to become chronic.

[29] Young men suffer from spitting of blood, consumption, acute fevers, epilepsy, and the other diseases, especially those mentioned above.

[30] Those beyond this age suffer from asthma, pleurisy, pneumonia, lethargic fever, phrenitis, causus, chronic diarrhoea, cholera,[1] dysentery, lientery, and haemorrhoids.

[31] Old men suffer from difficulty in breathing, catarrh accompanied by coughing, strangury, difficult micturition, painful joints, nephritis, dizziness, apoplexy, cachexia, pruritus of the whole body, sleeplessness, watery discharges from the belly, eyes, and nose, dim-sightedness, blindness from glaucoma, hardness of hearing.

---

[1] i.e. a disease in which the bilious humours of the body are violently discharged by vomiting and diarrhoea.

IX.7. [Hippocrates], *Breaths* 2, 4 (VI.92,16-19 & 96,1-33L = *CMG* I.1, pp. 92 & 93 Heib.)

This author, under the influence of Diogenes of Apollonia, seeks to reduce all diseases to the single principle, air, and maintains that they differ only by reason of their locality.

[2] Of all diseases the fashion is the same, but the location differs. Now diseases seem to be in no way like one another on account of their difference of location, but in reality they have a single essence and cause ....

[4] ... For mortals, too, <air> is the cause of life and the cause of disease in the sick ....

See, further, **V.9** above.

IX.8. [Hippocrates], *Affections* 1 (VI.208,7-15L)

The humours, bile and phlegm, are here identified as the primary cause of disease.

All human diseases arise from bile and phlegm. They produce diseases whenever <the one or the other of them> becomes too wet or too dry or too hot or too cold inside the body. They are affected in this way by food and drink, toil and wounds, from smell and sound and sight and sexual intercourse, and from heat and cold. They are affected whenever any of the aforementioned is applied to the body at the wrong time, contrary to custom, in too great an amount and too strong, or in too small an amount and too weak.

Diet and exercise were also regarded as highly important in maintaining the balance of the natural constituents of the body and so avoiding disease [see **XII.11-14**].

IX.9. [Hippocrates], *Regimen in health* I.2-3 (VI.76,1-8L = *CMG* I.1,3, pp. 208-10 Jou.)

In this treatise it is maintained that diet and exercise should be adapted according to age, time of year and bodily constitution.

Regimens must be formulated according to age, season, habit, country, and constitution, counteracting the prevailing heat or cold. For in this way they would be most healthy. [3] During the winter one should walk quickly, but in summer in a leisurely manner, unless one is walking in the heat of the sun. Fleshy people should walk faster, thin people in a more leisurely manner.

In addition to the Hippocratic Corpus the *Anonymus Londinensis* preserves important evidence of beliefs in the causation of disease. A great variety of theories is mentioned based upon one or more of the elements, the primary opposites or of the humours. There is no common agreement either about the number of these principles nor upon the roles they play in the causation of disease. Of these theories probably the most influential was the four element theory. Important evidence is preserved here in the *Anonymus Londinensis* of its subsequent adoption and adaptation by Philistion **[VI.16]**, who, in his turn, seems to have influenced Plato in the *Timaeus*.

PLATO'S THEORY OF DISEASE

Plato sets out in the *Timaeus* a tripartite classification of disease.

IX.10. Plato, *Timaeus* 81E-82A

According to the first of these classes diseases are due to the excess, deficiency, varietal unsuitability or displacement of the four elements.

The origin of diseases is, I suppose, plain to all. There are four forms from which the body is composed, earth, fire, water, air, and disorders and diseases arise from the unnatural excess or deficiency of these, or from their displacement from their proper place to an alien one; and, furthermore, since there happens to be more than one variety of fire and the other elements, the reception by the body of an inappropriate variety of one of them and all similar irregularities produces disorders and diseases.

IX.11. Plato, *Timaeus* 82B-83A

The second class results from disordered conditions of the tissues.

Again, as there are secondary formations in nature, there is a second category of diseases to be noted by one who is minded to understand them. Since marrow, bone, flesh, and sinew are composed of the elements – and blood also is formed of these bodies, though in a different way – most of the other diseases arise in the same manner as those previously described; but the most severe of them have dangerous results in this way: whenever the process of formation of these secondary substances is reversed, then they are corrupted. In the natural course of events, flesh and sinews arise from blood – sinew from the fibrin to which it is akin, flesh from the coagulation of what is left when the fibrin is removed. Furthermore, the viscous, oily substance that comes from the sinews and the flesh, not only glues the flesh to the structure of the bones, but also nourishes the growth of the bone itself around the marrow; while at the same time the purest part, consisting of triangles of the smoothest and oiliest sort, filtering through the close texture of the bones, from which it distils in drops, waters the marrow. When the process takes place in this order, the normal result is health. When the order is reversed diseases occur. For, whenever the flesh decomposes and discharges its decomposed matter back into the veins, then the blood in the veins, which is extensive and of every sort, mixing with the air, takes on a variety of colours and bitternesses, as well as acid and saline qualities. It develops bile, serum, and phlegm of all sorts. All these products of reversal and corruption first destroy the blood itself, and themselves providing the body with no further nourishment, are carried everywhere through the veins, no longer maintaining the order of their natural courses. They are in mutual conflict because they can derive no benefit from one another and they make war upon any constituent of the body that stands firm and stays at its post, spreading destruction and decay.

IX.12. Plato, *Timaeus* 84C-E

His third class is primarily concerned with afflictions of the various organs or parts of the body as a whole.

A third class of diseases must be conceived as occurring in three ways; from breath, from phlegm, or from bile: whenever the lung, which serves to distribute the breath to the body, is blocked by the rheums and does not afford clear passages, the breath, being unable to pass one way, but entering by another in more than its proper volume, causes on the one hand the parts deprived of respiration to rot, but in the other parts, by forcing its way through the veins and distorting them, it dissolves the body, and is cut off at its centre which contains the diaphragm. Thus are caused countless painful disorders, often accompanied by much sweating.

DIOCLES OF CARYSTUS

Diocles is also influenced by Philistion and bases his physiology upon the same four opposites Philistion had linked with the four elements [**VI.35**]. He integrates, however, this 'Sicilian' legacy with Hippocratic theory to form a comprehensive system that brought the four element theory into conformity with the theory of the four humours.

IX.13. Aëtius, *On the opinions of the philosophers* V.30.2 (Diels, 1879,
p. 443 = *Diokles* Fr. 30 Wellmann)

Diocles here is in agreement with Philistion and Plato that diseases are caused by an imbalance of the elements.

Diocles says that most diseases come about through the imbalance of the elements in the body and the climatic situation.

He also shared with them the belief that some diseases are due to blockage of the passage of *pneuma*. Other diseases were caused when its passage from the heart was blocked by an aggregation of phlegm [see **IX.16, 17 & 18**].

PRAXAGORAS OF COS

Praxagoras also subscribed to 'Sicilian' theories presumably under the influence of Diocles. On occasion, however, he rejects these doctrines. For example, he maintains that the purpose of respiration is not to cool the innate heat but to nourish the psychic *pneuma* [**VI.17**]. He seems to have subscribed to a variation of the humoral theory and believed that when heat was in due proportion in the organism it transformed nourishment into blood, but an excess or deficiency of heat engendered other humours regarded as morbid and productive of various pathological conditions.

IX.14. Galen, *On natural faculties* 2,9 (II.141K = *Scripta minora* III,
p. 203 Helmreich = *Praxagoras* Fr. 21 Steckerl)

According to Galen Praxagoras distinguished no less than eleven humours including the blood.

In another treatise I have written about Praxagoras, the son of Nicarchus's account of the humours. Even if he puts forward, assuredly, ten humours, excluding the blood (which would itself be the eleventh), he does not depart from the teaching of Hippocrates. He divides into certain classes and varieties the humours mentioned first of all by him with the proper demonstrations ....

IX.15. Galen, *On the differences of fevers* 2.18 (VII.404K = *Praxagoras*
Fr. 60 Steckerl)

Intermittent fevers caused by a 'putrefaction of the humours'.

The species of non-intermittent fevers, whose whole duration is characterised by a single, severe fit, either having the same intensity throughout, or diminishing or increasing until the time of crisis, has come about naturally from such a cause as Praxagoras postulated for all fevers, supposing that a putrefaction of the humours has coagulated in the 'hollow vein' <i.e. the vena cava>.

IX.16. *Anonymus Parisinus* 20 (*Anecdota medica* 20, p. 550 Fuchs = *Praxagoras* Fr. 75 Steckerl = *Diokles* Fr. 57 Wellmann)

Paralysis due to a blockage of the arteries caused by phlegm.

The cause of paralysis: Praxagoras and Diocles say that it is caused by thick, cold phlegm in the region of the arteries that branch off from the heart and the aorta, through which voluntary motion is transmitted to the body.

IX.17. *Anonymus Parisinus* 3 (*Anecdota medica* 3, p. 541 Fuchs = *Praxagoras* Fr. 70 Steckerl = *Diokles* Fr. 51 Wellmann)

A similar cause is given for epilepsy –

The cause of epilepsy: Praxagoras says that epilepsy is engendered in the region of the aorta by the agglomeration of phlegmatic humours in it .... Diocles also believes that there is an obstruction in the same place ....

IX.18. *Anonymus Parisinus* 4 (*Anecdota medica* 4, p. 542 Fuchs = *Praxagoras* Fr. 74 Steckerl = *Diokles* Fr. 55 Wellmann)

– and apoplexy.

The cause of apoplexy: Praxagoras and Diocles say that the condition originates in the region around the aorta and is caused by thick, cold phlegm since within the aorta no *pneuma* whatsoever can escape and thus there is danger of suffocation.

HEROPHILUS OF CHALCEDON

Herophilus seems to have accounted for health and disease upon the basis of the theory of the four humours [**IX.19 & 20**].

IX.19. Cornelius Celsus, *On medicine* Proem 14-15 (*CML* I, p. 19 Marx = *Herophilus* Fr. 133 von Staden)

For <those who profess rational medicine> do not believe that one who is ignorant of the origin of diseases can know how to treat them properly. They say that there is no doubt that there is need for a different form of treatment if, as certain teachers of wisdom have said, some excess or deficiency among the four principal elements produces an adverse state of health, and a different treatment again, if every defect lies in the moistures *<in umidis[1]>*, as it seemed to Herophilus ....

[1] For the persuasive argument that 'moisture' here is the equivalent of 'humour' and that *hygron* and *chymos* are used interchangeably in the Hippocratic *Corpus* see von Staden, 1989, p. 246.

IX.20. Galen, *On the doctrines of Hippocrates and Plato* 8.5.24 (V.684-
5K = *CMG* V.4,1,2, p. 510 De Lacy = *Praxagoras* Fr. 16 Steckerl
= *Herophilus* Fr. 132 von Staden)

Not only Plato, but also Aristotle, Theophrastus, and the other pupils of Plato and Aristotle, tried to emulate Hippocrates's account of the humours, as did also the most notable of the ancient physicians: Diocles ... Praxagoras ... and Herophilus.

See, too, *On diagnosing the pulses*, II.3 (VIII.870K) and Ps.-Galen, *Introduction or the Doctor* 9 (XIV.698-9K).

ERASISTRATUS OF CEOS

Erasistratus held that the main cause of disease was *plêthôra*, i.e. the flooding of the veins with superfluous blood engendered by excessive nourishment. This blood was ultimately discharged through fine capillaries into the arteries (*paremptôsis*) where it was compressed by the *pneuma* pumped from the left ventricle of the heart. This compressed blood caused local inflammations with attendant fever.

IX.21A. Ps.-Galen, *Introduction or the Doctor* 13 (XIV.728-9K =
Erasistratus Fr. 169 Garofalo)

According to Erasistratus ... there is just one cause of all disease ... it is the transfusion (*paremptôsis*) of blood into the arteries.

See also **VII.19**.

IX.21B. Galen, *On fullness* 6 (VII.537-8K = *Erasistratus*
Fr. 161 Garofalo)

The origin of *plêthôra* <Erasistratus says> is as follows: 'for when the nutriment that is being distributed is neither fully digested nor elaborated according to what is customary for each individual, nor secreted in some other way, of necessity the veins are filled by digestion and distribution operating in accordance with their natural processes. When, on the one hand, the nutriment already in the veins is not consumed in any way, and, on the other hand, more nutriment continues to come into being from food, the veins, too, in the body are stretched to an even greater extent. When the veins can no longer accept further accumulation and other nutriment is being conveyed from the stomach, the nutriment already in the veins rushes into the arteries that lie alongside them ....'

See, too, Galen *On the use of the parts* VII.8 (III.537-9K).

IX.22. Galen, *On venesection against the Erasistrateans living at Rome* 7 (XI.228K)

Starvation is recommended as treatment for *plêthôra*.

Erasistratus says: 'consequently we should give no food at the time of the inflammation, for the veins, when emptied, will more easily receive back the blood which has invaded the arteries'.

*

In the Heroic Age of Greece diseases were attributed to the wrath of the gods [see **I.8-15**]. Even the diseases which emerged from Pandora's jar and spontaneously attacked men were ultimately the deadly gift of the gods [**I.14**]. However, the advent of Ionian Rationalism brought about a new outlook whereby man was regarded as a product of his environment, made of the same substances, and subject to the same physical laws as the cosmos at large. And, as a corollary to this, the diseases to which he is prone were themselves subsequently defined in accordance with natural processes and held to be totally independent of arbitrary supernatural interference. An important fragment preserved from the work of the Crotoniate doctor, Alcmaeon, first reveals this philosophical influence upon medicine [**III.2**]. Here is displayed an entirely different outlook upon disease from that encountered in Greek Epic. Alcmaeon rejects the ontological conception revealed there and maintains that disease is due to the disturbance of the body's natural equilibrium. He thus regards disease as a part of nature and, in consequence, subject to the same laws that operate in the world at large. He divides the causation of diseases broadly into two distinct categories, internal and external, and among the external causes he mentions specifically environmental factors such as the quality of water and the local environment.[1]

A binary classification of diseases coupled with a similar rational outlook is found in the Hippocratic work *Diseases* I.2 [**IX.1**] which displays some striking affinities with Alcmaeon's views. Neither the Hippocratic author nor Alcmaeon, however, makes the origin of the heat and cold, which they both cite as activating disease, at all clear. It is not inconceivable, however, that they might have regarded these qualities primarily as due to seasonal influences. A much more elaborate correlation of diseases with seasonal effects is presented in the treatise, *Aphorisms*, which lists in some detail not only the diseases of summer and winter, but also those of spring and autumn [**IX.2**]. These seasonal complaints evidently were regarded as springing up and passing away in accordance with the cyclical change of the seasons as *Nature of man* makes plain [**IX.3**] – a work that similarly tightly links disease with environmental effects (see below).

In addition to this belief that seasonal factors were influential in the causation of disease, the role of environmental influences, adumbrated earlier by Alcmaeon, is extensively developed within the Hippocratic *Corpus* – especially in *Airs, Waters, Places*. In this treatise, after stressing the importance of seasonal factors, followed by the effects of different prevailing winds and the diverse properties of water, the author presents a classification of diseases based upon the orientation of a city according to the four cardinal points of the compass **[IX.4]**. This classification of diseases upon environmental factors, it may be noted, is carefully integrated with that based upon seasonal effects since a comparison is drawn between orientation and the seasons – a city with an easterly orientation, it is claimed, manifests conditions which resemble those of springtime, whereas one facing west has a climate comparable with autumn **[IX.5]**. Further classifications of diseases were based upon sex [see **XVI.1-5**] and age. *Aphorisms*, for example **[IX.6]**, presents a classification based upon the age of the patient which is every bit as detailed as its earlier classification upon a seasonal basis.

Although many such classifications were put forward, they failed to result in a generally accepted codification. No single dominant Hippocratic conception emerged. Some medical authors, revealing an even higher degree of philosophical influence than those mentioned above, sought, in the manner of their Presocratic forebears and contemporaries, for a unifying hypothesis to explain a multiplicity of medical phenomena. The author of the treatise *Breaths*, for example, strongly influenced by the philosopher Diogenes of Apollonia, sought to reduce all diseases to the single principle, air, and maintained that they differed only by reason of their locality **[IX.7]**. Again, the author of *Sacred disease*, under identical influence, put forward a comprehensive explanation of disease, including epilepsy, upon the basis of two theories, both held by Diogenes – the belief that the brain is the seat of the intelligence and that air is the source and principle of intelligence in the living organism **[III.19; V.10 & 11]**. Other Hippocratic authors founded similar theories upon what they conceived to be identifiable pathological entities within the human body. For example, both *Affections* 1 **[IX.8]** and *Diseases* I.2 **[IX.1]** identify the humours, bile and phlegm, as the primary causes of disease within the human body.

As has already been seen, attempts of this nature to deduce explanations of medical phenomena from general unifying hypotheses were not without their vigorous opponents within the Hippocratic *Corpus*. The author of *Ancient medicine*, for example, firmly rejects this use of what he regards as arbitrary and untestable hypotheses to account for the causation of disease **[V.1]**. (It was seen, however, that he is not himself entirely immune to the very criticisms that he levels at his opponents.) *Nature of man*, too, attacks philosophical intrusion into medicine. In this case, as we saw, his polemic is restricted and confined to those who attempt to base medicine upon the unitarian hypothesis that man, like the world at large, is composed of a single, basic substance **[V.9]**. His own highly influential theory, which he believes to be empirically justified, attempts to account for the causation of disease as part of a highly schematic and comprehensive system that draws elaborate correlations between four basic humours, the four primary opposites and the four seasons. Each of the humours is associated with a particular season and with two of the primary opposites. Blood, yellow bile, black bile, and phlegm are each held to predominate in turn according to the appropriate season. Blood, the dominant humour in spring, is, like that season, characterised by the qualities hot and moist. In similar fashion, yellow bile, like summer, is hot and dry; black bile, like autumn, is cold and dry, and phlegm, like winter, is cold and moist. Whenever these four humours stand in equal proportions to each other, health ensues, but, whenever any one of them is in a state of deficiency or excess, pain is the result **[III.4]**.

Despite, then, the very considerable differences regarding the causation of disease revealed within the Hippocratic *Corpus*, these medical writers nevertheless share a broad measure of agreement on the names and descriptions of the main ailments they encountered. These afflictions are generally identified by them upon the basis of the part of the body affected or by their most prominent signs or symptoms. Particular diseases, as has been seen, are commonly accepted to be correlated with particular seasons and climatic conditions. Diseases are also widely regarded as due to some sort of imbalance or disturbance of the natural state of the body brought about by external factors, such as those just described, or by internal factors. Of the latter those most commonly mentioned are diet and exercise. *Regimen in health* 1, for example, maintains that both diet and exercise should be adapted according to age, season and constitution [**IX.9**]. Eating the wrong kind of food (or too much or too little) disturbs the balance of the natural constituents of the body. Diet and exercise are regarded as having opposite effects and had to be made to work together to produce health. Disease is held to be hostile to the body and the doctor's role is conceived essentially as combating the disease and giving full play to the *vis mediatrix naturae* – the healing power of nature. Of all the views held in common by the Hippocratics the most important is their belief that diseases are definable strictly in accordance with natural processes and held to run their courses within set periods of time totally independent of any arbitrary supernatural interference.

In addition to the Hippocratic *Corpus*, the *Anonymus Londinensis* preserves evidence on the causation of disease including the belief of the Cnidian school that residues (*perittômata*) formed under abnormal conditions in the bowels and then spread to the rest of the body to cause disease in the other organs (*Anon. Lond.* 4.20 – 5.34). Here, too, one also finds a great variety of theories of disease based upon one or more of the elements, of the primary opposites or of the humours. It is again immediately apparent that the medical authors cited here were in agreement neither about the number of these principles nor upon the roles played by them in the causation of disease. Of these theories probably the most influential since its original formulation by Empedocles was the four element theory [see **Chapter VI**]. Important evidence is preserved in the *Anonymus Londinensis* of its subsequent adoption and adaptation by Philistion of Locri [**VI.16**].

Philistion's influence seems to have played in its turn an important role in Plato's adoption of this theory in the *Timaeus* [**VI.18**]. Towards the end of this work Plato sets out a tripartite classification of diseases. According to the first of these classes, diseases are due to the excess, deficiency, varietal unsuitability or displacement of the four elements [**IX.10**]. This theory is basically a blend of the view that disease is due to an excess of a bodily constituent and the Empedoclean four element theory. The third class contains diseases primarily caused by blockage of respiration [**IX.12**]. The correspondences between these two classes of disease and the first and third of the three classes attributed to Philistion [**VI.16**] are striking and suggest that Plato is here dependent upon the latter as an intermediary for much of his aetiology of disease. The second class of diseases described at [**IX.11**] comprises diseases of the tissues. Here, too, we have a further development upon the basis of Empedocles's biology since it rests upon the assumption that the blood is the ultimate nutriment of the body.[2] When the tissues, sinews, flesh etc. are formed in the proper order, health results. A reversal of this process, however, causes disease [**IX.11**]. The close and underlying parallels with Empedocles are here clearly apparent. Both Plato and Empedocles hold that blood is the ultimate nutrient of the body; blood is composed directly from digested food; blood is ultimately composed of the four elements and flesh is a secondary formation of blood. The theory of disease as a reversal of the normal process may itself, however, be Plato's own innovation. Plato, then, accounts for the physiological processes of the body upon the basis of his elementary physics. When these

119

processes become disordered, diseases ensue. According to his threefold classification of disease, the first class contains those due to excess or deficiency, varietal unsuitability or displacement of the four 'elements'. Here is presented Plato's basic conception of causation of disease, which underlies that of the second and third classes. Its priority is underlined by his emphasis that health can only be preserved by a uniform and proportionate replacement of the wastage that constantly occurs. Fevers, we are told at *Timaeus* 86A, are caused by an excess of one or other of the 'elements' and their periodicity is dependent upon the relative mobility of that 'element'. The second class of diseases results from disordered conditions of the tissues. The majority of these diseases are caused in the manner just described. Worse disorders, however, are caused by an unnatural reversal of the process by which the tissues were initially formed that results in the decomposition of the flesh and the discharge of the products of decomposition into the veins. These morbid secretions destroy the blood and are carried everywhere through the veins spreading destruction and decay. In his analysis of diseases of the tissues Plato describes the origin and nature of the humours, phlegm and bile, but discusses them only in so far as these products of corruption affect the normal functioning of the blood. In his third class of diseases he describes those caused by these morbid humours as well as those caused by *pneuma*. This third class is primarily concerned with afflictions of the various organs or parts of the body as a whole as distinct from those of the tissues. It includes pulmonary complaints like consumption, bronchial affections, pleurisy, and tetanus caused by *pneuma*; epilepsy, which is due to phlegm and black bile; psoriasis, eczema, and other skin diseases caused by phlegm, and diarrhoea, dysentery and other such disorders that are due to bile. Plato also believes that certain psychic disorders are due to physical causes and treats them as essentially no different from diseases of the body, tracing their causes to vapours arising from blood and phlegm when pent up within the body.

Diocles of Carystus, too, reveals indebtedness to Philistion and bases his physiology upon the same four opposites Philistion had previously linked with the four elements **[VI.35]**. His theories, however, are developed beyond what he adopted from Philistion and he integrates the 'Sicilian' legacy with Hippocratic elements to form a comprehensive system which brought the four element theory into explicit conformity with that of the four humours as it is expounded in *Nature of man*. Diocles's dietetic prescriptions suggest that, as in this Hippocratic work, the predominance of individual humours is closely linked with the seasons of the year **[XII.14]**. Upon the basis of these theories he puts forward a varied account of the causation of disease, holding with Philistion and Plato that they are caused by an imbalance of the elements **[IX.13]**. He also shared with these two the belief that some diseases occur when the passage of the *pneuma* through the pores in the skin is impeded. Such stoppages, he believes, were due to the influence of bile and phlegm upon the blood in the veins; whereas the latter cooled the blood abnormally and compacted it, the former caused it to boil and curdled it. In either event, the *pneuma* was unable to permeate throughout the body and fever ensued. According to the *Anonymus Parisinus* Diocles believed that epilepsy, apoplexy, and paralysis were due to the blocking of the passage of the psychic *pneuma* from the heart through the aorta by an accumulation of phlegm **[IX.16,17&18]**.

Praxagoras of Cos also subscribes to 'Sicilian' theories and it is likely that he, in his turn, was influenced by Diocles. However, he does, on occasion, reveal his independence of these doctrines and even stands in marked disagreement with some of them. For example, he rejects the view that the purpose of respiration is to cool the innate heat, claiming that its role is rather to provide nourishment for the psychic *pneuma* **[VI.17]**. He seems to have subscribed to a variation of the humoral theory and, according to Galen, distinguished eleven humours (including the blood) **[IX.14]**. Galen adds, however, that Praxagoras did not entirely depart from the teachings of Hippocrates here since he divided into different classes and varieties the humours first mentioned by Hippocrates. Health and disease are regarded by Praxagoras as ultimately dependent upon these humours. He believes that, when heat is present in the organism in due proportion, nourishment is transformed naturally by the digestive process into blood; but an excess or deficiency of heat gives rise to the other humours, which he regarded as morbid and ultimately productive of various pathological conditions **[IX.15]**. Like Empedocles and Diocles, Praxagoras considered the digestive process to be a kind of putrefaction. The blood produced as the end product of this process was restricted to the veins; the arteries, however, served as vessels for carrying the psychic *pneuma* that issued from the heart. Praxagoras is generally given the credit for this distinction between veins and arteries together with the theory that *pneuma* moves through the latter and blood through the former. Galen, however, attributes this differentiation also to Praxagoras's father, Nicarchus, and Diocles, too, seems to have subscribed to these views since both he and Praxagoras are credited with an identical explanation of paralysis as due to an agglomeration of thick, cold phlegm in the arteries and we are further told that both regarded arteries as channels 'through which voluntary motion is imparted to the body' **[IX.16]**. (The *pneuma* is the cause or agent of this motion.) Furthermore, both are said to have explained epilepsy and apoplexy also as due to the blocking of the passage of the *pneuma* from the heart by an accumulation of phlegm **[IX.17 & 18]**.

Herophilus, by contrast, seems to have been rather more traditional in his pathology. Our evidence is sketchy and by no means unequivocal, but it seems to suggest, on balance, that he accounted for health and disease upon the basis of the traditional theory of the four humours. Reports in both Celsus **[IX.19]** and Galen **[IX.20]** seem to support this view.

Erasistratus, however, adopted a corpuscular theory derived from the Peripatetic philosopher Strato of Lampsacus, and held that matter existed in the form of small, imperceptible, corporeal particles which were surrounded by a vacuum in a finely divided or discontinuous condition. (This theory he combined with the *pneuma* doctrine.) Upon this corpuscular basis he explained physiological processes such as nutrition. In the case of the latter, for example, he held that the supply of nutriment, in the form of blood, to each particular bodily part was effected by a process of absorption (*paremptôsis*) through extremely fine pores in the walls of the capillary veins contained within it. The particles of nourishment were drawn through these very fine branches of the venous system in accordance with his principle of *pros to kenoumenon akolouthia* (lit. 'following towards what is being emptied', or *horror vacui*) to fill those spaces being emptied by the emanations and evacuations that constantly occur in the living body.

Disease is explained by Erasistratus upon the basis of this theory of nutrition. Its main cause is held to be *plêthôra*, i.e. the flooding of the veins with a superfluity of blood engendered by an excessive intake of nourishment **[IX.21A&B]**. As *plêthôra* increases the limbs begin to swell, then become sore, more sluggish and harder to move. Should *plêthôra* increase still more, this superfluous blood is then discharged through the *sunanastomôses*, fine capillaries that were closed under normal conditions, into the arteries, which were believed by Erasistratus to carry *pneuma* not blood. In the arteries this blood is compressed by the *pneuma* being continually pumped from the left ventricle of the heart. This compressed blood collects in the extremities of the arteries and causes local inflammations accompanied by fever. Since the flow of the *pneuma* is impeded by the (unnatural) presence of this blood in the arteries, it cannot perform its normal functions. As examples of diseases brought about in this way by *plêthôra*, he mentions ailments of the liver, spleen, stomach, coughing of blood, phrenitis, pleuritis, and pneumonia.

As treatment for *plêthôra* Erasistratus, who, unlike many of his contemporaries, did not freely resort to phlebotomy, recommended primarily starvation on the grounds that the veins, when emptied of superfluous blood, would more easily receive back the blood that had been discharged into the arteries [**IX.22**].

[1] This aspect of Alcmaeon's theory of health seems to be overlooked by medical historians.

[2] See Longrigg, 1993, p. 110ff.

X

Epidemic disease

SUPERNATURAL CAUSATION

Homer preserves our earliest surviving literary account of epidemic disease when he describes the plague sent by Apollo upon the Greek army investing Troy [see **I.8**]. In similar fashion Hesiod describes a plague sent by Zeus [**I.13**]. In both these epic accounts those stricken are afflicted en masse by the action of an angry god. This belief in the supernatural causation of epidemic disease continued to be held by some even during the Fifth-Century Enlightenment – as may be inferred from Thucydides's account of the Athenian Plague [**X.6**] and even from Sophocles's portrayal of the plague at Thebes [**X.1 & 2**], which, although fictitious, doubtless reflects common beliefs regarding the causation of disease current at the time.

X.1. Sophocles, *Oedipus Tyrannus* 22-30

The Priest of Zeus at Thebes describes the impact of plague upon the stricken city.

Thebes, as you yourself see, already is excessively tempest-tossed and is able no more to lift up her head from the depths of the bloody surge. She perishes in the budding fruits of her soil; she perishes in the herds at pasture and in the unfruitful travail of her women. And moreover, the fire-bearing god, most hateful god of plague, has swooped upon the city and harasses it. By him the house of Cadmus is made empty and black Hades grows rich with groans and lamentations.

X.2. Sophocles, *Oedipus Tyrannus* 169-83

The Chorus of Theban Elders echoes his lament.

Woe, for countless are the ills we endure. Our whole host sickens and there is no spiritual resource with which to defend oneself. For neither do crops grow from our glorious soil nor do women with offspring cease from grievous pangs of childbirth. You might see one after another speeding like a well-winged bird faster than irresistible fire to the shore of the god of darkness.

The city perishes by the loss of countless hosts of them. Unpitied, children lie upon the plain pitilessly spreading death. Our wives and grey-haired mothers, from this place and that, raise beside the altar a shriek as suppliants from bitter pangs.

There are some points of resemblance between Sophocles's description here of the mythical plague at Thebes and Thucydides's account of the Great Plague of Athens [see **X.6**], which have prompted the speculation that the tragedian's portrayal was coloured by his experiences in plague-ridden Athens.

RATIONAL CAUSATION

X.3. [Hippocrates], *Nature of man* 9 (VI.52,11-54,20L = *CMG* I.1,3, pp. 188-90 Jou.)

Within the Hippocratic *Corpus* explanations of epidemic disease are sought in terms of physical and natural causes. The epic concept of causation with its religious and moral connotations is implicitly rejected. Here air is held to be the cause of epidemic disease.

Some diseases arise from regimen, others from air which we inspire to live. We should distinguish between the two in the following way. Whenever many are contemporaneously affected by a single disease, the cause must be attributed to that which is most common and which we all use most. This is what we breathe in. For it is clear that the regimen of each of us is not responsible, since the disease attacks all in turn, both younger and older, men and women alike, drinkers and teetotallers, eaters of barley and eaters of wheat, those who undertake much strenuous toil and those who undertake little. Regimen, then, could not be the cause when people following all manner of diets are afflicted by the same disease. But when all sorts of diseases occur at the same time, it is clear that in each case the particular regimen is responsible .... But whenever an epidemic of a single disease is prevalent, it is clear that regimen is not responsible, but what we breathe and that this causes †trouble†[1] through some unhealthy exhalation (*apokrisis*).

The last phrase, where the text appears to be defective, has been interpreted by some to entail some idea of infectious transmission. But there is no suggestion that the air in question has been exhaled by someone already affected by the disease, nor do the remedies subsequently recommended include advice to avoid those afflicted. The more likely implication is that the air itself contains some noxious quality. In that case *apokrisis* here would be synonymous with *miasma* in the next passage [**X.4**]. See, too, Hankinson, 1995, pp. 43ff.

[1] Reading ἀνίᾳ.

X.4. [Hippocrates], *Breaths* 6 (VI.96,23-98,13L = *CMG* I.1, p. 94 Heib.)

This Hippocratic author similarly attributes epidemic disease to air 'corrupted by some pollution'.

There are two sorts of fever: the one which is common to all is called plague (*loimos*), the other, due to bad regimen, is specific and attacks those who follow a poor regimen. Air is the cause of both. The common <i.e. epidemic> fever has this characteristic because everyone inhales the same air, and when similar air is mingled in similar fashion with the body, similar fevers occur. But perhaps someone will say, 'Why, then, do not such diseases attack all animals, but only a particular species?' I would reply that is because one body differs from another, one type of air from another, one nature from another and one form of nutriment from another. For the same things are not well- or ill-suited to all species of animals, but different things are beneficial or harmful to different sorts. So, whenever the air has been defiled with such pollutions (*miasmasin*)[1] which are hostile to human nature, then people fall sick, but whenever the air has become ill-suited to some other species of animals, then these fall sick.

[1] For sources of such pollution see Didorus Siculus at **X.7**.

X.5. [Hippocrates], *Nature of man* 9 (VI.54,20-56,12L = *CMG* I.1,3, pp. 190-2 Jou.)

How to avoid epidemic disease.

This is the advice that should be given to people <whenever an epidemic is prevalent>. They should not change their regimen, because it is not the cause of their disease, but rather see that the body is as thin and weak as possible by depriving it of its accustomed food and drink little by little ... then ensure that they inspire the least possible amount of air and from as far away as possible and by changes of place as far as is possible from the regions in which the disease is established and by reducing the body, for thus they would have the least need of deep and frequent respiration.

It is noteworthy that the concept of *miasma* in the three Hippocratic passages above differs from that found in the mythical account of plague described by Homer **[I.8]** and by Sophocles **[X.1]** in that there is no implication of religious pollution due to divine displeasure, nor is the disease transmitted by contagion to those in close proximity. The concept has been taken over and thoroughly rationalised so that it merely entails a general environmental condition productive of epidemic disease. The air serves as the general vector of the disease which is not directly communicated from one patient to another.

THE ATHENIAN PLAGUE

In the early summer of the second year of the Peloponnesian War (430 BC) the Lacedaimonians again invaded Attica and laid waste to the countryside, whose inhabitants had taken refuge within the Long Walls. Athens had consequently become seriously overcrowded. A few days after the invasion the Plague broke out – killing, it would appear, about one third of the population of the city. The impact of the disease upon Athens is described by the historian Thucydides in the second book of his *History of the Peloponnesian War*. He provides our only contemporary account, which has become a literary model for descriptions of plague by many subsequent authors [see, for example, **X.7**]. He himself fell victim to the disease. His rational detailed account of its symptoms is unparalleled outside the writings of the Hippocratic *Corpus* and there seems to be no good reason to doubt that

X. Epidemic disease

Thucydides was familiar with contemporary medical literature and had been influenced by the spirit of Hippocratic medicine. But, notwithstanding this influence, it would be unwise to conclude that his rationality of approach was itself derived from contemporary medicine. Thucydides is himself a child of the Enlightenment and the writing of History had itself, in any case, felt at an earlier date the influence of Ionian Natural Philosophy. Despite numerous attempts on the part of modern scholars to identify the disease, none can be regarded as convincing. For in each and every case there remains at least one vital factor irreconcilable with Thucydides's evidence.[1] The historian has recently been given credit for making two important observations not previously recognised in medical history. He has been held to be the 'first of extant writers to enunciate clearly the doctrine of contagion' and the first to have described the phenomenon of acquired immunity.[2] But, while Thucydides manifestly deserves praise for his accurate observation and detailed description of these particular effects of the plague, both of these claims overpress the evidence. Thucydides certainly observes and records the *fact* of contagion. However, this is not to say that he clearly enunciated the *doctrine* of contagion or possessed an '*understanding* of contagion and immunity' or had any conception at all of its true cause. In any case, by his own evidence Thucydides reveals that he was not unique in recognising the *phenomenon* of contagion. At 51.5 he states explicitly that a number of his contemporaries were afraid to visit one another and that those whose sense of moral obligation transcended their fear and drove them to nurse their friends were especially vulnerable to the disease. Although Thucydides may have been the first to describe in writing the phenomena of acquired immunity and of contagion, his own evidence reveals that the realisation that one could contract the disease from someone already affected by it and that it did not attack the same person twice – at least, not fatally – was a matter of general knowledge within the Athenian populace. Nor should it be overlooked that this standpoint is also not without affinity with traditional religious beliefs in the contagious transmission of pollution.

[1] See Longrigg, 1980, pp. 209-25.
[2] See Poole & Holladay, 1979, pp. 282-300.

X.6. Thucydides, *History of the Peloponnesian War* II.47-54, 58; III.87

[47] In the first days of summer in the second year of the war the Lacedaimonians and their allies, with two thirds of their forces as before, invaded Attica. (Their commander was Archidamus, king of the Lacedaimonians, son of Zeuxidamus.) They settled down in their positions and laid waste to the country. They had not been many days in Attica when the plague first began to appear among the Athenians. It was said to have struck even before this in many places, both in the vicinity of Lemnos and elsewhere. However, nowhere was a pestilence remembered as being so virulent or so destructive of life as it was in Athens. For neither were the doctors, who were the first to offer treatment in ignorance of the disease, able to ward it off; (their own mortality indeed was especially heavy inasmuch as they approached the afflicted most frequently). Nor was any other human skill of avail. Equally useless were prayers in the temples,

consultations of oracles and so forth. Finally, overcome by their sufferings, the sick ceased to resort to such practices.

[48] The plague first originated, so it is said, in Ethiopia above Egypt and then descended into Egypt and Libya and much of the Persian Empire. It fell suddenly upon Athens and attacked in the first instance the population of the Piraeus; giving rise to the allegation that the Peloponnesians had put poison into the reservoirs (there were not yet any wells there). Later it also arrived in the upper city and by this time the number of deaths was greatly increasing. The question of the probable origin of the plague and the nature of the causes capable of creating so great an upheaval, I leave to other writers, with or without medical experience. I, for my part, shall merely describe its nature and set down its symptoms by which it might be recognised if it should ever break out again. I caught the disease myself and observed others suffering from it.

[49] It is generally agreed that the year in question was particularly free from other kinds of disease. If anyone had an illness prior to the onset of the plague all its symptoms were resolved into it. Others, from no prior observable cause, but in good health, were suddenly attacked in the first instance by violent heats in the head; their eyes became red and inflamed; the inner parts, such as the throat and the tongue, immediately became blood-red and the breath unnatural and malodorous. These symptoms were followed by sneezing and hoarseness and in a short time the pain descended into the chest, producing a severe cough. Whenever it settled in the region of the heart, it upset it and there ensued evacuations of every kind of bile named by the doctors accompanied by great distress. Most patients then suffered an attack of empty retching, producing violent spasms; in some cases soon after the abatement of the previous symptoms, in others much later. Externally the body was neither excessively hot to the touch, nor pale in appearance, but flushed and livid with an efflorescence of small blisters and sores. Internally the heat of the body was such that the victims could not endure even the lightest coverings or linens; they preferred to go naked and would have liked best to throw themselves into cold water. Many of the sick who were not cared for actually did so, plunging into the water-tanks driven by their unquenchable thirst. It made no difference whether they drank little or much. They continually suffered distress through sleeplessness and their inability to rest. At the height of the disease the body did not waste away, but surprisingly withstood its ravages. Consequently the majority succumbed to the internal heat on the seventh or the ninth day before their strength was totally exhausted. Or, if they survived this critical period, the disease would descend to the bowels, where a severe ulceration occurred coupled with an attack of uncompounded diarrhoea, which in many cases ended in death from exhaustion. For the disease, seated at first in the head, began from above and passed throughout the whole body; if the patient survived its worst effects, it left its mark upon his extremities; it attacked the genitals, fingers and toes; many escaped with the loss of these, some also lost their

eyes. Some rose from their beds seized momentarily by a total loss of memory and failed to recognise themselves and their friends.

[50] The nature of the disease was beyond description: in general its individual attacks were more grievous than human nature could endure, and in the following particular respect, especially, it revealed that it was something out of the ordinary. Though there were many unburied corpses lying around, the birds and beasts that prey upon human bodies either did not go near them, or died after tasting them. As evidence for this: there was a conspicuous disappearance of such birds; they were not seen about the bodies, or indeed at all. But it was the dogs rather, being domestic animals, that provided an opportunity to observe this effect.

[51] If we pass over many other peculiarities as it manifested itself differently in individual cases, such was the general nature of the disease. Throughout the duration of the plague none of the ordinary diseases attacked the population as well: or, if any did, it ended in this. Some died in neglect, others in spite of being given every care. No single 'cure', as it were, established itself as the one which had to be applied to benefit the sick (for what helped one, harmed another). No bodily constitution, whether strong or weak, was conspicuously capable of resistance; but the disease carried off all alike, even those treated with every medical care. The most terrible aspect of the malady was the despondency of the afflicted when they realised that they were falling sick (for their minds immediately turned to despair and in the majority of cases they gave themselves up for lost instead of resisting). Most terrible, too, was the fact that having caught the infection through caring for one another they died like sheep. This was the cause of the greatest mortality. For, if they were afraid to visit one another, they expired with no one to look after them. (Many houses were emptied through lack of anyone to do the nursing.) Alternatively, if they did visit the sick, they also perished – especially those who made any claim to goodness. For their shame did not allow them to spare themselves from entering the houses of their friends at a time when even their relatives, overcome by the size of the disaster, were wearied of the funeral dirges for their dead. But still, it was those who had survived the disease who showed the more pity to the dying and the suffering because they themselves had previous experience of it and were themselves by this time confident of their immunity. For the disease did not attack the same person twice, at least not fatally. Such people both received the congratulations of the others and they themselves in the elation of the moment also entertained to some extent a vain hope that for the rest of their lives they would never die of any other disease.

[52] In addition to their existing distress, the crowding into the city of people from the country also caused the Athenians further hardship, and this especially affected the newcomers. Since there were no houses available for them and they had to live in stifling cabins in the hot season of the year, they perished in utter disorder: corpses and the dying lay one upon the other and half-dead people reeled about in the streets and around all

the fountains in their desire for water. The sacred places, too, where they had camped, were full of corpses of those who had died there. As the disaster pressed so overpoweringly upon them, men, not knowing what was to become of them, became contemptuous of everything, both sacred and profane. Burial customs, which had previously been observed, were all thrown into confusion and they buried their dead each as they could. Many, through lack of the necessary materials due to the fact that many members of their household had already died previously, resorted to shameful modes of burial; some would hurl their own dead upon another's pyre and set fire to it, forestalling those who had raised it; others would throw the corpse they were carrying on top of another that was already burning and depart.

[53] In other respects, too, the plague was responsible for first introducing a greater degree of lawlessness at Athens. Men ventured more readily upon acts of self-indulgence which had formerly been concealed. They saw rapid changes of fortune when the prosperous suddenly died and those who previously had nothing in a moment inherited their wealth. Regarding life and wealth alike as transitory they thought it right to live for pleasure and to enjoy themselves quickly. No one was eager to persevere in what was esteemed as honour, considering it uncertain whether he would live to attain it. But it was generally agreed that the pleasure of the moment and all that contributed to it was honourable and expedient. No fear of the gods or law of men restrained them. For, on the one hand, seeing that all perished alike, they judged that piety and impiety came to the same thing; and, on the other, no one expected that he would live to be brought to trial and punished. They believed the penalty that had already been passed upon them and was hanging over their heads to be far greater and that it was reasonable, before it fell, to get some enjoyment out of life.

[54] Such was the calamity that befell the Athenians and caused them great distress, with their people dying within the walls and their land ravaged without. In their distress they naturally recalled, among other things, this verse which the elders said had been uttered long ago: 'A Dorian war shall come and with it death.' There was controversy, however, whether the word used by the ancients had been 'dearth' and not 'death'. At the present time the view that the word was 'death' naturally prevailed. For people made their recollection fit their experience. But, I imagine, if ever another Dorian war should come upon us after the present one and a dearth should ensue, people will, in all probability, recite the verse accordingly. Those who knew of it, recalled, too, the oracle given to the Lacedaimonians in answer to their enquiry whether they should go to war; the god answered if they made war with all their might victory would be theirs and said that he himself would assist them. So they surmised that what was happening tallied with the oracle: the plague began immediately after the Peloponnesians had invaded; it did not enter the Peloponnese to any extent worth mentioning; it ravaged Athens most of all, then the other most populous places. Such was the history of the plague.

X. Epidemic disease

In chapter 58 Thucydides describes how this deadly disease was carried from the stricken city to infect the Athenian forces investing Potidaea:

[58] In the course of the same summer, Hagnon, son of Nicias, and Cleopompus, son of Cleinias, colleagues of Pericles, taking the forces which the latter had employed against the Peloponnese, immediately set out on an expedition against the Chalcidians in Thrace and against Potidaea. On their arrival they brought siege-engines to bear against Potidaea and tried every way to take it. But, in their attempts to take the city and in other respects, their success was incommensurate with the scale of their preparations. For the plague broke out there and sorely distressed the Athenians. It so ravaged the army that even the soldiers of the earlier expedition, who had previously been in good health, caught the disease from Hagnon's troops .... Hagnon, therefore, withdrew with his fleet to Athens, having lost by plague in about forty days one thousand and fifty hoplites from a total of four thousand. The soldiers of the previous expedition remained in position and continued the siege of Potidaea.

And in the following book [III.87] he records the return of the plague and estimates the military losses caused by it:

[87] During the following winter the Athenians suffered a second attack of the plague. It had never completely abated, but there had been some remission in its virulence. The second outbreak lasted no less than a year, the first lasted two. Nothing did more harm to Athenian power than this. For no less than four thousand four hundred heavy infantry in the ranks and three hundred cavalry died of it, as well as an indeterminable number of common folk.

For a discussion of the social impact of the disease upon Athenian society see Longrigg, 1992, pp. 21-44.

X.7. Diodorus Siculus, *World History* XII.45 and 58

In this later account of the of the Athenian Plague Diodorus attributes its cause to breathing polluted air.

[45] The Lacedaimonians together with the Peloponnesians and their other allies invaded Attica for a second time <i.e. in 430 BC> .... The Athenians did not venture to draw themselves up against them, but, confined within the walls, became involved in a crisis caused by plague. For a great multitude of all sorts of people had streamed together into the city and on account of the lack of space, as one might reasonably expect, fell victim to diseases as they breathed in polluted air.

Some chapters later on Diodorus takes up again his account of the plague and sets out what he conceives to have been its causes.

[58] At this time <i.e. 426 BC> the Athenians, who had enjoyed some period of relief from the plague, fell once again into the same misfortune. For they were so afflicted by the disease that, of their soldiers, they lost more than four thousand infantry and four hundred cavalry and, of the rest of their population, both free and slave, more than ten thousand. Since history seeks to ascertain the cause of the terrible nature of this disease, it is necessary to set them forth.

As a result of heavy rains the previous winter, the ground had become waterlogged and, having received a huge amount of water, many of the hollows had become lakes and contained stagnant water, as marshy areas do. When these waters became warm and putrefied in the summer, thick foul vapours formed which rose and corrupted the neighbouring air. (This phenomenon is also seen in marshes which have a pestilential nature.) The bad quality of the food-supply also aggravated the disease. For the crops throughout that year were completely watery and their natural qualities were corrupted. The failure of the Etesian winds by which most of the heat is constantly cooled throughout the summer proved to be a third cause of the disease. When the heat intensified and the air grew fiery, the bodies of the inhabitants, without anything to cool them, wasted away. Consequently it transpired that all the diseases at the time were accompanied by fever on account of the excessive heat. For this reason most of the sick threw themselves into the cisterns and springs in their desire to cool their bodies. The Athenians, because of the extreme severity of the disease, attributed the causes of the disaster to the deity. Consequently, in accordance with a certain oracle, they purified the island of Delos, which was sacred to Apollo but had seemingly been defiled by the burial of the dead there. They dug up, therefore, all the graves on Delos and transferred the remains to the neighbouring island called Rheneia. They also passed a law forbidding birth or burial on Delos. They celebrated, too, the festal assembly of the Delians,[1] which though held in former times, had been discontinued for a long time.

[1] The ancient festival of the Ionian Amphictiony held in honour of Apollo and Artemis (cf. Thucydides, *History of the Peloponnesian War* III.104).

X.8. Diodorus Siculus, *World History* XIV.70.4-71

Diodorus also used Thucydides's description of the Athenian plague as a model for his own description of a different epidemic that afflicted the Carthaginians investing Syracuse in 397 BC. It is illuminating to compare the two authors' accounts.

After the Carthaginians had captured the suburb and plundered the temple of Demeter and Core, a disease fell upon their army. This god-sent calamity was increased by the crowding of tens of thousands into the same place; by the fact that the time of year was very conducive to disease, and, in addition, by the extraordinary heats prevailing that summer. It seems probable that the place, too, had something to do with the intensity of the trouble; for when the Athenians had earlier occupied the same camp, many of them had perished from disease, the place being marshy and low-lying. At first, before sunrise, owing to the coldness of the air from the marshes, shivering was produced in the body, while the heat of mid-day naturally had a stifling effect upon such a crowd gathered together in such a confined space.

This malady, then, first attacked the Libyans, many of whom died; the dead were buried at first, but afterwards, when their numbers increased and those attending the sick were seized by the disease, none dared to approach the sufferers. Thus, aid being withdrawn, there was no more help against the trouble. Owing to the stench of unburied corpses and the putridity arising from the marshes, the disease began with catarrhs; later swellings supervened about the throat, succeeded shortly afterwards by fevers, muscular pains in the back, and heaviness of the legs. Thereafter followed dysenteries and small blisters over the whole surface of the body.

Such was the experience in the majority of cases. Others were afflicted by madness and a complete loss of memory; they would walk about the camp out of their minds striking anyone they met. In general, as it turned out medical assistance was of no avail, both because of the intensity of the disease and the suddenness with which death arrived; for the victims died on the fifth day, or on the sixth, at the latest, enduring terrible tortures so that those who had fallen in the war were universally regarded as blessed. For in fact those who attended upon the suffering fell victims to the disease; consequently the plight of the sick was terrible, since none would help them in their trouble. For not only did strangers desert one another, but brothers were compelled to abandon brothers and friends friends through fear for themselves.

The extent to which Diodorus models his account upon that of Thucydides is plain for all to see – notwithstanding his adoption of the miasmatic theory as evidenced above [X.7]. But, in sharp contrast to the rationality of Thucydides's account, which makes no attempt to account for the onset of the Plague in terms of the anger of affronted deities, Diodorus regards the Syracusan epidemic as a 'god-sent calamity' in retribution for the plundering of the temple of Demeter and Core.

X.9. [Hippocrates], *Epidemics* I.1 (II.598-604,2L)

Another contagious disease? Our Hippocratic author certainly seems to suggest that the epidemic he describes here was contagious.

In Thasos, during Autumn, about the time of the equinox, towards the setting of the Pleiades, there was abundant rain, soft and continuous, with southerly winds. The winter southerly, light north winds, droughts; on the whole the winter was spring-like. Spring was southerly, cool with light showers. Summer for the most part cloudy, no rain. Etesian winds were few, light and irregular.

All atmospheric conditions had been southerly with drought, but early in the spring conditions changed to their opposite and became northerly and a few people were stricken with remittent fevers which were very mild. A few had haemorrhages which were not fatal. Many had swellings around the ears, some on the one side, some on both; in most cases without fever and the patient was not confined to bed. Some also experienced a slight fever. In all cases the swellings subsided harmlessly. In no case was there suppuration such as is common with swellings from other causes. The character of the swellings was spongy, large and spread widely, without inflammation or pain. In all cases they disappeared without a sign. Boys, young men and men in their prime were afflicted – mainly those who frequented the wrestling-school and the gymnasia. (Few women were attacked.) Many had dry coughs without expectoration; their voices were hoarse. Soon after the onset of the disease, but in some cases after an interval, painful inflammations developed sometimes in one, sometimes in both testicles, sometimes with fever, sometimes not, causing much suffering to the majority of patients. But, in other respects, people were free from the sort of ailments that require medical assistance.

The symptoms described above, which include swellings in the regions of the ears and which, in the case of some males, were coupled with the added complication of a painful orchitis, strongly suggest that the disease was mumps. Our author tells us that few women were affected; its main victims were youths, young men and men in their prime – for the most part those who frequented the wrestling-school and the gymnasia. Despite the scepticism of Poole and Holladay (p. 298), it is very hard to believe that there is not, at least, an implicit recognition here of the fact of contagion. As has been seen above, the traditional Hippocratic view was that epidemics were 'miasmatic' in origin, i.e. were caused by air polluted by some unhealthy exhalation [see **X.3 & 4**] – a widespread belief which still survives in the term 'malaria' (bad air). But, to explain this disease upon such a miasmatic basis, it would be necessary to assume either that the gymnasia and wrestling school were all located in an insalubrious area or badly ventilated, and set apart from private dwellings. In the present instance the medical writer has evidently realised some males, who came into contact while taking exercise, picked up the infection from one another; whereas the women, who stayed at home, were less prone to catch the disease. It may be of some significance that the epidemic is described as having occurred at Thasos, the island where Thucydides was himself stationed in 424 BC. But, in view of the controversy regarding the dating of Hippocratic works – not to mention the difficulty in determining when the different parts of Thucydides's *History* were written, it would not be wise to go further and draw any firm conclusions regarding influence between medicine and history here.

Hippocrates and the Athenian plague

X.10. Galen, *On theriac to Piso* 16 (XIV.280-1K)

Galen records the legend that Hippocrates eradicated the Athenian Plague by purifying the air, (see, too, **IV.5**).

On this account I also commend Hippocrates, who deserves great admiration for curing the famous epidemic that first came upon the Greeks from Ethiopia, merely by altering the air so that it would no longer be inhaled in the same condition. He ordered fires to be kindled throughout the whole city, not simply composed of kindling wood, but also of the sweetest garlands and flowers. These, he advised, were to be fuel for the fire, and he urged that richest of sweet-scented unguents should be burned so that men might inhale for relief the air purified in this way.

*

Our earliest surviving literary description of epidemic disease is the account of the impact of plague[1] (*loimos*) upon the Greek army besieging Troy in the first book of the *Iliad* [I.8]. The disease is represented as being supernatural in origin, sent by Apollo in punishment for Agamemnon's arrogant treatment of his priest, Chryses, who had come to the Greek camp in an endeavour to ransom his captive daughter. Eventually, the Greeks, on the suggestion of Achilles, consulted the soothsayer, Calchas. He revealed to them that Apollo had sent the disease to avenge his priest and that the god would not lift the pestilence until the girl had been returned to her father, without a ransom and with a hecatomb of oxen for sacrifice. The Greeks concurred, purified themselves, cast the 'defilements' into the sea and sacrificed to Apollo. The god was appeased and the plague abated. In similar fashion, Hesiod describes in *Works and Days* 238-45 a plague, sent this time by Zeus, which killed the men and rendered the women barren [I.13].

In both of these epic accounts, it may be noted, the disease is not regarded as communicable from one victim to another. The stricken are represented as having been afflicted *en masse* by the action of a vengeful god. They do not infect one another by contact. While both of these accounts are, presumably, fictitious, their authors are doubtless reflecting common beliefs regarding the origins and operations of diseases current at their own time. This belief in the supernatural causation of disease was persistent [see, for example, **X.8**]. It was held by some even during the Fifth-Century Enlightenment – as may be inferred, for example, from Thucydides's account of the Athenian plague in *History of the Peloponnesian War* II.47 [**X.6**]. At the beginning of his tragedy *Oedipus Tyrannus* Sophocles puts into the mouth of the priest of Zeus a dramatic description of the impact of plague (*loimos*) upon Thebes [**X.1**] that is echoed a little later in the words of the Choir of Elders [**X.2**]. Petitioned to take action, Oedipus sends his brother-in-law, Creon, to consult the oracle at Delphi for advice as to what should be done. Creon returns to announce that Apollo commands that a *miasma* (source of pollution), which is defiling the city, must be expelled. Oedipus himself, polluted by the killing of his own father, Laius, is the source of that *miasma* which he is transmitting by contagion to those in proximity (see, too, *Oedipus Coloneus* 226-36, 1132-6).

Within the Hippocratic *Corpus* [**X.3 & 4**], however, although the term *miasma* is retained, the concept of religious contagion is now stripped of all moral and religious connotations and thoroughly rationalised. Here one finds no suggestion of individual culpability. No appeals are made to gods or oracles. Physical and natural explanations are sought upon which therapy is based [**X.5**]. Although Thucydides displays the same rational standpoint found in the Hippocratic writings, he does not himself, unlike Diodorus in his later description [**X.7**], resort to this miasmatic theory of disease in his account of the great Plague of Athens [**X.6**]; but subscribes to the belief that the disease was transmitted by contagion and thus has seemingly reverted to a highly rationalised version of the religious belief revealed by Sophocles in the *Oedipus Tyrannus*. [see **X.1 & 2**]. Although it has been denied that transmission of disease by contagion occurs in the Hippocratic *Corpus*, *Epidemics* I.1 seems to suggest otherwise [**X.9**].

It may also be noted here that in his description of the Athenian plague Thucydides makes no mention of the legend which later attributed its cessation to the intervention of Hippocrates. (see, for example, Galen, *On theriac to Piso* 16 at **X.10**).

[1] In modern times the term 'plague' is commonly used to denote bubonic plague, *Yersinia pestis*, the Black Death. Here, however, this term is used to denote any widespread epidemic disease.

XI

Prognosis and diagnosis

Hippocratic prognosis was concerned not only with the future course of a patient's illness, but also with his past and present state of health.

XI.1. [Hippocrates], *Prognostic* 1, 2, 25 (II.110-118,6; 188,6-14L)

In the following passage the Hippocratic doctor is given detailed instructions as to how he should proceed in his initial examination of the patient.

[1] It seems to me that it is an excellent thing for a physician to practise prognosis. For, if he has foreknowledge and declares beforehand at his patients' bedside both the present, the past and the future, filling in the details they have omitted, it will be believed that he has a better understanding of their cases so that they will have the confidence to entrust themselves to him as their doctor. Furthermore, he would carry out treatment most effectively from foreknowledge derived from the present symptoms of what will be the future course of the disease. It is impossible to cure all the sick – that would be better even than forecasting future developments. But, since men do die, some owing to the severity of the disease before they have summoned the doctor, others immediately after summoning him – some living a single day, other a little longer, before the physician by his art can combat each disease, it is therefore necessary to learn the natures of such <i.e. swift-acting> diseases, whether there is something divine in these diseases,[1] the extent to which they exceed the strength of the body and how to predict them. In this way one would be justly admired and be a good physician. For the longer one makes plans to meet each contingency, the greater one's capacity to save those who still have a chance of survival, and, by realising and announcing beforehand which patients will die and which will be saved, one would be free from blame.

[2] In acute diseases one must pay attention to the following: first, one must examine the face of the patient to see whether it is like that of the healthy, and, especially, whether it is as normal. Such likeness is the best sign; the greatest divergence is the most dangerous. The latter is as follows: nose sharp, eyes hollow, temples sunken, ears cold and contracted with their lobes distorted, and the skin about the face hard and stretched and dry; the colour of the whole face being yellow or black.[2] If at the beginning of the disease the face is like this and if it is not yet possible from the other symptoms to make a prognosis, one must enquire whether the

patient has suffered from insomnia or from severe diarrhoea, or is at all hungry. If he admits to any of these, his case should be considered less severe. If the facial appearance is on account of any of these causes, crisis occurs in a day and a night. But if he admits to none of these things, and the condition does not settle within the prescribed time, know that this is a sign of death. If the face assumes this appearance when the disease is of longer standing than the third day, ask the same questions as I ordered previously and examine the other symptoms, both of the whole body and of the eyes. For if they shun the light or weep involuntarily or squint, or if one becomes smaller than the other, or the whites are red or livid or have black veins or bleariness appears round the eyeballs, or if they wander or protrude or have become deeply sunken, or the complexion of the whole face is changed – all these symptoms must be considered bad, indeed fatal. The appearance of the eyes in sleep should also be considered. For if some part of the white appears when the lids are closed, and it is not due to diarrhoea, drug-taking, nor is it the normal habit in sleep, it is a bad sign and especially fatal. If, the eyelid or the lip or the nose becomes swollen or livid together with one of the other symptoms, you must know that death is close at hand. It is also a fatal sign if the lips are parted and hang loose and have become cold and very pallid.

[25] Any one who is going to make accurate forecasts as to who will recover and who will die, for whom the disease will continue for more days and for whom less, must be thoroughly acquainted with all the symptoms and be able to form his judgement by estimating their comparative powers, as has been described in speaking of urine, sputa and other matters. The physician must be quick to recognise the trends of epidemic diseases that constantly occur and not to let climatic conditions escape his notice ....

[1] For the implications of this expression see **II.16 n.1 & II.26**.
[2] Here we have the famous 'Hippocratic face' portending imminent death.

XI.2. [Hippocrates], *Epidemics* I.10 (II.668,14-670,15L)

This treatise, too, lists signs crucial for the prediction of critical periods of disease so that appropriate action can be taken to restore the balance of health.

The following were the attendant circumstances of the diseases from which I formed my diagnoses, learning from the common nature of all, and the particular nature of each individual, from the disease, the patient, from what is prescribed, from the person making the prescription – for from these things diagnosis is rendered easier or more difficult; from the constitution, both as a whole and in respect of the parts, of the weather and each region; from the custom, mode of life, habits and age of each patient; from his words, mannerisms, silence, whims, sleep or sleeplessness, nature and time of dreams, pluckings, scratchings, tears; from paroxysms, excrement, urine, sputa, vomit, and what kind of developments take place in succession from and into what sort of diseases, and their prolongation to a fatal issue or a crisis, sweating, shivering, chill, cough, sneezes, hiccoughs, breathing, belchings, flatulence, farting, silent or noisy, haemorrhages and haemorrhoids. From these must we consider what their consequences also will be.

XI.3. [Hippocrates], *Humours* 2 (V.478,6-13L)

The author of this treatise also provides a comprehensive list of conditions to be observed and acted upon.

These things must be considered: symptoms that disappear of their own accord, ... things that are harmful or beneficial, shapes, movement, swelling, subsidence, sleep, wakefulness, anticipation of what must be done or prevented from being done. The lessons to be learnt from vomiting, evacuation below, sputum, mucus, coughing, belching, hiccuping, flatulence, urine, sneezing, tears, itchiness, pluckings, touchings, thirst, hunger, satiety, sleep, pains, absence of pain, body, mind, learning, memory, voice, silence.

XI.4. [Hippocrates], *On the art* 11 (VI.18,14-20,3L = *CMG* I.1, p. 16 Heib.)

Here it is recognised that there are hidden conditions which must be investigated by the intellect.

It is impossible for anyone who sees only with his eyes to know any of the things that have been here described. In consequence they have been called by me obscure, even as they have been judged to be by the art. They have not prevailed over us by their obscurity, but have been mastered where possible. It is possible to do so in so far as the dispositions of the sick afford opportunities for being examined and those of investigators have a natural capacity for research. They are discerned with a greater degree of effort and no less an amount of time than if they were seen with the eyes; for what escapes the sight of the eyes are mastered by the eye of the mind.

'CRITICAL DAYS'

It was widely believed that in acute diseases crises occurred as a general rule at fixed and regular intervals.

XI.5. [Hippocrates], *Epidemics* I.12 (II.678,5-682,2L)

Here is presented a double series of critical days: diseases that become exacerbated on even days also have crises on even days; those that become exacerbated on odd days have crises on those days.

When symptoms become exacerbated on even days, crises occur on even days. Those diseases whose exacerbations occur on odd days have their crises on odd days. The first period of those diseases that have their crisis on even days is the fourth, then the sixth, the eighth, tenth, fourteenth, twentieth, twenty-fourth, thirtieth, fortieth, sixtieth, eightieth, one hundred and twentieth. Of those that have their crisis on the odd days, the first period is the third, then the fifth, seventh, ninth, eleventh, seventeenth, twenty-first, twenty-seventh, thirty-first. So one must pay attention and know that at these times there will be crises resulting in recovery, or death, or turns for the better or worse. Further, one must know that if these crises occur other than on the days indicated, there will be relapses and fatalities might occur. One must also consider in what periods the crises occur of irregular fevers, of quartans, quintans, septans and nonans.

XI.6. [Hippocrates], *Diseases* II.47 (VII.70,4-11L)

Auscultation and succussion are both employed as diagnostic aids in the treatment of a patient suffering from pus in the pleural cavity (empyema).

When the fifteenth day has arrived after the pus has broken forth into the <pleural cavity>, wash the patient with much hot water, seat him on a steady stool, have someone else hold his hands, and shaking him yourself by his shoulders, listen to determine on which side the sound occurs. Choose to make the incision on the left for it is less lethal. If, because of the thickness and abundance of the pus, there is no sound – for this happens sometimes – make the incision on the side that is swollen and more painful, as low down as possible, behind the swelling rather than in front of it so that your exit for the pus offers an easy flow.

XI.7. [Hippocrates], *Diseases* II.47 (VII.72,1-4L)

Prognosis in such cases.

A sign that the patient is going to recover: if the pus is white and pure and there are strands of blood in it, the patient generally recovers; but, if, for example, it flows out on the first day like pease-pudding, or, on the next day, thick, greenish and smelly, these patients die.

XI.8. [Hippocrates], *Diseases* II.48 (VII.72,6-21L)

Diagnosis and prognosis in cases of consumption. See, too, *Internal affections* 10 (VII.188-90L).

When there is lung-disease thick, greenish, sweet sputum is coughed up, there is grinding of teeth and pain occurs in the chest and the back. There is a light whistling sound in the throat, which becomes dry. The hollows beneath the eyes become red and the voice deep. The feet become swollen and the nails curve.[1] The patients become thin, their upper body wasted. The sputum is disgusting when it remains in the mouth after the throat has been cleared. Coughing occurs most early in the mornings and in the middle of the night, but also at other times. The disease affects younger women more than older ones. If the patient's hair is by this time falling from his head and the head is already becoming bald as if from disease, and if, when he spits upon coals, the sputum has a heavy odour,[2] declare that he is about to die within a short time and that what kills him will be diarrhoea. For, when the pus about the heart is already putrefying, it smells of fat upon coals;[3] and the brain, on being heated, pours forth a salty fluid, which sets the cavity in motion; this is a symptom: hair falls from the head.

When the circumstances are such, do not treat this patient.[4]

[1] The curving of the nails is still regarded as an important and reliable diagnostic sign.

[2] See, too, *Aphorisms* V.11 (IV.536L): 'In patients troubled with consumption, if the sputum they cough up onto burning coals has an offensive smell and if their hair falls out from their head, then it is a fatal sign.'

[3] See, too, *Coan prenotions* 426 (V.680L) where, in a similar context, it is added that 'there is a strong smell of burnt meat'. By this procedure the Hippocratic doctor is able to detect the presence of pulmonary tissue in the sputum.

[4] For the recommendation that treatment should not be attempted under certain circumstances see **VIII.4.**

PULSATION

Although the throbbing of certain blood vessels had been observed earlier by several Greek authors, the first to regard pulsation as a constant and normal phenomenon occurring in all blood vessels seems to have been Aristotle. He did not, however, distinguish between the venous and arterial systems. The first to assign a diagnostic role to the pulse was Praxagoras, who drew a clear distinction between veins and arteries and restricted pulsation to the arteries alone.

XI.9. Galen, *On trembling, palpitation, convulsions and cramps* 5
(VII.598K = *Praxagoras* Fr. 27 Steckerl)

Praxagoras attributes pulsation to the arteries ....

XI.10. Galen, *On the differences of the pulses* 4.2 (VIII.702K =
Praxagoras Fr. 28 Steckerl = *Herophilus* Fr. 155 von Staden)

According to Galen, Praxagoras believed that the arteries possessed the power to pulsate independently of the heart. Herophilus, however, rejected this view and maintained that the arteries' power of pulsation was derived from the heart.

Concerning the arteries there arose a still greater disagreement among the physicians from olden times. Some of them, including Praxagoras, too, thought that they pulsated by themselves, possessing, like the heart, an innate capacity of such a sort. Others, on the other hand, while recognising that they pulsate because the arterial coat itself dilates and contracts, just like the heart, did not believe that they possessed an innate capacity which enabled them to do this, but rather derived this capacity from the heart. Herophilus, too, was of this opinion ....

XI.11. Galen, *On the differences of the pulses* 4.3 (VIII.723-4K = *Praxagoras* Fr. 27 Steckerl = *Herophilus* Fr. 150 von Staden)

Praxagoras failed to differentiate pulsation from other cardiac and arterial movements, whereas Herophilus isolated it as a specific physiological reaction.

There was no small disagreement between Herophilus and his teacher Praxagoras concerning these affections <spasm, tremor, palpitation>, since Praxagoras had stated incorrectly that palpitation, tremor, and spasm are an affection of the arteries, differing not in kind, but in size from the pulsating motion in them. For pulsation, Praxagoras said, occurs when the arteries are in a natural condition without any difficult circumstance. But when their motion is increased to an unnatural extent, first spasm is caused; next, in consequence, tremor; thirdly, palpitation. All these affections differ from one another in size. For this reason, then, Herophilus, right at the beginning of his treatise *On pulses,* tries to overturn his teacher's opinion.

See, too, Galen, *On trembling etc.* 1 (VII.584K).

XI.12. Galen, *On diagnosing the pulses* 4.3 (VIII.959K = *Herophilus* Fr. 162 von Staden)

Herophilus's classification of the different types of pulse.

... What more reliable witness of Herophilus's opinion do you wish than Herophilus? 'One pulse', he says, 'appears to differ from another, as has been said, in rhythm, size, speed and vehemence.'

XI.13. Ps.-Rufus, *Synopsis on the pulses* 4 (pp. 223-5 Daremberg/Ruelle = *Herophilus* Fr. 177 von Staden)

Herophilus distinguishes certain cardiac rhythms as characteristic of different ages.

Herophilus says <the pulse of new-born children> is irrational in its composition <i.e. it has no definable ratios>. He calls the pulse that is without some ratio 'irrational', for it neither has a double ratio, nor a ratio of one and a half to one, nor any other proportion, but is very short and occurs, in our view, similar in size to a prick of a needle. Consequently, Herophilus first properly called it 'irrational'. But with the advance of age and the body's coming to full growth, the pulse, too, increases with reference to ratio and acquires a dilation that is proportionately more extended than the contraction. As for the rest, their ratios are capable of adaptation to a demonstration derived from the scansion of grammarians.

For the first pulse discovered in the case of new-born children will have the rhythm of the short-syllabled foot, since it is short both in dilation and contraction and, on account of this, is conceived as consisting of two <short> time-units, whereas the pulse of children who are growing up is analogous to the foot known among grammarians as a trochee. This pulse consists of three <short> time-units, holding its dilation for two time-units, but its contraction for one. The pulse of those in the prime of life is equal in both, that is, in dilation and contraction, and is comparable to the so-called spondee, which is the longest of the disyllabic feet. It is composed of four <short> time-units. This pulse Herophilus calls 'in equal quantity'. The pulse of those who are past their prime and almost old is itself also composed of three time-units, holding its contraction for twice as long as its dilation or longer.

XI.14. Galen, *Synopsis of his own books on the pulses* 14 (IX.470K = *Herophilus* Fr. 175 von Staden)

He identifies three main kinds of abnormal pulse.

In comparing the time of the dilation <of the pulse> to the time of its contraction, as Herophilus required, it can be recognised that the sick person has a pulse-rate contrary to nature, and in addition that it is greatly or slightly contrary to nature. For great deviations from the natural rhythms into that which is contrary to nature indicate great harm, whereas lesser deviations indicate smaller harm. Pararhythmic pulses, then, reveal a small deviation, heterorhythmic a greater and ecrhythmic the greatest of all.

XI.15. Marcellinus, *On pulsation* 31 (pp. 468-9 Schöne = *Herophilus* Fr. 170 von Staden)

Other types of abnormal pulse are defined by Herophilus in metaphorical terms derived from their resemblance to the gait of animals.

Herophilus, who was the first to name the 'gazelle-like' (*dorkadizôn*) pulse, says that he observed it once in the case of a certain eunuch ....

XI.16. Galen, *Synopsis of his own books on the pulses* 8 (IX.453K = *Herophilus* Fr. 180 von Staden)

Disagreement regarding the 'ant-like' pulse.

Archigenes says that the 'ant-like' (*myrmekizôn*) pulse is fast, whereas Herophilus says that it is not fast.

XI.17. Marcellinus, *On pulsation* 11 (p. 463 Schöne = *Herophilus* Fr. 182 von Staden)

Herophilus attempts to measure the pulse by means of a portable water-clock.

Herophilus demonstrated that a man has a fever when his pulse becomes more frequent, larger and more forceful, accompanied by great internal heat. If the pulse loses its forcefulness and magnitude, an alleviation of the fever ensues. He says that the increased frequency of the pulse is the first symptom of the beginning of a fever and extends equally until the complete remission of the fever. There is a story that Herophilus was so confident in the frequency of the pulse that, using it as a reliable symptom, he prepared a clepsydra capable of containing a specified amount for the natural pulses of each age. He then went to the patient's bedside, set up the clepsydra, and took hold of the fevered pulse. And in so far as a greater number of pulse-beats occurred than was natural, relative to the time required to fill the clepsydra, to this degree was the greater frequency of the pulse revealed – that is to say, the patient had more or less fever.

XI.18. Galen, *On the differences of the pulses* 4.2 (VIII.714K)

Erasistratus, too, regards pulsation as a regular physiological phenomenon.

Erasistratus says that the pulse is a movement of the arteries arising by dilation and contraction through the agency of a vital and psychic faculty, and it occurs for the sake of keeping full the arteries, which contain vital pneuma.

*

When summoned to undertake a case the Hippocratic doctor was less concerned to provide his patient with an explanation of the cause of his complaint than to provide a 'prognosis' which covered the past and present as well as the future of his disease. This prognosis was based upon a very thorough examination of the patient. The treatise, *Prognostic*, presents detailed instructions as to how the doctor should proceed [**XI.1**]. At a time when there were no universally recognised professional medical qualifications and success as a doctor was dependent upon reputation acquired in practice, Hippocratic prognosis, with its primary emphasis upon foreknowledge, upon predicting the future course of a disease, also performed an important social function in that the successful description of the patient's past medical history together with a prediction of the future course of his disease by the (usually) itinerant doctor would impress that patient and do much to win his confidence and acceptance of future treatment. Careful prognosis, too, would provide the means whereby the Hippocratic doctor would be able to identify those cases that were hopeless and so enable him to protect his reputation. The author of *Prognostic* in the passage translated at **XI.1** alludes to this situation when he stresses the necessity to determine and announce beforehand which patients are going to die and so absolve oneself from any blame. (See also *The Art* 3 and *Fractures* 36). As well as employing prognosis to secure the confidence and trust of his patient, the doctor relied upon it to avoid any repercussions deriving from unsuccessful treatment.

The most favoured method of treatment for the Hippocratic doctor was by means of diet (see **Chapter XII** below), since disease was widely regarded as an imbalance of the constituents of the body, frequently of one or other of the four humours [**IX.3**]. (The widespread prevalence of malarial fever in Classical Greece, with its regular patterns of development and seasonal onset must have contributed greatly to the predominance of this medical theory.) The aim of dietetic medicine was to devise a regimen that would correct the imbalance and restore health. Prognosis, therefore, was necessary to pick out the crucial signs and predict the critical periods of the disease so that appropriate action could be taken to restore the balance of health. Crises were believed to occur on what were termed 'critical days': diseases were supposed to reach a crisis on a fixed day (or on fixed days) after their commencement [XI.5]. (The times varied in the case of different diseases.) A crisis that occurred at a time other than on a critical day was believed to indicate the likelihood of a fatal outcome. A comprehensive list of perceptible signs is provided in the passages from *Prognostic*, *Epidemics* and *Humours* translated here [XI.1, 2 & 3]. In the treatise *On the art*, however, it is recognised that there are hidden ailments and conditions that must be investigated by the intellect [XI.4].

Auscultation coupled with succussion is recommended as an aid to diagnosis in the treatment of a patient suffering from empyema [XI.6] and signs are described in both this disease [XI.7] and in consumption [XI.8] to enable the doctor to determine whether his patient will live or die. One important diagnostic aid, pulsation, however, is conspicuous by its absence in the Hippocratic *Corpus*. Although the beat of the heart and the throbbing motion of certain blood vessels had been remarked upon by various Greek authors,[1] in these instances the connotation is that of violent emotion not that of the normal vital function of the pulse. The author of the Hippocratic treatise *On places in man* 3 (VI.280L) explicitly recognises that a pair of vessels in the temples always pulsate and do not do so only under abnormal conditions. However, our author here cannot be credited with any general pulse-theory, but has merely recognised a limited and highly localised pulsation of blood vessels.[2]

Aristotle seems to have been the first to regard pulsation as a constant and normal phenomenon occurring in all blood vessels, but made no distinction between the two vascular systems, the venous and arterial. It was Praxagoras who first gave the pulse an important role in diagnosis and therapy. Having drawn a clear distinction between veins and arteries, he restricted pulsation to the arteries alone [XI.9 & 10] (which, he maintained, contained not blood but air).

These pioneering investigations were subsequently developed by Herophilus. Galen, who is our main source of information, clearly regards Herophilus's work as inaugurating a new era. Although indebted to Praxagoras, Herophilus departs markedly from his master's teaching in several respects. For example, Praxagoras's belief that the arteries possessed the capacity to pulsate independently of the heart was rejected by Herophilus along with the latter's conception of air-filled arteries. He reaffirmed the arteries' connection with the heart and held that they derived their power of pulsation from that organ [XI.10]. He failed, however, to recognise that their pulsation was caused by the pumping action of the heart. (Erasistratus later recognised this.) Although Praxagoras's discovery that only arteries pulsate was an important innovation, pulsation was still not differentiated by him from other cardiac and arterial movements [XI.11]. Herophilus, however, distinguished the pulse from these and similar phenomena and, having isolated it as a specific physiological reaction, thereby became the first to recognise its full importance as a clinical sign in diagnosis and prognosis. He developed a systematic (but largely fanciful) classification of the different types of pulse employing the four main indications of size, strength, rate and rhythm [XI.12] and adopted a musical terminology derived, some have thought, from his contemporary, Aristoxenus of Tarentum, to differentiate the numerous sub-divisions of these four main groups. He produced an elaborate theory of a tetrapartite development of human pulse rhythms, distinguishing certain cardiac rhythms as characteristic of different periods of life, namely childhood, adolescence, maturity, and approaching old age **[XI.13]**.

Herophilus was also interested in deviations from normal rhythms and identified three main types of abnormal pulse – the 'pararhythmic', the 'heterorhythmic' and the 'ecrhythmic'. Of these the first indicates merely a slight divergence from normality, the second a greater and the third the greatest **[XI.14]**. For other types of abnormal pulse he devised metaphorical terms derived from their supposed resemblance to the gait of certain animals **[XI.15 & 16]**. Herophilus is also credited by Marcellinus, a physician of the first century AD, with the first known attempt to measure the frequency of the pulse by means of a portable water-clock or clepsydra. It is hard to envisage how the apparatus could have been calibrated with sufficient sophistication to cater accurately for various age groups. The absence of any record of subsequent use of this device might seem to suggest that the innovation was not successful **[XI.17]**.

According to Galen, Erasistratus shared with Herophilus this view of the pulse as a normal and consistent physiological function **[XI.18]**. He recognised, however, that it was caused by the pumping action of the heart (Galen, *On the doctrines of Hippocrates and Plato* 6.7 (V.562K)).

See, generally, Edelstein, 1967b.

[1] See, for example, Homer, *Iliad* 22.452; Plato, *Phaedrus* 251D.

[2] Pulsation is recognised as a sign of health or disease in the Hippocratic treatises, *On nutriment* 48 (IX.116L) and *On the heart* 1 **[XIV.14]**, but these works are generally considered to be late.

XII

Dietetics and regimen

Dietetics appears to have been a relatively late development in Greek medicine.

XII.1. Porphyry, *Homeric Enquiries* (on *Iliad* 11.515), p. 165, 12 Schräder (= *Praxagoras* Fr. 36 Steckerl)

According to Porphyry, Homer did not mention anyone being treated by diet. He claims that dietetic medicine was introduced by Herodicus of Selymbria in the fifth century.

Herodicus began dietetic medicine. Hippocrates, Praxagoras and Chrysippus perfected it .... But, if he <viz. Homer> did not introduce someone being treated by diet, it is not strange, for he omits treatment by diet because of its unseemliness.

XII.2. Cornelius Celsus, *On medicine* Proem 3-4 (*CML* I, p. 17 Marx)

Celsus endorses this view when he points out that the sons of Asclepius gave no aid when pestilence struck the Greek army besieging Troy.

After him <viz. Aesculapius> his two sons Podalirius and Machaon, who followed Agamemnon as their leader to the Trojan War, gave no inconsiderable help to their comrades. Homer stated that they did not give any aid in the plague nor in the various kinds of diseases, but were only wont to treat wounds by the knife and by medication. Hence it appears that only these parts of medicine were attempted by them and that these were the most ancient. From the same authority, indeed, it can be learned that diseases were then attributed to the anger of the immortal gods, and that from them help was customarily sought. It is probable that with no aids against ill health, health was nevertheless generally good on account of good habits.

XII.3. Eustathius, *Commentaries on Homer's Iliad* 11.514 (van der Valk, III, 1979, pp. 243-4)

According to post-Homeric legend, however, Podalirius was later identified as a specialist in internal disease [see also **XV.6**].

Observe that this noble Greek physician <i.e. Machaon> gave his attention to the treatment of wounds. The poet does not mention diet. For they say that only surgery and pharmacy were invented by the ancients, but dietetics was begun by Hippocrates and completed by Herodicus, Praxagoras and Chrysippus. Some hold that Machaon practised surgery, but that Podalirius, who was also a warrior himself, ... practised dietetics. Proof of this is that the king summoned Machaon, but not Podalirius, to treat the wounded Menelaus. Evidence for this is also given in the epic accounts of the *Sack of Troy* in which it is related of Podalirius and Machaon that both were the sons of Poseidon, but one of them he manifestly made more renowned than the other. For 'to the one he gave more agile hands to draw the darts from the flesh and to heal all wounds. To the other[1] he gave the power to know accurately in his heart all matters that are unseen, and to heal things incapable of being healed .... '

[1] i.e. Podalirius.

XII.4. Galen, *Thrasybulus* or *Whether the art of health is part of medicine or gymnastics* 33 (V.869K = *Scripta minora* III, pp. 78-9 Helmreich)

Galen, too, raises the question of the origin of dietetics, but defers to Plato's authority.

I cannot guess whether another third part of medicine called dietetics also was in existence in Homeric times. But one who is older than I and is more likely to be credible about Greek matters, the philosopher, Plato, says that the Asclepiads of old did not use quite so much this part of the art; but that there are these three parts of medicine and the art that treats bodies that are in disorder is called by all the Greeks the art of medicine. Hardly anyone denies this. The name of the gymnastic art was not yet found in Homer. Nor was anyone at all called a trainer of athletes as one is called a doctor, seeing that even in Plato it is not possible often to find the name of the gymnastic art. He calls, however, the practitioner of this art a physical trainer rather than a trainer of athletes; for a little before the time of Plato the art of the trainer of athletes began when the training of athletes also came into being ....

XII.5. Plato, *Republic* III.406A-B

Socrates is here depicted contrasting the simple medicine of the Heroic Age with the modern medical fad of cosseting illness invented by Herodicus of Selymbria.

The Asclepiads did not use this modern, coddling treatment of disease before Herodicus's time. Herodicus was a trainer who became chronically ill and combined the art of physical training with medicine into a means of tormenting first and foremost himself and then many others later on. 'How?' he asked. 'By prolonging his death,' I replied. For, although he cosseted his illness, which was fatal, he was unable to cure himself. He spent his life doctoring himself with no time for anything else, tormenting himself if he departed a whit from his usual regimen, and, thanks to his cleverness, reached old age struggling against death all the time.

XII.6. *Anonymus Londinensis* 9.20-33 (Jones, 1947, p. 48)

Some further evidence of Herodicus's views on regimen is preserved in the *Anonymus Londinensis*: no pain, no gain.

Herodicus of Selymbria thinks that diseases arise from regimen. Regimen, he says, is in accordance with nature when exercise is included together with the necessary amount of pain. Thus nourishment is digested and bodies grow as the nourishment is distributed naturally. For he thinks that health ensues when bodies have a natural regimen, and disease when the regimen is unnatural. For those who are in an unnatural condition the medical art, when called in, prescribes exercise and so, as he himself says, brings them into the natural condition. It is said that he called the art of medicine 'artistic guidance to the natural condition'.

XII.7. [Hippocrates], *Epidemics* VI.3.18 (V.302,1-4L)

Herodicus's regime is criticised by this Hippocratic author.

Herodicus used to kill fever-patients with running, much wrestling, and with vapour baths: bad policy. Wrestling, walking, running and massage are inimical to the febrile. For them it is to add suffering to suffering in the form of distension of the veins, redness, lividity, jaundice, and slight pains in the sides.

XII.8. Iamblichus, *Life of Pythagoras* 163 (DK 58D1)

Iamblichus's testimony here to Pythagorean interest in dietetics also seems to entail that it was a post-Homeric innovation.

<The Pythagoreans> especially approved of the dietetic form of medicine and were most precise practitioners of it. In the first place they endeavoured to learn thoroughly the indications of symmetry between drink, food, and rest. Secondly, they were just about the first to try to treat systematically and to make distinctions concerning the preparation of foods offered to patients. They employed plasters to a greater extent than their predecessors; they had a lower regard for drugs and of these they employed especially those used for ulcers. Least of all they approved of surgery and cautery.

XII.9. [Hippocrates], *Ancient medicine* 3 (I.574,8-576,4L = *CMG* I.1, p. 37 Heib.)

This Hippocratic author, however, seems to suggest that dietetics was conterminous with the art of medicine.

The art of medicine would not have been discovered originally, nor would any medical research have been carried out – for there would have been no need for it – if the sick had benefited from the same food and regimen that the healthy eat and drink and otherwise adopt. But, as it is, sheer necessity caused men to search for and discover medicine because the sick did not benefit from the same diet as the healthy, just as they do not benefit from it today. To go back further still, I maintain that the regimen and nutriment, which the healthy now use, would not have been discovered if man had been satisfied with the same food and drink as an ox, or horse, and every animal except man....

XII.10. [Hippocrates], *Regimen in acute diseases* 1 (II.224-226,7L)

If the polemic by the author of this treatise may be regarded as historical, we would then have some further evidence to support the view that dietetics was an innovation of the fifth/fourth century.

The authors of the work called *Cnidian opinions* have correctly described the experiences of patients suffering individual diseases and the outcome of some of these diseases. To this extent, even a layman could make a correct description if he carefully inquired of each patient the nature of his experiences. But much of what the doctor should know in addition, without his patient telling him, they have omitted ....

[2] Whenever their interpretation of the symptoms leads them to prescribe treatment in each case, in these matters my own judgement is in many respects different from their exposition. Nor is this the only criticism I make, but also because the remedies they employed were few in number ....

[3] Now, if these remedies were good and suited to the diseases for which they recommended their use, they would be more worthy of praise, in that, though few, they were sufficient....

XII.11. [Hippocrates], *Regimen* I.2 (VI.468,6-470,10L = *CMG* I.2,4, pp. 122-4 Jo.)

It is recommended that before writing upon regimen, one should first acquire a thorough knowledge of the nature of man generally as well as the qualities of various foodstuff and the effect of different types of exercise. Here dietetic theory is based upon a physiological system which was itself influenced by philosophical theory.

I declare that he who is intending to write correctly about human regimen must first acquire knowledge and discernment of the nature of man as a whole – knowledge of his original constituents and discernment of the components by which he is controlled. For, if he is ignorant of the original constitution, he will be unable to gain knowledge of their effects; if he is ignorant of that which is prevailing in the body, he will be incapable of administering suitable treatment to the patient. These things, therefore, the author must know, and, further, the power possessed severally by all the food and drink of our diet, both that derived from nature and that from human art. For it is necessary to know how one ought to take away the power of those that are naturally strong and how one ought to add strength through art to those that are weak, whenever the opportunity for each might occur. But even when men understand what has been said, the treatment of a patient is not yet sufficient in itself because eating alone cannot keep a man healthy if he does not also take exercise. For food and exercise, while possessing opposite qualities, contribute mutually to produce health. For it is the nature of exercise to use up material, but of food and drink to make up deficiencies. And it is necessary ... to discern the power of the <various types> of exercise ... to know which of them tends to increase flesh and which lessen it ... to know also the correspondence between exercise and the bulk of the food, the constitution of the patient, the age of the individuals, the seasons of the year, the situations of the regions in which the patients live, the changes of the winds, and the state of the year.

For the claim that this passage reveals the same methodology as that attributed by Plato·to Hippocrates and may, therefore, be identified as having been written by the latter, see **IV.12**.

XII.12. [Hippocrates], *Regimen in health* I.1 (VI.72-74,9L = *CMG* I.1,3, pp. 204-8 Jou.)

Diet, it is urged, should be employed to counter adverse seasonal effects.

Laymen ought to order their regimen in the following way: in winter eat as much as possible and drink as little as possible ... when spring comes, one should then increase drink and make it very diluted and less in quantity and use softer foods, less in quantity ... in summer the barley-cake should be soft, the drink diluted and copious and all the meats boiled ... in autumn make food more abundant and drier and the meats in proportion, while drinks should be fewer and less diluted.

XII.13. Plato, *Timaeus* 88B-C

A successful regimen, it is held here, requires the balanced exercise of both mind and body.

... neither exercise the mind without the body nor the body without the mind so that they both may become equally matched and healthy. So, anyone engaged in mathematics or any other strenuous intellectual pursuit must also provide his body with exercise by taking part in physical training; while he who is assiduous in keeping his body in shape must, correspondingly, take mental exercise by taking up besides cultural and all manner of intellectual pursuits ....

XII.14. Oribasius, *Medical collections* 3.168ff. (Daremberg/Bussemaker = *CMG* VI.2,2, Vol. IV, pp. 141ff. Raeder = *Diokles* Fr. 141 Wellmann)

In a long fragment preserved by Oribasius, physician to the Emperor Julian, the Apostate, Diocles expounds his dietetic theory by presenting his detailed recommendations for a single day's routine. He distinguishes what is suitable for the various ages and makes adjustments for changes of season. He begins with prescriptions for a summer's day and then adds his modifications for spending a day in winter followed by the other seasons. (Since this fragment is far too long to include in its entirety, a précis is provided here.) Diocles makes his prescriptions for regimen from the moment of awakening which he places shortly before sunrise.

One should not arise immediately upon wakening, but wait until the heaviness of sleep leaves the limbs. Then the neck should be rubbed to counter any stiffness caused by the pressure of the pillows. Next, one should rub the entire body lightly with oil (mixed with water in summer). In some cases, even before emptying the bowels. One should then stretch the whole body and flex the joints. Thereupon the hands and face should be washed in pure, cold water and the teeth, gums, nose, ears, hair and scalp should be cared for. After this, those with work to do should attend to it; those who have not, should take a walk either before or after breakfast. The length of the walk should be in accordance with one's constitution and state of health. If taken before breakfast, long walks make one more receptive of nutriment and more able to digest it; after breakfast, when slow and of moderate length, they mix the food and relax the stomach. Long, swift walks after eating, however, are not recommended for they separate the food and cause indigestion.

After walking, one should sit down and deal with one's affairs until it is time to take exercise. The young should go to the gymnasium; the older and more infirm to the baths or some other warm place and anoint themselves with oil. Massage should preferably be self-administered since one also derives benefit from the exercise involved.

After the morning's exercise, one should take lunch, which should be neither warming nor drying in summer, nor cooling and moistening in winter and should occupy a mean position in spring and autumn. Directly after lunch, one should take a short siesta in a cool, shady place free from draughts. Upon awakening, one should attend to one's affairs and take a walk. After the walk, followed by a short rest, one should go to the gymnasium. The younger and stronger should take a cold bath after exercise; the older and weaker should oil and massage themselves and wash in warm water.

Dinner should be taken in summer shortly before sunset when the stomach is empty. The food and drink consumed should be appropriate both to the season and the individual constitution. After dinner, those with poor digestion should go to sleep immediately; the others should take a short, slow walk and then rest. In winter, walking and other corporeal exercises should be more vigorous than in summer. In spring and autumn, a regimen that steers a mid-course is the most appropriate. In general, one should modify one's regimen gradually to keep in accordance with the seasons.

With regard to sexual activity one should not indulge in it often or continuously. While it is most suitable for those of cold, moist, melancholic and flatulent dispositions, it is least so for those who, by nature, are thin, narrow-chested, and lean in the hips and loins, and for those who, in age, are moving from childhood to adolescence or are old. In the case of those who indulge excessively and inopportunely physical damage occurs in the region of the bladder, kidneys, lungs, eyes, and the spinal marrow. Those who are not otherwise naturally unsuited for such an activity, who always engage in it moderately and not excessively, and take good and abundant nourishment, are least harmed and remain sexually potent for the longest time.

Finally, it is better for those who live well-ordered lives and are still accustomed to physical exercise not to resort to vomiting – nature herself has provided outlets for any excess of food, drink, and other natural excretions.

XII.15. Cornelius Celsus, *On medicine* III.9.2 (*CML* I, p. 116 Marx)

The Alexandrians, like the Hippocratics, employed treatment by contrary remedies.

Nor, by Hercules, is that treatment new – treatment by contrary remedies – by which nowadays they occasionally cure the sick handed over to them after protracted treatment under more cautious doctors. If indeed, among the ancients, too, before Herophilus and Erasistratus and especially after Hippocrates, <this treatment was frequently used>.

In Hellenistic times, too, medicine is primarily concerned with the dietetics of the healthy.

XII.16. Sextus Empiricus, *Against the mathematicians* XI.50
(= *Herophilus* Fr. 230 von Staden)

In a work whose main emphasis seems to be aimed at the preservation of health through preventive care, Herophilus enumerates values jeopardised by the absence of health.

Herophilus says in his *Regimen* that, when health is absent, wisdom cannot be shown, science is obscure, strength not tried in contest, wealth useless, and reasoning impossible.

XII.17. Ps.-Galen, *Introduction or the Doctor* 8 (XIV.692K)

Erasistratus, too, preferred prevention to cure and considers regimen to be more important than healing the sick.

Regimen is not only considered to be a part of medicine but is also classed as being superior to therapeutics. For it is far better not to allow sickness to develop in the first place than to get rid of it. Just as it is preferable for a helmsman to complete his voyage before encountering a storm than to escape it after being storm-tossed and in danger.

XII.18. Galen, *On habits* (*Scripta minora* II, p. 16 Müller = *CMG* Suppl. III ed. Schmutte & Pfaff, 1941, p. 12, 5 = *Erasistratus* Fr. 247 Garofalo)

According to Erasistratus here regimen should be regulated to suit individuals.

Erasistratus in the second book of his work 'On paralysis' has written as follows: 'It is necessary for one who is intending to practise medicine systematically to consider very carefully familiarity and unfamiliarity. I mean in the following way. Those, on the one hand, who are performing many customary labours continue to do so without feeling fatigue, but they become tired after a short spell of unaccustomed work. Some people more easily digest indigestible food to which they are accustomed than more digestible food to which they are not accustomed. The body requires habitual excretions which, even if they are in themselves unprofitable, have come to be customary and, if it is deprived of them, it falls into disease.

XII.19. Galen, *Thrasybulus or Whether hygiene is a part of medicine or gymnastics* 38 (= *Scripta minora* III.86 Helmreich = *Erasistratus* Fr. 156 Garofalo)

In this passage Erasistratus complains that many doctors of his time were not interested in hygiene, the art of preserving health. He himself wrote a work on this subject in two books and, in general, preferred prevention to cure. Here Galen quotes from the first of these books:

Plato did not distinguish hygiene <the art of health preservation> from the art of medicine, as did all of those mentioned above. Let us, if you like, mention one of these, since his writings are readily accessible to all. Erasistratus, then, says in the first of his books *On hygiene*, 'it is not possible to find a doctor who has dedicated himself to the practice of health preservation'. Then, next: 'attacks of indigestion come about from some bodily state and their treatment falls to the medical art and not to those who practise the art of health-preservation'. Then again, going further on, he says, 'if there should be some bodily corruption which will continually contaminate its food and thus will bring it to the same unhealthy state as its present sustenance, it is the role of the doctor not the hygienist to resolve such a disposition.' Then, in succcession to this, he says: 'discussion of these issues and resolving them falls to doctors and not those who practise hygiene'.

XII. Dietetics and regimen

*

Dietetics, in any sophisticated sense, appears to have been a relatively late development in Greek medicine. In a scholion on *Iliad* 11.515 (written in the Hellenistic era) Porphyry observes [XII.1] that Homer did not introduce anyone being treated by diet (adding by way of explanation that he omitted such treatment because of its 'unseemliness'). (See, too, Eustathius, *Commentaries on Homer's Iliad* II.514. at **XII.3**.) The Roman encyclopaedist, Cornelius Celsus, endorses this view regarding the absence of dietetics in Homer when he points out [XII.2] that the two sons of Asclepius, Machaon and Podalirius, gave no aid during the pestilence sent upon the Greek army investing Troy. They only relieved wounds by the knife and by medication, he says, and concludes that only these parts of the art of medicine (i.e. *cheirourgia* and *pharmakeutikê*) were attempted and that these were the oldest. Celsus goes on to add, presumably by way of explanation, that diseases were at that time ascribed to the anger of the gods and from them help was sought. (He conjectures that, with no aids against bad health, general levels of health were probably high because of good habits.)

Thus the picture that emerges in Homeric times is that of the doctor who heals flesh wounds, mends fractures, and, in general, confines his treatment to manipulation and external application of medicaments. Internal medicine, where it existed, seems to have been limited to a few simple remedies. This relative neglect of internal medicine can be explained, as Celsus suggests above, by the tendency to regard non-traumatic illness as sent by the gods and, therefore, not considered curable by human agency. It should be noted, however, that in post-Homeric legend Podalirius is later identified as a specialist in internal disease and medicine is subsequently divided between the two sons of Asclepius, with the one now portrayed as a surgeon and the other treating internal complaints. The earliest mention of this division seems to have been Arctinus (seventh century BC?) in his epic, *The Sack of Troy* [XII.3]. Upon the basis of Arctinus's testimony here Podalirius was subsequently held to have 'treated diseases by diet' or 'practised dietetics'. But none of our sources who record this view seems to have been persuaded by it and the only evidence reported by them in support of it, namely that, when Menelaus was wounded, Agamemnon summoned only Machaon to treat him, is manifestly weak.

Our ancient scholiast goes on to declare [XII.1] that dietetics was inaugurated by Herodicus and brought to perfection by Hippocrates,[1] Praxagoras and Chrysippus. Galen, too, raises this question of the origin of dietetics and defers to the authority of Plato [XII.4]. His reference is patently to *Republic* III. 406A-C, whose dramatic date is *c.* 410 BC. Here Socrates is depicted contrasting the simple medicine of the heroic age with 'the modern medical technique of pampering illness' which, it is implied, has recently been invented by the gymnastic trainer Herodicus of Selymbria [XII.5]. According to this account Herodicus, suffering from a chronic disease, devised for himself a complicated regime which subsequently became fashionable. In the sixth book of the *Epidemics* [XII.7], however, this (presumably the same) Herodicus is castigated for having killed fever-patients with exercise. Thus physical training must have been a main feature of his system; but, as the evidence of Plato entails, gymnastic training must have involved some attention to diet as well as physical exercise.

According to Iamblichus [XII.8], the Pythagoreans were deeply concerned with dietetics. He says here that they were 'virtually the first to inquire into distinctions in the foods administered to the patient', which also seems at least to suggest that dietetics was a relatively late, i.e. post-Homeric, innovation. Dietetic texts in the Hippocratic *Corpus* appear to confirm a fifth-century origin. Although the author of *Ancient medicine* regards the administration of diet as virtually conterminous with the art of medicine [**XII.9**] and this view has been widely accepted by modern scholars, it is difficult to determine precisely at what time he conceived the inception of the art of medicine to have taken place, and allowance here must be made for polemical exaggeration. It may be significant that the theory of health adopted by him can be traced back as far as Alcmaeon and beyond [see **III.2**] The author of *Regimen in acute diseases*, it may be noted, in criticising the therapy expounded in *Cnidian sentences* adds that 'the physicians of old wrote nothing worth mentioning about diet' [**XII.10**]. If this criticism is regarded as historical[2] rather than, as is usually the case, as an attack upon the assumptions of a particular 'school', then this remark is consistent with the evidence that dietetics was an innovation in fifth-/ early fourth-century medicine. These dietetic treatises all share a common denominator in their association of dietetics with physiological theories that were themselves underpinned by cosmological theories familiar to us from the sixth and fifth centuries BC. They also share a common characteristic with the Presocratic philosophers in drawing parallels between constituent elements in man and the same or similar elements in nature outside man, not only in his nutriment but also in the air, water, and earth which make up his environment. The author of *On regimen*, for example, maintains that anyone intending to write about human regimen must first have a thorough knowledge about the nature of man in general, of his primary constituents and of the parts by which he is controlled [**XII.11**]. Our author explicitly bases his dietetic system on a physiological theory in which the elemental components of man are fire, which is hot and dry, and water, which is cold and wet, and in which the effects of food, drink and exercise upon the body are explained in terms of their capacities to heat and cool, to dry and moisten. Here, as Lonie well points out,[3] may be seen evidence of the great change which occurred in the second half of the fifth century, when the treatment of internal disease was, thanks to the influence of Ionian rational philosophy, no longer regarded as the result of supernatural causation and came to be based upon dietetics, which was itself based upon physical (i.e. philosophical) theories involving elements and their qualities.

The favourite method of treatment for the Hippocratic doctor was by means of regimen, which entailed for him not just our modern conception of diet but rather one's whole life-style, how one slept, exercised and, generally, interacted with one's environment. Disease was regarded as essentially an imbalance among the constituents of the body (frequently one or other of the four humours) and the purpose of dietetic medicine was to devise an appropriate regimen to restore the original balance. Since the seasons were held to affect man's constitution, diet was employed as the means to counterbalance adverse seasonal effects by keeping the body hot and dry in the winter and cool and moist in the summer. The treatise *Regimen in health,* for example, in its opening chapter prescribes how one should live during the various seasons [**XII.12**] and, at a later date, Diocles of Carystus provides very detailed recommendations as to how one should conduct oneself throughout the course of a single day [**XII.14**]. In the *Timaeus* it is maintained that a successful regimen must include the balanced exercise of both mind and body [**XII.13**] and, adopting an attitude previously displayed by the Pythagoreans [**XII.8**], Plato warns against the dangerous practice of resorting to drugs, which, he believes, should be administered only in extreme circumstances [see **XIII.8**]. Although Praxagoras is one of those credited with having brought to perfection dietetic medicine [**XII.1**], virtually nothing has survived of his dietetic theory apart from some scanty evidence of his views upon the dietetic qualities of some foodstuffs and drink. In common with their earlier predecessors, both the Alexandrians employed treatment by contrary remedies **[XII.15]**. Herophilus also believed that health care should include a prophylactic element **[XII.16]** to ensure the preservation of health through exercise and a sound diet, and Erasistratus, too, preferred prevention to cure **[XII.17 & 19]**. Rejecting violent remedies, especially purgatives, the latter recommended exercise and diet, which he believed had to be carefully regulated to suit the requirements of the individual patient **[XII.18]**.

Greek attitudes towards dietetics, generally, are well summarised in the following aphorism found at the very end of the Hippocratic treatise, *Regimen in health* (Ch. 9), but which has seemingly strayed from the very beginning of *Affections*: 'An intelligent man must understand that health is his most valuable possession and he must know how to help himself by his own thought in the case of illness' (*Affections* 1).

¹ Eustathius reverses the order here: see **XII.3**.
² See, especially, Lonie, 1977, p. 241.
³ Op. cit., p. 236.

XIII

Pharmacology

Our earliest literary evidence for the medical use of plants and their properties in Ancient Greece comes from Homeric Epic.

MEDICAL USE OF PLANTS IN HOMER

XIII.1. Homer, *Iliad* 11.844-8

Here Patroclus applies a pain-killing and styptic drug to Eurypylus's arrow wound.

Then Patroclus stretched him out and with a knife cut from his thigh the sharp, piercing arrow, and from the wound washed away the black blood with warm water. He cast upon it a bitter pain-killing root, after rubbing it in his hands, which stayed all his pains. The wound dried up and the blood ceased.

XIII.2. Homer, *Iliad* 5.900-4

The divine healer treats the god, Ares, with pain-killing drugs when wounded by Diomedes.

Paëon spread pain-killing drugs upon his wound and healed him. For he was in no respect mortal. Even as when the juice of the fig speedily congeals the white milk, though it is liquid ... even so swiftly he healed furious Ares.

XIII.3. Homer, *Odyssey* 4.220ff.

Helen gives her guests a powerful Egyptian tranquilliser.

Into the wine of which they were drinking Helen cast a drug that banished sorrow and anger and made one forgetful of all ills. Whoever drank it down, when it had been mixed in the wine-bowl, could not shed a tear that day down his cheeks, not even if his mother and his father died, not even if his brother or beloved son was slain by the sword in his presence, and he saw it with his own eyes. Such were the helpful and potent drugs possessed by the daughter of Zeus that the wife of Thon gave her, Poly-damna from Egypt, where the fertile soil produces the greatest number of

157

drugs, many good in compounds, but many poisonous. Every man is a doctor there and skilled beyond all men.

Egyptian drugs continued to be employed in classical and Hellenistic times.

XIII.4. Homer, *Odyssey* 10.286ff.

The magical powers with which some drugs were invested are most clearly evident in the *Odyssey*. Here Hermes provides Odysseus with an antidote to Circe's drugs.

Come, then, I'll get you out of your troubles and save you. Here, take this good drug and go into Circe's house. It will give you power against an evil day. I shall tell you all the malevolent guiles of Circe. She will make for you a pottage and put drugs in the food. But even so she will not be able to enchant you, for this good antidote that I shall give you will not allow her .... So spoke Argeïphontes, and he gave me a herb he had plucked from the ground and explained its nature to me. It was black at the root, but had a milky-white flower. The gods call it moly. It is hard for mortal men to dig up; but the gods have power to do all things.

HIPPOCRATIC PHARMACOLOGY

Significantly the Hippocratic writers do not mention the superstitious beliefs and rituals which invested the collection of plants for medical use. Nowhere are these plants invested with supernatural or magical properties.

XIII.5. [Hippocrates], *Places in man* 39 (VI.328,16-340,1L)

Here mandrake is recommended for use in the treatment of the sick and depressed, those who contemplate suicide, and in the treatment of spasms –

One should give the sick and depressed and those who wish to hang themselves an infusion of mandrake-root to drink early in the day of a lesser dosage than would cause delirium.

One should treat spasm in the following manner: kindle a fire on either side of the bed and give the patient to drink an infusion of mandrake-root, less in dosage than would cause delirium, and apply to the Achilles tendons hot poultices. If fever supervenes from the spasm, it ceases on the same day, on the next day or on the day after.

XIII.6. [Hippocrates], *Diseases* II.43 (VII.60,6-21L)

– and here as an ingredient, along with hellebore, in a compound to be administered in cases of quartan fever.

Whenever a quartan fever takes hold, if it attacks someone unpurged of another disease, give him a medicine to drink to purge him downwards. Then to purge his head. Then give him another draught to purge him downwards again. If the fever does not abate when he has done these things, leaving an interval of two seizures after the downward purging, wash him in copious hot water and give him to drink as much of the fruit of henbane as is the equivalent of a single grain of millet seed, an equal amount of mandrake, three beans of fig-juice, and a like amount of trefoil in unmixed wine. If he is vigorous and seems to be in good health, but has fallen into a fever as a result of fatigue or a journey, and the fever becomes quartan, give him a vapour-bath and then garlic dipped in honey. Then let him drink afterwards a mixed potion of lentils, honey, and vinegar. When he is full, let him vomit. Then, wash him in warm water and when he has cooled down, let him drink a posset in water. Towards evening let him take soft foods in small amounts. On the next seizure wash him in warm water, pile cloaks upon him until he perspires, then give him to drink straight-away the equivalent of three fingers' length of the root of white hellebore, a drachma's size of trefoil and two beans of fig-juice in unmixed wine ....

XIII.7. [Hippocrates], *Nature of woman* 2 (VII.312,14-314,13L)

A variety of drugs is here employed in the treatment of dropsy in the womb.

If dropsy occurs in the womb, menstruation becomes less and causes more trouble; then it ceases suddenly and the stomach becomes swollen and the breasts dry; the woman is in other respects in a bad state and imagines she is pregnant. By these symptoms you will recognise that she is suffering from dropsy. The *os uteri* also provides an indication: for it appears dry to the touch. Fever and dropsy take the patient. Pain of ever-increasing severity takes hold of the lower belly, the loins and the flanks. This disease comes about especially after a miscarriage, but also from other causes. Whenever this is the case, one should wash the woman with warm water and apply warm fomentations where she has pain. One should administer a purgative and, after the purgative, fumigate her womb in a cow-dung vapour-bath. Then insert a pessary made with cantharid beetle, and, after three days, a pessary made of bile. After an interval of one day, let her douche herself with vinegar for three days. Then if her belly empties and the fevers have ceased and menstruation supervenes, let her lie with her husband. If not, let her repeat the same procedures until menstruation occurs and employ some suppositories. In the intervening days let her drink a potion of samphire-bark and black seeds of peony and the fruit of elder in wine on an empty stomach. Let her eat as much garden-mercury as possible, and garlic, both boiled and raw. Have her eat soft foods, octopus and other soft animals. If she gives birth she recovers her health.

For drugs used to treat dislocation of the womb, see **XVI.12** below.

PHARMACOLOGY IN THE FOURTH CENTURY

Plato

XIII.8. Plato, *Timaeus* 89B-D

Plato's hostility towards the use of drugs.

Diseases, except where they are very dangerous, should not be irritated by drugs. For every disease has a structure that resembles in a certain manner the nature of living creatures. For the composition of these living creatures has prescribed periods of life for the species as a whole .... It is the same with the constitution of diseases: whenever anyone destroys this by drugs, contrary to the allotted period of time, many serious diseases are wont to arise from those that are few and slight. Consequently, so far as leisure permits, one should control all such diseases by regimen, instead of irritating a troublesome evil by administering drugs.

Diocles

Diocles seems to have been the first to write a herbal on the medical use of plants. Unfortunately only very brief fragments of this work have survived.

Theophrastus

The important botanical research carried out by Theophrastus was influential throughout antiquity.

XIII.9. Theophrastus, *History of plants* 9.5

Unlike the Hippocratics, Theophrastus explicitly cites botanical folk-lore. Here he records the dangers attendant upon the collection of thapsia.

<Herbalists and root-cutters> enjoin that in cutting some roots one should stand to windward, for example, in cutting thapsia among others, and that one should first anoint oneself richly with oil; for, if one stands to leeward, one's body will swell up.

XIII.10. Theophrastus, *History of plants* 9.6

And the perils in peony-collecting.

<They say> that the peony, which some call the *glycyside*, should be dug up at night, for, if one does it in the day-time, and is observed by a woodpecker while gathering the fruit, one risks the loss of one's eyesight, but if one is cutting the root at the time, one gets prolapse of the anus.

XIII.11. Theophrastus, *History of plants* 9.8

He records some procedures recommended for the collection of mandrake.

One should thrice draw circles round the mandrake and cut it facing west. One should dance in circles round the second piece cut and say as much as possible about sex.

XIII.11B. Dioscorides, *On medical materials* IV.75 (Vol. II, pp. 233-7 Wellmann, 1906-14)

Dioscorides of Anazarbus (fl. AD 50-70) wrote during the reign of Nero a *Materia medica* that superseded all earlier botanical treatises. It was translated into Latin at least by the sixth century and into Arabic by the ninth, and exercised a great influence upon Islamic, Mediaeval, and Renaissance botany and therapy. Here is Dioscorides on the mandrake. (Although strictly outside the chronological parameters of this book, in view of the importance attached to this plant in the ancient world this context has been included on grounds of general interest.)

Some call it animimon, bombchylon or circaea for the root seems to be good for making philtres. There is a female variety which is black called thridacias. It has leaves that are narrower and smaller than those of the lettuce. They have a foul and heavy odour, and spread out over the ground. Along the leaves there are fruits that resemble the sorb-apple, being yellow and of pleasant smell. In them is the seed, which is like that of the pear. The roots are large, two or three in number and intertwined, black on the surface, white within. The bark is thick and there is no stalk.

The white male variety, which some have called morion, has large, flat, and smooth white leaves, like those of the beet. Its fruit is twice as large, saffron in colour, and of pleasant, but heavy, odour. Shepherds eat it and become somewhat drowsy. The root is like that just described, but larger and whiter. The variety is also without a stalk.

The bark of the root, when tender, gives juice when beaten and placed under a press. The juice must then be fermented in the sun and, after being condensed, must be stored in an earthen vessel. The fruit also gives juice in a similar way, but the juice extracted is diluted. The bark of the root is stripped off, pierced with a thread, and hung up for storage. Some boil down the roots in wine to a third of their original size, and after filtering it, store away the product. They administer a cyathos[1] of it to insomniacs, to those in severe pain, or to those whom they wish to anaesthetise during an operation involving cutting or cautery.

Two obols[2] of the juice, when drunk with melicraton,[3] brings up phlegm and bile, as hellebore does. It is fatal if drunk in larger quantities. It is used as a component in eye medicines, anodynes, and soothing pessaries. But an application of as much as half an obol of it unmixed brings on menstrual flow and expels the embryo. Inserted as a suppository in the anus it causes sleep ....

Fresh leaves of this plant when applied as a plaster with barley are good for inflammations of the eyes and those upon ulcers. It disperses all hardness and abscesses, glandular swellings, and tumours. If rubbed on gently for five or six days it causes branded marks to disappear without ulceration. Its leaves preserved in brine are set aside for the same purposes. The root, rubbed smooth with vinegar, heals erysipelas, but for snake bites is used with honey or oil. It disperses glandular swellings and tumours when used with water, and, in combination with barley, gives relief from pains of the joints.

Wine from the bark of the root is also prepared without boiling. One should place three minas into a metretes[4] of sweet wine and give three cyathoi of this preparation to those who are about to be operated upon with knife or cautery, as has been said. For, being overcome by sleep, they do not feel the pain. Again, the fruit, when eaten or smelled, causes drowsiness, as does the juice of the fruit. Taken in excess it causes loss of speech.

When drunk the seed of the fruit purges the womb; applied as a pessary with native sulphur it stops the red discharge. A muddy liquor is extracted when the root is grooved around, and the flow is caught in the hollow. But the <pressed out> juice is stronger than this liquor. Roots, as experience reveals, do not yield liquor at every point.

Some record another variety called morion growing in shady places and around caves, with leaves like those of white mandragora but smaller, about a span in length, white, and falling in a circle around the root which is tender and white, a little longer than a span, and the thickness of a thumb. They say that when so much as a single drachma[5] of this is drunk or eaten with barley on a cake or in a sauce it causes stupefaction. For, in whatever form a person consumes it, he remains asleep and unconscious of everything for three or four hours from the time it was taken. Physicians use this, too, when they are about to cut or cauterise. They say that the root, when drunk together with thorn-apple, is also an antidote against what is called madness.

[1] About half a pint.

[2] An obol was about one fortieth of an ounce in the Attic system; about one thirtieth in the Aeginetan.

[3] A mixture of honey and milk or water.

[4] The mina was about a pound in the Attic system; the metretes about nine gallons.

[5] About a sixth of an ounce.

XIII.12A. Theophrastus, *History of plants* 9.8

The collection of black hellebore was also considered to be fraught with danger as is recorded here by Theophrastus.

One should draw a circle round the black hellebore and cut it facing east and saying prayers and one should look out for an eagle both from right and left; for there is a danger to the cutters of dying within the year, if the eagle should come near.

XIII.12B. Theophrastus, *History of plants* 9.10

Here Theophrastus provides a detailed description of hellebore and its effects. The name, as he points out here, is applied to two unrelated plants: Black hellebore (*Helleborus cyclophyllus*), better known as the Christmas Rose, which is a Ranunculacea, and White hellebore (*Veratrum album*), a member of the lily family. Both are poisonous. Black hellebore served as an all-purpose drug for the Greeks and was employed especially for its emetic and diarrhoetic effect. The danger of hellebore was recognised by the Hippocratics (see *Aphorisms* IV.16, IV.506L).

The black and the white hellebore seem as it were to have the same name. But there is disagreement concerning the appearance of the plants. Some say that the two are alike, except that they differ only in colour, the root of the one being white and of the other black. Some say that the leaf of the black resembles that of the bay and that of the white is like that of the leek, but the roots are alike except for their colours. Those, then, who say that they are alike describe their appearance as follows: the stem is like that of asphodel and is very short; the leaf has broad divisions, and is very like that of the ferula, but is long; it has radical leaves flat on the ground; it has many roots, the slender ones are very useful.

They say that the black is fatal to horses, oxen and pigs, on which account none of these animals feeds upon it. The white, however, is eaten by sheep and from this its property was first observed; for they are purged by it. It is in season in the autumn and out of season during the spring. However, the people from Mt. Oeta gather it about the time of the meeting of the Amphictyons[1] at Pylae, for it grows there best and in greatest abundance, but at one place only in Oeta ....

Black hellebore grows everywhere. It grows in Boeotia, in Euboea, and in many other places. The best is that from Mt. Helicon – the mountain, in general, is rich in herbs. The white is found in few places. The best and most used comes from four places, Oeta, Pontus, Elea and Malea. They say that from Elea grows in the vineyards and makes the wine so diuretic that those who drink it are very emaciated.

Best of all these and the rest is that from Oeta. That from Parnassus and from Aetolia (for it grows there too and many buy and sell it in their ignorance) is bitter and excessively harsh. These plants, then, though resembling the best in their appearance, differ in their properties.

Some call the black 'Melampus's hellebore' on the grounds that he was the first to cut and discover it. They also purify houses and sheep with it, chanting some incantation at the same time. They also employ it for several other purposes.

[1] These meetings were held regularly in the autumn and sometimes in the spring. The spring meeting is implied here.

XIII. Pharmacology

ALEXANDRIAN PHARMACOLOGY

XIII.13. Cornelius Celsus, *On medicine* V.1 (*CML* I, p. 190 Marx = *Herophilus* Fr. 251 von Staden)

The Alexandrians maintained this interest in the healing properties of drugs.

I have spoken about those ills of the body for which the regulation of diet is especially helpful; now I must pass on to that part of medicine that counters them more by drugs. The ancient authors attributed much to these drugs, both Erasistratus and those who call themselves Empiricists, but especially Herophilus and the followers of that famous man, to such an extent that they did not treat any kind of disease without drugs.[1] They also handed down many things about the properties of drugs such as are found in the works of Zeno or Andreas or Apollonius surnamed Mus.

---

[1] Celsus's claim here is somewhat exaggerated since we learn elsewhere ([Galen], *On easily acquired remedies* 2.13 XIV.444K) that Herophilus treated consumption solely by dietary means.

XIII.14. Marcellus, *Letter of Cornelius Celsus On remedies* (*CML* V.36 Niedermann/Liechtenhan = *Herophilus* Fr. 248b von Staden)

Drugs as 'the hands of the gods'.

Herophilus, who was once held to be among the greatest physicians, is held to have said that drugs are the hands of the gods, and indeed, not without reason, in my opinion. For, in a word, what divine touch can effect, drugs tested by use and experience also accomplish.

XIII.15. Pliny, *Natural history* 25.23.57-8 (= *Herophilus* Fr. 255 von Staden)

The effects of hellebore.

<Herophilus> used to liken hellebore to a very brave captain; for, when it has stirred up everything within, it sallies out first in the van.

Elizabethan superstitions

The Elizabethans shared the same superstitions regarding the collection of certain drugs.

XIII.16. *Romeo and Juliet* Act IV, Scene 3

The dangers attendant upon the picking of mandrake ...

> And shrieks like mandrakes torn out of the earth,
> that living mortals, hearing them, run mad.

XIII.17. John Gerarde, *The Herball or Generall Historie of Plants*, 1597, p. 281

... were such that a dog was used to pull out the plant.

They fable further and affirm that he who woulde take up a plant <i.e. of mandrake> thereof must tie a dogge[1] thereunto to pull it up, which will give a great shrike at the digging up; otherwise if a man should do it, he should certainly die in a short space thereafter.

[1] An illustration in the Juliana Anicia Codex (sixth century AD) depicts the nymph Discovery presenting a mandrake to Dioscorides. The mandrake is still tied to a dog whose life has been sacrificed to obtain it.

*

The use of inorganic and organic substances, particularly of plants, for medical purposes antedates recorded history. Information concerning drugs had been accumulated over many centuries by collectors of herbs and root-cutters, who had tested many plants, assessed their various powers and devised elaborate means for their collection. Doubtless these prescriptions and rituals that attended their gathering were intended as much to invest these plants with a particular mystique (which would thereby accentuate the placebo-effect) as to increase their value in the market-place by stressing the difficulties and dangers involved in their collection. Mandrake,[1] for example, was invested with a superstitious ritual that remained in vogue at least until Elizabethan times. See, for example, *Romeo and Juliet* Act IV Scene 3 **[XIII.16]**, where is recorded the belief that the plant screamed when dragged from the earth. Such was the danger attendant upon picking it that it had to be done by tying it to a dog, whose life was forfeit **[XIII.17]**. Theophrastus preserves tales recording similar dangers investing the gathering of herbs, for example, the cutting of thapsia **[XIII.9]**, the peony **[XIII.10]**, mandrake **[XIII.11]**, and hellebore **[XIII.12]**. The properties of many plants, then, were known by root-cutters (*rhizotomoi*) and herbalists who, while observing all manner of superstitious practices in their work, nevertheless transmitted to posterity a rich treasury of herbal lore.

Our earliest literary source of evidence for the medical use of plants and their properties (real or imaginary) is, again, Homeric Epic. Many passages, especially in the *Iliad*, refer to the application, of pain-killing drugs – often derived from plants – to wounds sustained in battle. For example, at *Iliad* 4.210-19 **[XV.3]** Machaon spreads upon Menelaus's arrow-wound soothing drugs (*pharmaka*) that Chiron once gave to his father, and at *Iliad* 11.822-36 **[XV.2]** the wounded Eurypylus asks Patroclus to sprinkle upon his wound healing drugs he has learned from Achilles. Patroclus, we are told, after cutting out the arrow from Eurypylus's thigh, applied to the wound a bitter pain-killing root, which dried up the wound and stopped the blood **[XIII.1]**. Even when the gods were wounded their treatment was not dissimilar. When Ares was wounded by Diomedes, he was treated by the divine healer, Paëon, who spread pain-killing drugs upon his wound that acted 'like rennet curdling milk' and swiftly cured him **[XIII.2]**. In the *Odyssey* **[XIII.3]** Helen, the wife of Menelaus, laced the wine she gave to her guests, Telemachus and Peisistratus, the son of Nestor, with a powerful Egyptian tranquilliser. The magical power with which some drugs were invested is clearly apparent in

XIII. Pharmacology

Odysseus's encounter with Circe in the eleventh book of the *Odyssey*. Here Odysseus is given an antidote by Hermes to counter the drug used by Circe to turn men into animals **[XIII.4]**.

It is clear from the title of a play by Sophocles, of which only fragments survive, that the term *rhizotomoi* ('root-cutters') was applied by the fifth century, at least, to those concerned with the collection of plants for medicinal purposes. The root-cutters are also frequently associated with drug-sellers (*pharmakapôlai*) and it seems likely that the same individuals engaged in both the collecting and selling of medicines derived from plants, which were by far the most frequently employed in Greek pharmacology. The doctors, too, seem to have compounded their own drugs, and the treatise entitled *rhizotomikon* attributed later to Diocles of Carystus (see below) seems also to point to the likelihood of overlapping activity here.

The Hippocratic *Corpus* preserves much evidence of the medical use of plants. Many of the pharmacological texts appear as appendages to the gynaecological treatises. It is significant that these Hippocratic writers refrained from mentioning in their accounts of particular plants the superstitions and folk-beliefs so frequently in evidence elsewhere and, on no occasion, are these plants invested with supernatural or magical properties. Mandrake, for example, is recommended in several gynaecological treatises for use as a potion, pessary or clyster **[XIII.5]**, and in *Diseases* II.43 it is prescribed as part of a compound of several ingredients for cases of quartan fever **[XIII.6]**; but nowhere do we find any indication of the superstitious rituals to be followed during its collection, which can be found in other authors. This silence is in strict conformity with the rationalist outlook that pervades the *Corpus* generally. However, as Lloyd points out,[2] the Hippocratics' use of particular plant substances and the manner in which they used them may reflect existing folklore.

Plato reveals himself in the *Timaeus* more hostile to the use of drugs and maintains that one should resort to them only at times of dire necessity, preferring treatment by means of exercise and regimen **[XIII.8]**. The Lyceum, in contrast, provides valuable information concerning plants and their uses acquired as part of the programme for the systematisation of knowledge carried out there. Although there are numerous botanical references in Aristotle's works and he himself on two occasions refers to his own botanical work, there are no extant studies to match those of his zoological treatises.[3] (Because of its Peripatetic style and structure, the treatise *On plants* in two books, which has survived via an Arabic translation from Syriac, subsequently translated into Latin by Alfred of Sareshel, and then re-translated into Greek by Maximus Planudes in the thirteenth century, was erroneously regarded by the majority of Renaissance botanists as having been written by Aristotle himself. Its true author, however, is now generally accepted to have been Nicolaus of Damascus. Apart from the herbals deriving from Dioscorides and Pseudo-Apuleius, this work became the most important single source for later mediaeval botany.)

The first herbal on the medical use of plants seems to have been composed by Diocles of Carystus. The work has been lost but surviving fragments suggest that it contained short descriptions of plants[4] and their natural habitats together with a listing of their medical applications. However, the most important and influential botanical research carried out at the Lyceum, and, indeed, throughout antiquity, was that of Theophrastus, whose works were written within a similar framework to that of Aristotle's zoological treatises. The *Causes of plants,* which corresponds to Aristotle's *Parts of animals,* deals with aitiology, while the *History of plants* is concerned with description, analysis and classification. The ninth book of the latter work reveals Theophrastus's interest in the medical use of plants, and much of the information assembled there seems to have been derived from earlier herbals – perhaps including that of Diocles, as some scholars have suggested. This book differs from the rest in that it contains a mass of folk-lore **[XIII.9-12]** and much more information concerning the herb-gatherers or rhizotomists, some of whom are mentioned by name. Although well aware of the unreliability of these drug-sellers and root-cutters, Theophrastus was disinclined to reject their stories about the potent effects of drugs out of hand and was prepared to accept the possibility that, however fanciful, they might contain at least a grain of truth. Here he stands in marked contrast with the seemingly rational pharmacologies of the Hippocratics, who, as Lloyd well points out,[5] had professional reasons for seeking to distance themselves from other sorts of healers.

As Celsus records **[XIII.13]**, the Alexandrians continued this interest in the healing properties of drugs, both simple and compound. Herophilus is said to have described them as 'the hands of the gods' **[XIII.14]**. His *bon mot* preserved by Pliny describing the effect of hellebore is worth recording here **[XIII.15]**. Among later Herophileans interested in herbals were Zeno, Mantias, Andreas of Carystus and Apollonius Mus.[6] Although our surviving evidence of early Alexandrian pharmacology is only fragmentary, it is sufficient to reveal that, unlike the Hippocratics who are exasperatingly vague in the amounts of the ingredients they prescribe, the Alexandrians were much more precise in specifying the measures to be employed.

[1] The resemblance of the mandrake root to the human form, both male and female, doubtless fostered the superstitions that surrounded it. It contains atropine and was used as an anaesthetic. It was also used in compounding aphrodisiacs [see **XIII.11**].

[2] See Lloyd, 1983, p. 132.

[3] Alexander, referring (*Commentary on Aristotle's treatise On sensation* 183) to a work by Theophrastus *On plants,* declares that there was no botanical work by Aristotle extant. (On this matter, which has aroused some controversy among scholars, see, especially, Senn, 1930, pp. 113-40 and Regenbogen, 1937, pp. 474-5.)

[4] The first illustrations of plants seem to have been introduced by Crateuas, personal physician to Mithridates VI of Pontus. Since illustrated diagrams were employed in zoology within the Lyceum (see, for example, *Generation of animals* 746a14ff. and *History of animals* 510a30ff.), it is surprising that they do not appear to have been adopted in botany, too.

[5] Op. cit., p. 134.

[6] For all of these see von Staden, 1989.

XIV

Anatomy

Homeric Epic provides our earliest literary evidence of the level of anatomical knowledge in ancient Greece.

ANATOMY IN THE HEROIC AGE

The accuracy of anatomical detail in the description of some of the wounds sustained in the fighting around Troy has given rise to claims that Homer was an army surgeon or had learned anatomy from the dissecting-table.

XIV.1. Homer, *Iliad* 5.65ff.

Here Phereclus is killed by a spear-thrust which pierces his bladder.

Meriones pursued Phereclus and, when he caught up with him, he struck him in the right buttock. The spear point passed right through to the bladder beneath the bone. He fell to his knees with a groan and death enshrouded him.

XIV.2. Homer, *Iliad* 16.345ff.

The unfortunate Erymas is stabbed through the mouth. The impact of the blow is exaggerated.

Idomeneus stabbed Erymas in the mouth with the pitiless bronze. The bronze spear passed straight through beneath the brain and shattered the white bones. His teeth were shaken out and both eyes were filled with blood. Up through mouth and down through nostrils he spurted blood as he gasped and a black cloud of death enshrouded him.

XIV.3. Homer, *Iliad* 22.322ff.

Hector is slain by a thrust through the throat.

All the rest of Hector's flesh was covered by bronze armour, the fine armour that he had stripped from mighty Patroclus, when he slew him. But, where the collar-bones part the neck and shoulders, there was an opening, at the throat, where the destruction of life is swiftest. There, as he rushed upon him, god-like Achilles thrust with his spear and the point went right through the tender neck. But the ashen spear, heavy with bronze, did not cleave the wind-pipe so that Hector could respond to and address his foe.

ALCMAEON OF CROTON

XIV.4. Chalcidius, *Commentary upon Plato's Timaeus* 246, pp. 256.22-257.15 Waszink (*Corpus Platonicum Medii Aevii: Plato Latinus* IV = pp. 279ff. Wrobel (DK 24A10) = *Herophilus* Fr. 86 von Staden)

It has been claimed on the basis of this late source (fourth century AD) that Alcmaeon was the first to employ human dissection as a general method of investigation. But Chalcidius's reference is not confined solely to Alcmaeon and there is otherwise no evidence of human dissection until Hellenistic times. It is, therefore, highly unlikely that Alcmaeon dissected or vivisected humans and more probable that the reference here is to a surgical operation upon a human subject.

The nature of the eye, therefore, must be demonstrated. Concerning its nature very many others have brought many things very clearly into the light – especially Alcmaeon of Croton, who, well trained in natural philosophy, was the first to dare to approach the excision of the eye, and Callisthenes, Aristotle's pupil, and Herophilus: namely that there are two narrow passages containing natural *pneuma*, which pass from their seat in the brain, wherein is situated the highest and principal power of the soul, to the cavities of the eyes. Although these passages proceed for a while from a single beginning and from the same root, they are joined in the innermost parts of the forehead, but, when they arrive at the concave abodes of the eyes, where the cross-ways of the eye-brows are stretched obliquely, they are separate like the forks of a road. There the two passages curve and there, where the 'lap' of the tunics receives natural moisture, they fill the eyeballs, protected by the covering of the eyelids. For this reason they are called 'orbs'.

Furthermore, dissection, indeed, primarily shows that the light-bringing passages proceed from a single location, yet this is recognised no less from the fact that each eye moves in unison with the other and neither could move without the other.

Furthermore, they noted that the eye itself is contained in four membranes[1] or tunics of unequal thickness. If one should wish to pursue the diffences and peculiarities of these, he would undertake a greater labour than the subject-matter set forth here.

[1] For Herophilus's discovery that the eye had four tunics see **VII.14A & B**.

HIPPOCRATIC ANATOMY

Although a fair degree of knowledge of the human skeleton and the main vessels of the vascular system is revealed in the Hippocratic *Corpus*, in the main knowledge of the anatomy of the internal organs is poor.

XIV.5. [Hippocrates], *On wounds in the head* 1-2 (III.184,9-188,12L)

Knowledge of the anatomy of the skull was evidently derived from observation of accidental injuries and those sustained in war.

The skull is double along the middle of the head. The hardest and most dense part of it is both the uppermost part, where the smooth surface of the bone comes under the scalp, and the lowest, the part close to the membrane, where the smooth surface of the bone is beneath. Passing from the uppermost and lowest layers of bone, from the hardest and most dense parts to the softer and less dense, it is also more porous right on to the diploe.[1] The diploe is extremely hollow and soft and particularly porous. The whole bone of the head, except a very little of the uppermost and of the lowest, is like a sponge. The bone contains many moist fleshy particles all alike. If one were to rub them with the fingers, one would get blood out of them. There are also rather thin, hollow vessels full of blood in the bone.

Such is the state of the skull with regard to its hardness, softness, and porosity.

[2] Its thickness and thinness, however, is as follows: Of the whole head the bone is thinnest and weakest at the bregma,[2] and has the least and thinnest covering of flesh in this part of the head where there is the most underlying brain.

[1] The porous substance between the double plates in the bones of the skull.
[2] The front part of the top of the head, where the skull remains open longest.

XIV.6. [Hippocrates], *On fleshes* 5 (VIII.590,6-23L)

Here the heart is correctly held to be the central source of the blood vessels. All vessels run into the 'artery' (aorta) and the 'hollow vein' (vena cava), both of which proceed from the heart.

The heart contains a lot of the glutinous and the cold. Heated by the hot it became hard, viscous flesh enclosed within a membrane. It was made hollow, but in a different way from the veins. It is situated at the head of the most hollow vein. For there are two hollow veins from the heart. One is called 'artery'; the other one, to which the heart is attached, is called the 'hollow vein'. The heart has the most heat where the hollow vein is situated and it dispenses the *pneuma*. In addition to these two veins there are others throughout the body. The most hollow vein, to which the heart is attached, runs through the whole of the belly and the diaphragm and divides towards each of the kidneys. In the loins it branches and shoots up to the other parts and into each leg. But also above the heart in the neck some <vessels> go to the right, some to the left. Then they lead to the head and at the temples each vessel divides. It is possible to enumerate the greatest veins, but, in a word, from the hollow vein and from the artery other veins branch off throughout the whole body. The most hollow veins are those near the heart and the neck, those in the head and those beneath the heart as far as the hip-joints.

It is generally agreed that this treatise antedates Diocles. Although the term 'artery' is here applied to the aorta, which might suggest that the treatise should be regarded as later than Diocles (or the father of Praxagoras), in the rest of the work no distinction is drawn between these two different types of vessel: arteries and veins alike – including branches of the artery – are elsewhere all called 'veins'.

XIV.7. [Hippocrates], *On anatomy* 1 (VIII.538,1-16L)

Here in this little work are described the windpipe, liver, bladder, and the kidneys as well as the heart and lungs. *Pace* Harris our author does not appear to have differentiated between veins and arteries and, in general, the anatomical knowledge displayed here seems inferior to that of Aristotle.

The windpipe, originating from either side of the throat, ends at the top of the lung. It is composed of similarly shaped rings whose circular parts are in contact with one another at the surface. The lung itself, inclined both to the left and the right, fills the thoracic cavity. It has five projections called lobes. It has an ashen colour, stippled with dark spots and is spongy by nature. The heart is situated in the middle of the lung. It is rounder than that of all other animals. From the heart a large vessel (*bronchiê*) reaches down to the liver and with it the vessel called the 'great vein' through which the whole body is nourished. The liver bears a resemblance to <that of> all the other animals, but is more suffused with blood than those of the others. It has two projections called 'gates' and it is situated on the right. From the liver a slanting vein extends to the parts below the kidneys. The kidneys are similar in shape and in colour are like apples. From the kidneys oblique channels lead to the very top of the bladder. †The bladder is all sinewy and large. On each side of the bladder urine is conveyed <through the ureters>†.[1] These six organs constitute the internal nature of the body.

---

[1] The text is corrupt. I suggest: κύστις δὲ νευρώδης οὔλη καὶ μεγάλη. Ἑκασταχόθι δὲ κύστιος μετοχέτευσις πέφυκε.

ANATOMY IN PLATO

The heart

XIV.8. Plato, *Timaeus* 70A-D

Plato's knowledge of internal anatomy is of a very low order. His description of the anatomy of the heart here is patently not based on dissection and is clearly conditioned by the constraints of his tripartite psychology.

The gods stationed the heart, the knot of the veins and well-spring of the blood, which moves vigorously throughout all the limbs, in the guard-room, so that, when passion was roused to boiling point at a message from reason that some wrong was taking place in the limbs ... every sentient part should quickly perceive through all the narrow channels the commands and threats and obediently follow in every way and so allow the noblest part to have command. The palpitation of the heart is caused by the expectation of evil and the excitement of passion. The gods, then, foreseeing that all such passion would come about by means of fire, devised support for the heart in the structure of the lung, making it soft and bloodless, perforated by cavities like a sponge, so that by absorbing breath and drink, and cooling by respiration, it might also provide relief in the heat of passion. For this reason they cut air-channels to the lung and set it around the heart as a cushion, so that when passion was at its height, the heart might beat against a yielding body, be cooled down and, being less distressed, might be able to aid the spirited element in the service of reason.

ANATOMY IN ARISTOTLE

The heart

XIV.9. Aristotle, *History of animals* 496a4ff.

In sharp contrast to Plato, Aristotle's description of the heart is much more sophisticated and is manifestly based upon frequent dissection of animals. He may even have derived some knowledge of the shape and position of the human heart from aborted human embryos.

The heart has three cavities. It lies above the lung at the point where the wind-pipe (*arteria*) divides into two. It has a fat, thick membrane where it attaches to the Great Vein and the Aorta. It lies with its apex upon the aorta. The apex lies towards the chest in all animals that have a chest. In all animals, whether they have a chest or not, the apex of the heart is towards the front. This often escapes notice owing to the change of position of the parts under dissection. The convex end of the heart is above. The apex is largely fleshy and compact in texture and there are sinews in its cavities. In animals – other than man – that have a chest, its position is in the middle of the chest; in man it is more on the left, inclining a little from the division of the breasts towards the left breast in the upper part of the chest. The heart is not large; its shape as a whole is not elongated but somewhat rounded, except that its extremity comes to a point. As has been said, it has three cavities, the largest is that on the right hand side, the smallest that on the left, and the medium sized one is in the middle. All of them, even the two small ones, have a connection leading into the lung. This is clearly visible in respect of one of them. Below, from the point of attachment at the largest cavity, there is a connection to the Great Vein.

Passages also lead into the lung from the heart. They divide, as the windpipe does, and follow closely those from the windpipe throughout the whole of the lung. Those from the heart are uppermost. There is no common passage, but through their contact they receive the *pneuma* and transmit it to the heart. For one passage leads to the right cavity, and the other to the left.

Although Aristotle parts company with Plato and takes what the anatomical investigations of the Alexandrians were subsequently to reveal to be a retrograde step in identifying the heart as the seat of the intellect, his recognition here of the heart as the organ from which all the blood vessels arise is of greater precision than Plato's vague description of it as the 'knot of the veins'. All vessels (except those of the lung), he believed, were connected with the vena cava or the aorta, which have the heart as their origin. He also seems to have been the first to recognise that the heart consists of more than one chamber, although he makes a celebrated error, much debated since Galen, in maintaining that the hearts of all large animals (including humans) have three chambers. Aristotle briefly describes the structure of the heart elsewhere: see *History of animals* 513a28ff. and *Parts of animals* 666a6ff.

The brain

XIV.10. Aristotle, *History of animals* 494b25-495a18

Although Aristotle misconceives some major physiological functions of the brain, believing that its main functions were to serve as a refrigerant and cool the innate heat of the blood, and to produce sleep, he gives a good account of its membranes and distinguishes between the cerebrum and the cerebellum.

First of all, then, the brain has its position in the front portion of the head. This is also the case with all those other animals that possess this organ. All blooded animals have a brain, and so have the Cephalopods. For his size man has the largest brain and the most fluid one. Two membranes surround the brain: the one round the bone <i.e. the *dura mater*> is the stronger, the one round the brain itself <i.e. the *pia mater*> less so. In all animals the brain is double. Beyond this, at the far end, is the *parenkephalis* as it is called <i.e. the cerebellum>. It has a different shape from that of the brain, as can both be seen and felt ....

  In all animals the brain is bloodless. It does not have a single blood-vessel in it and is naturally cold to the touch. The brain of most animals has a certain small hollow in the middle. The membrane surrounding it is full of veins. This membrane is the skin-like membrane enclosing the brain. Above the brain is the finest and weakest bone in the head, called the *bregma*.

  From the eye three passages lead to the brain: the largest and second largest <trigeminal and optic nerve?> to the *parenkephalis*, the smallest <ocular motor nerve?> to the brain itself: this last is the one nearest to the nostril. The two largest run parallel and do not coalesce; the two second-largest do coalesce. (This is clear particularly in the case of fishes.) For these are also much nearer the brain than the large ones are. The smallest ones are the most distant from one another and do not coalesce.

XIV. Anatomy

DIOCLES OF CARYSTUS

The heart

It is impossible to reconstruct Diocles of Carystus's views upon the anatomy of the heart with any high degree of certainty. Our evidence is scanty, controversial and has been subjected to doxographical distortion. If Diels's emendations are accepted in the two contexts translated immediately below, it would appear that Diocles followed 'Sicilian' precedent and believed that the heart is the seat of the intellect.

XIV.11. Aëtius, *On the opinions of the philosophers* IV.5.6-8 (at Theodoret 6.8 = Diels, 1879, p. 204 n.1)

Empedocles and Aristotle and Diocles[1] and the Stoic sect allotted the seat of intellectual activity to the heart.

[1] Reading with Diels ʿΑριστο<τέλης, Διο>κλῆς' to replace the otherwise unknown ʿΑριστοκλῆς'.

XIV.12. Aëtius, *On the opinions of the philosophers* IV.5.7 (at Plutarch, *Epitome* IV.5 = Diels, 1879, p. 391)

Diocles[1] located the governing principle in the 'arterial', <i.e. the pneumatic> cavity of the heart.

[1] Following Diels in substituting 'Διοκλῆς' for 'Διογένης'.

XIV.13. [Vindicianus], *On the seed* (Fragmentum Bruxellense) 44 (= Wellmann, 1901, p. 234)

If Wellmann is correct in his claim (1901, 3-14) that what follows is a genuine report of Diocles, then the latter's view of the heart was more accurate and sophisticated than the three-chambered model envisaged by Aristotle. Although the number of ventricles is not stated above, it may be inferred from the context that the author conceived the heart to comprise two ventricles immediately beneath the two auricles.

He <Diocles?> said the phrenetic passion was caused by a tumour in the heart, which cuts off the blood supply and normal heat by which the brain supplies perception and intelligence. For it is due to one side of the brain that understanding takes place and sensation to another. And so there are thus formed in the head two parts of the brain, one providing intelligence, the other sensation. The right part provides sensation, the left, intelligence.

ANATOMY AFTER DIOCLES

XIV.14. [Hippocrates], *On the heart* 1, 4-8, 10 (IX.80,1-6; 82,14-86,6 & 86,13-88,8L)

This Hippocratic treatise because of its impressive descriptions of the auricles, ventricles and valves of the heart is generally regarded as Hellenistic in date (see Lonie, 1973, *passim*).

[1] The heart has the shape of a pyramid and is dark-red in colour. It is surrounded by a smooth membrane that contains a small amount of liquid resembling urine so that you might think that it moves within a vessel. The purpose of this liquid is to enable the heart to beat vigorously in safety. It has just sufficient liquid to cool it when it becomes over-heated ....

[4] ... The heart is a very strong muscle – not because of sinews but because of the compactness of its flesh. It has two 'bellies' <ventricles>, separate but contained within a single envelope .... They are quite dissimilar: the one on the right lies on its mouth <i.e. face-downwards>, and fits against the other ... this chamber is more capacious and much larger than the other. It does not extend to the extremity of the heart, but leaves the apex solid, being as it were stitched on outside.

[5] The other chamber lies largely underneath and just about in line with the left nipple, where the pulse is discernible. It has a thick surrounding wall and is hollowed out to a cavity in the shape of a mortar. It is softly enclosed by the lung, and being surrounded it moderates the excessive temperature of heat. For the lung is both naturally cold and is chilled by the intake of breath.

[6] Both the ventricles are rough inside as though slightly corroded, the left more than the right. For the innate heat is not located in the right ventricle. Thus it is not surprising that the left ventricle has become the rougher as it breathes in untempered air. Internally, too, this ventricle has a thick construction to withstand the force of the heat.

[7] The mouths of the ventricles are not exposed unless one cuts off the tops of the auricles and the top of the heart. On this excision, two mouths upon the two ventricles will be apparent ....

[8] Close by the origin of the blood-vessels soft and spongy bodies envelop the ventricles. Although they are called 'ears' <auricles> they do not have the perforations of ears. For they do not hear any sound. They are the instruments by which nature catches the air – the creation, I believe, of a good craftsman, who, having recognised that the heart would be a solid structure on account of the compact nature of its material and without any power of attraction, set bellows beside it, as coppersmiths do at their furnaces, so that through these <the heart> might control its respiration. As evidence for this you can see the heart beating in its entirety, while the auricles expand and contract separately.

[10] The rest of my description of the heart concerns the hidden membranes – a structure most worthy of description. There are membranes in

the cavities, and fibres as well,[1] spread out like cobwebs, girdling the mouths in every direction and implanting fibres into the solid wall of the heart. These seem to me to be the guy-ropes of the heart and its vessels and the beginnings of the aortas. There is a pair of these aortas < i.e. the aorta and the pulmonary artery>, and on the entrance of each three membranes have been devised rounded from the extremity and approximately semi-circular. When they come together they close the mouths in a wondrous fashion as a limit of the aortas (?). And if someone who fully understands their original arrangement, removes the heart of the dead <animal/man?>[2] and props up the one membrane and leans the other against it, he will find that neither water nor air forced in will penetrate into the heart. This is particularly true in the case of the left chamber; for there the membranes are constructed more precisely as it is right that they should be. For man's intelligence is situated in the left ventricle ....

[1] The author seems to have recognised the *chordae tendineae* with the *musculi papillares*, and the *trabeculae carneae*.

[2] The text seems to suggest that the point of reference is the human heart; but the cadaver in question could be that of the pig vivisected earlier with the information derived from that dissection extrapolated to the human context. The description of the shape and position of the heart seems to suggest human dissection; but it should be noted that Aristotle gives an accurate description of the shape and inclination of the human heart, which he may have derived from observation of aborted human foetuses.

*

In the *Iliad* the deadly wounds sustained by the heroes locked in combat around Troy are at times described by Homer in a manner that reveals some detailed anatomical observation [**XIV.1-3**]. Despite this accuracy of detail, which has led to extravagant over-assessment – even to the claim that Homer could only have derived such knowledge from the dissecting-table[1] – it is clear that the anatomical and physiological knowledge of Homeric times was extremely limited, as the situation revealed both by the fragments of the Presocratic philosophers and by the Hippocratic treatises several centuries later attests.

It has been claimed upon the basis of a late source [**XIV.4**] that Alcmaeon of Croton was the first to employ human dissection as a general method of investigation. Most scholars, however, rightly reject this suggestion on the grounds that our source here (Chalcidius) does not confine his reference solely to Alcmaeon, but includes Callisthenes and Herophilus, and that there is no evidence of human dissection before the third century BC. It has also been suggested that Chalcidius's reference is to an anatomical investigation performed upon an animal; but, viewed against the background of a culture wherein animals were regularly slaughtered for purposes of divination, the claim is not convincing. Chalcidius's Latin – *ausus est* – ('dared') strongly suggests a human subject, and we are left with the remaining possibility of a surgical operation upon a human subject for a therapeutic purpose, which Chalcidius could well have considered an important contribution towards the 'demonstration of the nature of the eye'.

Although certain of the Hippocratic treatises reveal a fair degree of anatomical knowledge of the skull [**XIV.5**], the limbs and skeleton generally, some acquaintance with the main vessels of the vascular system [**XIV.6**], in the main, the knowledge of internal organs revealed in the *Corpus* is of a very primitive level [**XIV.7**][2] and is clearly based upon experience gained from the actual treatment of patients, from opportunities for observation afforded by those injured in war, from the kitchen, butcher's shop or at sacrifice; sometimes it is even based upon analogies drawn between internal organs and external objects such as cupping-glasses. The great bulk of the treatises affords no evidence to suggest that their authors had sought to increase their anatomical knowledge by the systematic dissection of animals or man.

Plato's knowledge of internal anatomy is also of a very low order and is obviously not based upon any human, or even animal, dissection. In his description of the heart in the *Timaeus*, for example, [**XIV.8**] he neither describes the chambers of the heart nor gives an account of its operation. There is no suggestion here that the heart is the cause of the movement of the blood. Although some vascular connection is recognised between the heart and the lungs, which are given the dual function of keeping the heart from being injured by its violent throbbing when excited and of cooling the innate heat of the heart through respiration, it is evident that his views are conditioned by the constraints of his tripartite psychology and not by the results of any anatomical investigation.

Aristotle's zoological treatises display, by and large, a much more sophisticated level of knowledge than that attained by his predecessors. He gives, for example, a good account of the membranes of the brain and distinguishes between the cerebrum and the cerebellum [**XIV.10**]. Aristotle reveals himself as a competent comparative anatomist and has evidently dissected and even vivisected different types of animals. Diocles of Carystus seems to have been the first to have written a special treatise on animal anatomy (Galen, *On anatomical procedures* 2.1 = II.282K = *Diokles* Fr. 23 Wellmann) and his influence may have contributed substantially to the great advances made in the knowledge of animal anatomy in the Lyceum generally. Although Aristotle may have been the first to recognise that the human heart consists of more than one chamber, he made a notorious error in supposing that it was three-chambered [**XIV.9**]. There is some evidence to suggest that it was Diocles who recognised that it was a vessel of four chambers [**XIV.13**]. While it is possible that Aristotle derived some knowledge of the shape and position of the human heart from aborted human foetuses, religious scruples, veneration of the dead and the dread of the corpse had all combined to bring about a powerful taboo within Ancient Greek culture that effectively prohibited systematic human dissection. As has been seen in **Chapter VII**, it was not until the Hellenistic period, when dissections were at last performed on human beings upon a systematic basis, that the most striking advances in the knowledge of human anatomy occurred.

[1] See Körner, 1922, p. 1484ff.

[2] *Places in man, On fleshes* and *On the heart* are exceptional in that they display higher levels of anatomical knowledge. The two former works contain, for example, descriptions of the anatomy of the eye which could indicate dissection – although, it should be noted, in each case evidence from lesions is explicitly cited. The last named treatise exhibits so sophisticated a level of anatomical knowledge of the heart and its valves [**XIV.14**], apparently based upon dissection, that it can hardly be dated much earlier than the early Hellenistic period.

XV

Surgery

The Greek word for surgery, *cheirourgia*, denotes all healing by the operation of the hand, as opposed to medication taken internally. No distinction was drawn between these activities. The Greek doctor was a surgeon as well as a physician.

SURGERY IN THE HEROIC AGE

Homeric Epic provides our earliest literary evidence of surgical practice amongst the Ancient Greeks. The heroes fighting at Troy were prepared to treat both themselves and one another.

XV.1. Homer, *Iliad* 11.397-400

Diomedes treats himself before withdrawing from combat.

Diomedes sat down ... and drew the sharp arrow from his foot. Then he leapt upon his chariot and ordered his charioteer to drive to the hollow ships for his heart was grieved.

XV.2. Homer, *Iliad* 11.822-36

Eurypylus turns to Patroclus for aid.

The wounded Eurypylus answered him in turn: 'No longer, Zeus-born Patroclus, will there be any defence of the Achaeans, but they will fling themselves upon the black ships. For all that were bravest before, lie among the ships smitten by arrows or wounded by spear-thrusts at the hands of the Trojans, whose strength ever increases. But save me by leading me to my black ship. Cut the arrow from my thigh. Wash the black blood from it with warm water and sprinkle upon it gentle drugs that heal, which, men say, you have learned from Achilles, whom Chiron taught, the most righteous of the Centaurs. For the physicians, Podalirius and Machaon, the one, I think, lies wounded among the huts, needing himself a peerless physician, while the other on the plain endures sharp battle with the Trojans.'

XV.3. Homer, *Iliad* 4.210-19

Machaon, son of Asclepius, treats Menelaus's arrow wound.

When they came to where fair-haired Menelaus was wounded, and those who were chieftains were gathered in a circle around him, the god-like hero stood in their midst and straightaway pulled out the arrow from the clasped belt. As it was being extracted, the barbs were broken backwards. He loosened the glittering belt and the drawers beneath and the guard fashioned by the coppersmiths. But when he saw the wound, where the bitter arrow had struck, he sucked out the blood and with sure knowledge spread on soothing salves, which once Chiron with kindly thoughts gave to his father.

XV.4. Scholium on Pindar, *Pythian Odes* 1.51ff.

Here he cures Philoctetes.

Washed clean by the oracles of Apollo <Philoctetes> fell asleep; then Machaon, removing the gangrenous flesh from the festering ulcer and deluging it with wine, sprinkled over the wound a herb which Asclepius got from Chiron, and in this way the hero was cured.

XV.5. Homer, *Iliad* 11.505-15ff.

When Machaon is himself wounded by Paris, Idomeneus is moved to express his regard for doctors.

... Alexander, husband of lovely-haired Helen, stopped Machaon, excelling in valour and shepherd of the host, striking him on the right shoulder with a three-barbed arrow. Then sorely did the Achaeans, breathing might, fear for him lest somehow the enemy should kill him in the battle's reversal. Forthwith Idomeneus addressed noble Nestor. 'Nestor, son of Neleus, great glory of the Achaeans, come on, get on your chariot and let Machaon get on beside you and drive as quickly as possible to the ships your uncloven-hooved horses. For a healer (ἰητρός) is worth many other men for cutting out arrows and spreading soothing salves.'

XV.6. Arctinus, *Sack of Troy* (scholium on *Iliad* 15.515)

Machaon and Podalirius, considered here by Arctinus to be the sons, not of Asclepius, but of Poseidon, are here described as having different specialisms. The former is held to be a surgeon, whereas the latter treats internal disease [see also **XII.3**].

For their father himself, the glorious Earthshaker, gave them both honours, but one he made more renowned than the other. To the one he gave more agile hands to draw the darts from the flesh and to heal all wounds. To the other he gave the power to know accurately in his heart all matters that are unseen, and to heal things incapable of being healed.

SURGERY IN THE SIXTH/EARLY FIFTH CENTURIES

XV.7. Herodotus, *Histories* 3.129-30

Herodotus records the superiority of Greek over Egyptian surgery when he describes Democedes's successful treatment of Darius.

While hunting, Darius, in dismounting from his horse, twisted his foot so violently that the ball of the ankle-joint (*astragalus*) was dislocated from its socket. He employed some Egyptian doctors, who had the reputation of being foremost in the art of medicine. But they, by their violent twisting of the foot, made the damage worse and for seven days and nights Darius could get no sleep because of the pain .... Then someone, who had previously heard when he was still in Sardis of the skill of Democedes of Croton, told the king of him. Darius ordered him to be brought to him as quickly as possible ... and they brought him dragging his chains and dressed in rags. When he was brought before him, Darius asked him if he had knowledge of the art of medicine. But he denied it, fearing that, if he revealed the truth about himself, he would never be allowed to return to Greece. But it was clear to Darius that he was versed in the art of subterfuge. He ordered those bringing him to display whips and goads. Thereupon he confessed, declaring that he did not have precise knowledge but, having associated with a physician, he had a slight knowledge of the art of medicine. Darius then entrusted himself to him and Democedes, employing Greek remedies and applying gentle instead of violent techniques rendered him able to sleep and in a little while restored him to health, though the king never expected to have his foot made sound.

Despite Herodotus's description of Democedes's successful treatment of Darius's astragalus, this bone is only mentioned incidentally in a human context on a single occasion in the Hippocratic *Corpus* (*Epidemics* V.48 (V.236,4L)).

XV.8. Herodotus, *Histories* 3.133-4

Democedes also successfully treats Darius's wife, Atossa.

A short time after this ... Atossa, the daughter of Cyrus and wife of Darius, developed an abscess (*phyma*[1]) on her breast that burst and was spreading. For as long as it was quite small she concealed it and through shame told no one. But when it was in a bad state, she sent for Democedes and showed it to him. He promised to cure her, but made her swear that she would repay him by granting whatever he might request of her, saying that he would ask for nothing shameful .... His treatment restored her to health.

[1] Some scholars translate *phyma* as 'tumour' and believe that Atossa was suffering from breast cancer, but it seems more likely that her affliction was an inflammatory mastitis. See Sandison, 1959, pp. 317-22 and Grmek, 1989, pp. 350ff.

SURGERY IN THE CULT OF ASCLEPIUS

There is good evidence that the god was believed to employ secular surgical techniques.

XV.9. *Inscriptiones Graecae* IV².1 Nos. 121-2 (Edelstein, *Asclepius* Vol. I, No. 423 A IV p. 222)

Here the god is said to have successfully treated the diseased eye of Ambrosia.

Ambrosia of Athens, diseased in one eye. She came as a suppliant to the god. As she walked about in the temple, she laughed at some of the cures as incredible and impossible that the lame and the blind should become cured merely by having a dream. Falling asleep in the temple, she had a vision: the god seemed to stand over her and said that he would cure her; however, she would be required to set up in the temple as payment a silver pig as a memorial to her ignorance. After saying this, he opened up the diseased eye and poured in some drug. When day came, she left cured.

HIPPOCRATIC SURGERY

XV.10. [Hippocrates], *On joints* 51 (IV.224,6-226,4L)

Dislocation of the femur.

If the head of the thigh-bone becomes dislocated from the hip, the dislocation comes about in four ways: far most frequently inwards;[1] and of the other ways, most frequently outwards. Dislocation backwards and forwards occurs, but rarely. In those cases where the dislocation is inwards, the leg appears longer when placed beside the other, and naturally so for two reasons, for the head of the femur bears upon the bone which springs from the hip and passes up to the pubes, and the neck of the femur is supported by the cotyloid cavity. Again, the buttock appears hollow on its outer side because the head of the femur is inclined inwards. Again, the end of the femur at the knee is compelled to turn outwards, and the leg and foot correspondingly. Hence, owing to this outward inclination of the foot, physicians, on account of their inexperience, bring the sound foot to it, instead of bringing it to the sound foot. On account of this, the damaged foot looks much longer than the sound one, and this sort of thing causes misapprehension in many other instances. Moreover, the patient is unable to bend at the groin as in the normal condition. But, on palpating the head of the femur, it is manifest as it forms an undue prominence at the perineum.

[1] Although our author has here the support of antiquity in this belief that the inward dislocation of the femur is the most frequent, modern evidence is to the contrary.

XV.11. [Hippocrates], *On joints* 70 (IV.288,11-292,3L)

Reduction of the femur.

Dislocation of the thigh-bone at the hip-joint should be reduced as follows, if it is dislocated inwards. This reduction is good, precise and in accordance with nature, and, indeed, also has something striking about it, which pleases, at any rate, the sophisticated in such matters. One should suspend the patient by the feet from a cross-beam by a strong, but soft and broad, fastening. The feet should be about four fingers' breadth apart, or even less. He should also be bound round above the knees with a broad, soft strap, stretching up to the beam. The damaged leg should be extended about two fingers' breadth more than the other. Let the head be about two cubits, or a little more or less, from the ground. Let the patient be bound with something soft with his arms extended along his sides. Let all these preparations be made with the patient lying on his back so that he may be suspended for as short a time as possible. When he is suspended, a well-trained and strong assistant should insert his forearm between the patient's thighs and then place it between the perineum and the head of the dislocated thigh-bone. Then, grasping the inserted hand with the other and standing erect beside the body of the suspended patient, he should suddenly suspend himself from him and keep himself aloft as evenly balanced as possible. This mode of reduction provides everything that is necessary in accordance with nature. For the body, when suspended, itself makes an extension by its own weight; and the assistant, who is suspended from it, contemporaneously with the extension forces the head of the thigh-bone to be lifted up over the socket of the hip-joint and at the same time levers it out with the bone of his forearm and forces it to slide into its old natural place.

XV.12. [Hippocrates], *On joints* 62 (IV.262,10-266,8L)

Treatment for club-foot.

There are some congenital displacements which, if they are slight, are capable of being brought back to their normal position. Congenital club-foot is for the most part curable if the dislocations are not very great or the child is not too far advanced in growth. It is best to treat such cases as soon as possible before there occurs any very great deficiency in the bones of the foot and a corresponding deficiency in the flesh of the leg. Now there is not one but many kinds of club-foot; in most cases there is not complete disarticulation, but deformities are due to a habitual contraction of the foot. In the course of treatment attention must be paid to the following factors: to push back and straighten the bone of the leg at the ankle inwards from without and make counter-pressure outwards upon the external part of the heel so as to bring together the bones projecting at the middle and side of the foot; again, bend, or rather force round, all the toes together, including the big toe. Dress with cerate <a salve> well mixed with resin and with not a few pads and soft cloths of linen – but without too much pressure; make the turns of the bandage correspond with the manual correction of the foot so that there is rather a slight discernible inclination towards splay-footedness. A sole should be made of not too stiff leather or of lead and this should be bound on, not in immediate contact with the skin, but just when you are going to put on the last dressings.

The above account is concerned with the type of club-foot known technically as talipes varus in which the outer border of the foot, rather than the sole, touches the ground. The condition here is attributed to a form of contraction or habit-spasm rather than to any structural abnormality.

XV.13. [Hippocrates], *On joints* 69 (IV.282,13-284,11L)[1]

Gangrene – a laissez-faire policy.

Gangrene of the tissues: when it occurs in wounds with supervening haemorrhage or from tight constriction, and in fractures that are compressed more than is opportune, and in other cases of tight bandaging, the blackened parts come away in many instances. The majority of such cases survive – even when part of the thigh comes away with the tissues and the bone ... when the forearm or leg comes away, they survive still more easily. In cases of bone-fracture, constriction and blackening set in straightway, the mortified flesh swiftly breaks away all round, and the parts that come away do so swiftly, the bones having already given way. In cases where blackening occurs when the bones are healthy, the flesh dies rapidly here also, but the bones separate slowly at the borders of the blackening and the denudation of the bone. Those parts of the body that are below the limits of the blackening, when they are quite dead and insensitive, should be taken off at the joint, taking care not to wound any living part. For, if the patient suffers pain during the amputation and the limb happens to be not yet dead at the place where it is cut off, there is great danger of the patient fainting from pain. Such collapses often are immediately fatal.

[1] See, too, *Instruments of reduction* 35 (IV.376-8L).

XV.14. [Hippocrates], *On wounds in the head* 21 (III.256,11-258,13L)

Trepanation.

As to trephining, whenever it becomes necessary to trephine a patient, keep the following in mind. If you operate having taken on the treatment from the beginning, you should not straight away excise the bone down to the membrane, for it is not beneficial for the membrane to be denuded of bone and be exposed to harmful influences for a long time and end up becoming fungoid in some way.[1] There is also another danger that, if you immediately remove the bone by trephining down to the membrane, you may in the operation wound the membrane with the trephine.[2] You should rather stop trephining when there is very little left to be sawn through and the bone is already beginning to move and allow it to separate of its own accord. For no harm would ensue in the trephined bone or the part left unsawn; for that which is left is now thin. For the rest, the treatment should be as might seem beneficial to the lesion. While trephining you should frequently take out the saw to avoid heating the bone and immerse it in cold water. For the saw becomes heated by the rotation and, by heating and drying the bone, cauterises it and makes a bigger piece of bone surrounding the trephined part come away than was going to. If you want to trephine down to the membrane right away and then remove the bone, you must, in like manner, frequently take out the trephine and immerse it in cold water.

[1] Reading with Withington: τελευτῶσα πη καὶ διεμύδησεν.

[2] For a description of a crown trephine, a hollow cylindrical instrument with serrated lower edges and with a fixed pin in the middle, see Celsus *On medicine* VIII.3.

XV.15. [Hippocrates], *Diseases* II.47 (VII.70,11-72,1L)

Treatment of a patient suffering from pus in the pleural cavity (empyema). A rigid tube is inserted to facilitate drainage. (This passage continues from **XI.6**.)

First cut the skin between the ribs with a knife with a rounded blade. Then take a sharp-pointed knife wrapped in a strip of cloth with its tip exposed a thumb-nail's length and make an incision. Next, having drained away as much pus as seems appropriate, drain the wound with a drain of raw linen, attached to a cord. Let out the pus once a day. On the tenth day, after having let out all the pus, drain the wound with a piece of fine linen. Then inject warm wine and oil through a small tube so that the lung accustomed to being moistened by the pus might not suddenly be dried out. Let out the morning's infusion towards evening, and the evening one in the morning. When the pus becomes thin like water, sticky to the finger when touched, and scanty, insert a hollow, tin drainage-tube. When the <pleural> cavity is completely drained, gradually cut the drain shorter, and allow the wound to heal until you finally take out the drain.

For prognosis in such cases see **XI.7**.

XV.16. [Hippocrates], *In the surgery* 2-4 (III.274-288,3L)

General recommendations for surgical practice.

[2] Operative requisites in the surgery (*iatreion*): patient, surgeon, assistants, instruments, light, source and position ....

[3] The surgeon, whether seated or standing, should be positioned conveniently to himself, to what is being operated upon and to the light.

Now there are two kinds of light, natural and artificial. The natural is not in our power but the artificial is. Each may be used in two ways, either as direct or as indirect light. Indirect light is rarely used and the right amount is obvious. With direct light, from what is available and beneficial, turn the part being operated upon towards the brightest light .... Thus, while the part being operated upon faces the light, the surgeon faces the part, but not so as to overshadow it. For the surgeon would in this way have a good view, and the part under treatment would not be exposed to general view.

Regarding the surgeon himself: when seated his feet should be in a vertical line below the knees, having come together with a slight interval between. Knees a little higher than the groin with the interval between them sufficient for the positioning and juxtaposing of the elbows ... when standing, he should make his examination with the weight fairly equally balanced upon both feet, but operate with the weight upon the one foot (but not the one on the side of the hand in use); height of the knees in the same relation to the groin as when seated .... Let the patient assist the surgeon with the other part of his body either standing, sitting or lying down so that he continues to maintain the easiest necessary posture, guarding against the flesh falling away, settling down, being displaced or hanging downwards so that the position and form of the part under treatment may be properly preserved during presentation and during the operation ....

[4] The nails should neither exceed nor fall short of the finger tips. Practise using the finger ends, especially with the forefinger opposed to the thumb, with the whole hand held palm downwards, and with both hands opposed. Good formation of fingers: wide intervals between the fingers, and the thumb opposed to the forefinger .... Practise all operations, performing them with either hand and with both together – for they are both alike.

XV.17. [Hippocrates], *On joints* 72 (IV.296-300,1L)

Included among the instruments contained in the *iatreion* may have been the infamous Hippocratic 'bench' (*scamnus*), which was basically a device for stretching patients with winches (see, too, [Hippocrates], *Fractures* 13). There is no evidence to suggest that Hippocrates himself invented it. According to Celsus this rack-like contraption could rupture the muscles and ligaments (*On medicine* VIII.20).

It has already been said before that it is worthwhile for one who practises medicine in a populous city to obtain a rectangular plank about six cubits long, or rather more, and about two cubits broad, while a span[1] is sufficient thickness. Next, it should have an incision on either side along its length so that the mechanism might not be higher than is suitable.[2] Then, it should have short, strong posts, securely fitted in, one either side of the bench, each with a windlass. Next, it is sufficient to cut into one half of the board – though there is nothing to prevent them from extending its whole length – about five or six grooves about four fingers' breadth apart; but it is enough if they are three fingers broad and of the same depth. The board should also have a deeper incision in the middle, square and about three fingers' breadth. Into this incision, whenever it seems to be needed, insert a post, rounded in its upper part, fitting it into the whole. Insert it whenever it seems useful between the perineum and the head of the thigh-bone. This post, when in position, prevents the body from yielding to the pressure of the traction towards the feet. For sometimes this post is itself a sufficient substitute for the counter-extension upwards. Sometimes, too, when the leg is being stretched on this side and that, this same post, when loosely inserted to give play on either side, would be suitable for levering the head of the thigh-bone outwards. It is for this purpose, too, that the grooves are cut so that a wooden lever might be inserted wherever it might fit and bring pressure to bear either alongside the heads of the joints or, by pressing fully down upon them, simultaneously with the extension – whether it is advantageous to apply leverage outwards or inwards and whether the lever should be rounded or broad. For one suits one joint, another, another. This leverage in combination with the extension is very effective in the case of all reductions of the leg-joints.[3]

[1] i.e. the space one can embrace between the thumb and little finger.

[2] i.e. the supports are recessed into the board and do not project unduly above it.

[3] Herophilus's pupil, Andreas, personal physician of Ptolemy IV Philopator (*c.* 244-205 BC), is later credited with the invention of an instrument for reducing dislocations of the larger joints that seems to have employed the more sophisticated Alexandrian technology. (See Celsus, *On medicine* VIII (*CML* I, p. 407 Marx); Galen, *Commentary upon Hippocrates On joints* 4.47 (XVIIIA.747K) and, for the fullest account, Oribasius, *Medical collections* 49.6 (*CMG* VI.2.2 = Vol. IV, p. 12 Raeder).

A FOURTH-CENTURY SURGICAL INNOVATION

XV.18. Cornelius Celsus, *On medicine* VII.5.3 (*CML* I, pp. 309-10 Marx = *Diokles* Fr. 191 Wellmann)

The spoon of Diocles.

If a broad weapon has been embedded, it is not expedient to extract it from the other side lest a second large wound is added to one already large. It should therefore be pulled out by a certain type of instrument which the Greeks call the Dioclean *kyathiskos* because it was invented by Diocles, whom I have already ranked amongst the greatest of medical men of old. The instrument[1] consists of a thin piece of iron or even of bronze. At one extremity it has two hooks turned downwards on both sides; at the other it is bent double at the sides and is slightly inclined at the end towards that part which is bent. Moreover, it also has a perforation there. The instrument is lowered <into the wound> alongside the weapon, then, when the very bottom of its point has been reached, it is twisted a little so that it takes hold of the missile in its hole. When the point is in the cavity, two fingers placed under the hooks of the other part draw out the instrument and missile simultaneously.

[1] For a convenient illustration of this instrument see Majno, 1975, p. 361. Its operation has been rendered obscure by poor translation from the Latin (see, for example, Spencer in his Loeb edn. (1935-8, Vol. 3 ad loc.).

SURGICAL PRACTICE AT ALEXANDRIA

XV.19. Caelius Aurelianus, *On chronic diseases* III.4 (p. 752 Drabkin = *Erasistratus* Fr. 184B Garofalo = *CML* VI.1, Vol. II, p. 716 Bendz)

A risky surgical intervention on the part of Erasistratus.

In cases of those suffering from ailments of the liver, Erasistratus cuts the skin and the membrane covering the liver and applies drugs extensively to the organ itself; then he draws aside the stomach and boldly lays bare the part that is affected.

Surgical instruments used at Alexandria

XV.20. Tertullian, *On the soul* 25.5 (p. 36 Waszink = *Herophilus* Fr. 247 von Staden)

According to Tertullian both Herophilus and Erasistratus followed Hippocrates in using an embryotome to cut the embryo to pieces inside the womb. We learn further from Galen that Erasistratus was credited with the invention of a catheter to drain the bladder.

And so, among physicians' tools, along with an instrument <a dilator> by which parts previously hidden are forced to become manifest by means of a winding adjustment, and an annular surgical knife by which the limbs <within the womb> are cut with anxious direction, and a blunt hook by which a whole crime is eradicated by a violent delivery, there is also a bronze, pointed instrument by which the actual slaughter is managed with secret theft. From its infanticidal function they call it a 'foetus-slaughterer' (*embryosphaktês*). In the case of the living infant it is certainly lethal. Hippocrates possessed this instrument, as did Asclepiades, Erasistratus, Herophilus – that dissector even of adults – and the milder Soranus himself.

*

Our earliest evidence of surgical practice amongst the Ancient Greeks is afforded by the epic poems of Homer, especially, of course the *Iliad*, where, as has been seen above **[XIV.1-3]**, the wounds sustained by the heroes fighting outside Troy are described at times with a striking accuracy of detail. It is evident that these heroes treated both themselves and one another. Diomedes, for example, himself extracted an arrow that had pierced his foot [XV.1] and the wounded Eurypylus is assisted by Patroclus [XV.2]. Achilles, we also learn from this passage, had been instructed in healing techniques by the Centaur, Chiron. However, two of the warriors fighting on the Greek side, Podalirius and Machaon, the sons of Asclepius, were regarded as especially skilled in the healing art and are actually described here as ἰητροί (doctors or healers). Although Podalirius is never actually mentioned in the *Iliad* exercising his healing craft,[1] Machaon is mentioned frequently. At *Iliad* 4.210-19 for example, he is depicted treating Menelaus's arrow-wound [XV.3]. A scholion on Pindar's *Pythian Odes* describes his treatment of Philoctetes's festering wound [XV.4]. At *Iliad* 11.504ff., when Machaon himself is wounded in the shoulder by Paris, Idomeneus exhorts Nestor to get him out of the battle and back to the ships, remarking that 'a healer is worth many other men in cutting out arrows and spreading soothing salves' [XV.5]. Both brothers are mentioned in a later epic, *The Sack of Troy*, associated with the poet Arctinus of Miletus (seventh century BC?). Here [XV.6] a distinction is drawn between them that is nowhere apparent in the *Iliad* in that Machaon is depicted primarily as a surgeon, whereas Podalirius is held to be an expert in internal medicine. This distinction similarly appears in a variety of later sources where Podalirius is portrayed as a physician 'who worked on the subject of diet' or who 'treated diseases by diet' as opposed to his brother, the surgeon. More reliable evidence, however, suggests that dietetics was a much later development in the history of Greek medicine [see **Chapter XII**].

In contrast to the *Iliad*, the *Odyssey* affords little evidence of surgical treatment. In Book 19.455-8, as has already been seen [I.20], Odysseus, while hunting on Mt. Parnassus, was wounded by a boar and sustained a gash above the knee. His cousins, the sons of Autolycus, we learn, 'bound the wound skilfully and checked the dark blood with an incantation'. Here may be seen explicit evidence of the underlying use of magic in the treatment of wounds.

Before the end of the sixth century BC the reputation of Greek surgeons had spread as far as Persia. Herodotus, as has already been seen above, records how Democedes of Croton, the son of Calliphon and 'the best physician of his day', successfully treated the Persian king, Darius and his queen, Atossa [XV.7 & 8]. Surgery seems also to have been employed within the healing cult of Asclepius. It is evident from the beautiful ode that Pindar addressed (*c.* 473 BC) to Hiero, tyrant of Syracuse, that the god was believed to employ surgical techniques (Pindar, *Pythian* III.46-55 [see I.22]. Further testimony to this belief may be found in the *iamata*: for example, on Stele 1, Case 4 [XV.9] the god is described cutting into and successfully treating the diseased eye of Ambrosia of Athens. (Here, it may be noted, Asclepius is conceived as operating in the manner of a mortal physician.)

A whole group of surgical works is preserved in the Hippocratic *Corpus*. They were for a long time attributed to Hippocrates himself. Galen included them in his first, or most genuine, band of Hippocratic writings. Some ancient commentators even attributed two of them, *Joints* and *Fractures*, to Hippocrates's grandfather, Hippocrates the son of Gnosidicus (see Galen, *Commentary on Hippocrates Regimen in Acute Diseases* I.17 (XV.456K)). Three of them, *Joints*,[2] *Fractures*, and *Instruments of reduction*, deal with dislocations and fractures. The first two of these, which were almost certainly written by the same author, once formed a single work. The third is, for the most part, an abstract from the other two. In the course of time, the text of these three treatises became disarranged so that their order is not invariably logical and fractures and dislocations are discussed in all of them. *Joints* and *Fractures* also contain full descriptions of necessary apparatus and of bandages, splints and leverage, including the infamous Hippocratic 'bench' [XV.17]. Experience derived by the physician from the palaestra and gymnasium, where accidents to limbs and joints must have been frequent, is most probably reflected here. The femur, we learn, presented particular problems in that it could be dislocated from the hip in four different ways [**XV.10**]. Detailed directions for the reduction of the thigh at the hip are given [**XV.11**]. Congenital club foot is also discussed [**XV.12**]. This complaint is held to be curable provided the deviation is not too great and the child is not too advanced in years. In cases of gangrene, however, the Hippocratic doctor seems generally to have adopted a *laissez-faire* policy and simply waited until the affected limb slowly dropped off, occasionally removing bits of dead tissue [see **XV.13**].

The treatise, *On wounds in the head*, however, suggests experience derived from the battlefield. Here wounds are described together with the clinical symptoms they produce, the complications that may be expected, and their treatment, which includes a remarkably modern method of trepanning and a discussion of cases where trepanning is recommended and where it is better to abstain [**XV.14**]. Two other short treatises concentrate on ailments commonly given surgical treatment by the physician, viz. *On haemorrhoids* and *On fistulae*. This group of surgical treatises also includes the work, *In the surgery*, which is a collection of notes regarding the physician's surgery and the apparatus and instruments it should contain [**XV.16**]. Some general principles of surgery are also discussed and there is a detailed account of the use of various types of bandaging and dressings. Other types of surgical operation are described elsewhere in the *Corpus*. *Diseases* II.47, for example, describes the introduction of a rigid tube into the pleural cavity of a patient to facilitate the drainage of pus that had accumulated there [**XV.15**].

Outside the Hippocratic *Corpus,* little evidence of surgical practice and technique has survived. Diocles of Carystus had evidently read the Hippocratic treatise *Joints* and, according to Apollonius of Citium (II.13.2 = *Diokles* Fr. 188 Wellmann), had made reference to the reduction of the finger-joint described there in Chapter 80. He also seems to have maintained the Hippocratic interest in elaborate bandaging (see Oribasius IV.289 = *Diokles* Fr. 190 Wellman) and he is credited with the invention of the 'Diocles spoon' – a device for the extraction of missiles of the larger type [**XV.18**]. In the Hellenistic period, when surgical practice must surely have benefited from the Alexandrians' greater knowledge of human anatomy, Erasistratus seems to have been particularly bold and is even said to have opened up the abdomen of a patient suffering from dropsy in order to apply remedies directly to the liver [**XV.19**].

Some evidence of the Alexandrians' use of surgical instruments has survived [**XV.20**]. Herophilus and Erasistratus are both said to have followed Hippocrates in employing an embryotome to cut the foetus to pieces within the womb. Like his distinguished Alexandrian counterpart, Erasistratus was also interested in the development of technical aids and is credited with the invention and introduction into surgery of a catheter for draining the bladder. This catheter, which was named after him, was shaped like the Roman letter S (Ps.-Galen, *Introduction or the doctor* 13 = XIV.751K). Herophilus's pupil, Andreas, is later credited with the invention of an instrument for reducing dislocations of the larger joints that seems to have exploited some of the more sophisticated elements of Alexandrian technology. (For further details see **XV.17 n.3**.)

---

[1] He is, in fact, mentioned only twice: in the Catalogue of Ships (*Iliad* 2.729-33) and at *Iliad* 11.822-36 [**XV.2**], where he is described as being in the thick of the fighting when Eurypylus was wounded. In post-Homeric epic, however, he is portrayed curing wounds by stitching and spreading on salves (see Quintus of Smyrna, *Posthomerica* 4.396ff.).

[2] In the first century BC the Alexandrian physician Apollonius of Citium wrote a commentary on this book which has survived in a manuscript of the ninth or tenth century containing illustrations of the various ways of reducing dislocations.

XVI

Gynaecology

The bulk of our knowledge of gynaecology for the period under survey is provided by the Hippocratic *Corpus*. The gynaecological works preserved here are probably among the oldest.

DISEASE AND GENDER

The belief that the effect of disease is gender-specific is first encountered in Hesiod *Works and Days* [I.13], where, describing the impact of the plague sent by Zeus, Hesiod tells us that 'the men perished, the women were barren'. This view is prevalent throughout the Hippocratic *Corpus*.

XVI.1. [Hippocrates], *Diseases* I.22. (VI.182,22-184,2L)

Recovery from disease is here held to differ also according to the sex of the patient.

Among those that have these and similar diseases, *a man differs from a woman in the greater ease or difficulty he has in recovery;* a younger man differs from an older man, and a younger woman from an older woman. In addition, the season in which they have fallen ill makes a difference as does whether or not their disease has followed from another disease.

XVI.2. [Hippocrates], *Airs, Waters, Places* 3-4 (II.14,21-22,9L= *CMG* I.1,2, pp. 26-32 Di.)

It is suggested here that even when men and women catch the same disease their symptoms are quite different.

[3] A city that lies exposed to the hot winds between the winter rising of the sun and its winter setting .... These are the endemic diseases ... the women are unhealthy and prone to fluxes ... many are barren through disease and not naturally so. Miscarriages are frequent .... The men, on the other hand, suffer from dysentery, diarrhoea, ague, chronic fevers in winter, frequent pustules, and piles....

[4] Cities facing the cold winds that blow from between the summer setting and the summer rising of the sun ... these are the endemic diseases. Pleurisy is frequent, as are those diseases considered to be acute. This must necessarily be the case, whenever the intestines are hard. And many suffer abscesses from the slightest cause ... inflammations of the eyes eventually occur ... men under thirty suffer violent epistaxis during

the summer .... For the men these diseases are endemic ... for the women, on the other hand, in the first place many become barren on account of the water being hard, costive, and cold. Their menstrual discharges are not regular but are few and painful. Next childbirth is difficult, but miscarriage is rare. When they bear children, they cannot rear them, for their milk is dried up from the hardness and costive nature of the water. There are frequent cases of phthisis after parturition ....

XVI.3. [Hippocrates], *Diseases of women* I.62 (VIII.126,14-19L)

Women's diseases, it is stressed here, require different treatment from those of men.

Doctors are in error in not ascertaining accurately the cause of a <woman's> disease and treating it as if they were dealing with men's diseases (*ta andrika nosêmata*). I have already seen many women destroyed by such experiences. It is necessary straightway to inquire into the precise cause. For the treatment of women's diseases differs greatly from that of men's.

This belief that disease was gender-specific, however, became a controversial issue and was rejected by later authors.

XVI.4. Soranus, *Gynaecology* III Proem 2 (*CMG* IV, pp. 94-5 Ilb.)

Soranus at a later date cites the main protagonists in this controversy.

The inquiry is very useful for the sake of learning whether women also need treatment particular to them. But disagreement has arisen. Some suppose that conditions occur that are peculiar to women, as do the Empiricists, Diocles in the first book of his *Gynaecology*, and Athenion among the Erasistrateans .... Some deny that they do, for example, according to most people, Erasistratus and Herophilus ....

XVI.5. Soranus, *Gynaecology* III Proem 3.4 (*CMG* IV, p. 95 Ilb.)

Herophilus's standpoint is described in greater detail.

In the *Midwifery* Herophilus asserts that the uterus is woven from the same things as the other parts, is regulated by the same faculties, and has the same substances at hand, and suffers diseases from the same causes, such as excess, thickness and disagreement among similars. Therefore *there is no affection peculiar to women*, except conceiving, nourishing what has been conceived, giving birth, 'ripening' the milk, and the opposites of these.

XVI.6. Soranus, *Gynaecology* IV.1.4-5 (*CMG* IV, pp. 130-1 IIb. = *Herophilus* Fr. 196 von Staden)

Although Herophilus believed that no disease was peculiar to women, he did accept that there were certain conditions peculiar to the female. He concerned himself with them in his treatise *Midwifery*. This single surviving fragment preserves his views on the causes of difficult labour.

In his treatise *Midwifery* Herophilus says:

'Difficult labour occurs because a woman has had many troublesome pregnancies, for example three to five .... Difficult labour occurs when the foetus grows in a transverse position or when the neck of the uterus or even its mouth is not sufficiently distended, or when the membrane surrounding the embryo, where the water collects, is too thick and cannot be broken before the birth.' He says that foetuses have been seen born without the breaking of the membrane, but such foetuses still are delivered with difficulty.

Difficult labour, he says, also occurs because the uterus or its mouth lacks elasticity. The uterus's lack of elasticity is a problem inherent in the body.

'But difficult labour occurs also because of external factors – things that befall one, things consumed, things done – and because too much blood-like moisture is excreted from the body. Difficulty also arises through pains of child-birth because the uterus is distended by the foetus and because of cold or heat or a tumour or an abscess in the intestines or in the abdomen. A hollowness in the loins and the spine[1] also becomes a cause of difficult labour. On account of an accumulation of fat in the abdomen and in the hips difficult labour also occurs when the uterus is squeezed, and because the foetuses are dead.'

[1] It has been pointed out that here we have the first definite reference to a skeletal anomaly as a factor in dystocia (Fasbender, 1897, p. 23).

MENSTRUATION

The Hippocratic Corpus

The female body is held to be softer and more loosely-textured than the male and so attracts more fluid in the form of blood from the stomach. The female is unable to utilise all this food she has ingested and in order to remain healthy needs to evacuate this excess blood each month.

XVI.7. [Hippocrates], *Diseases of women* I.1 (VIII.12,6-21L)

Failure to menstruate results in pain and ill-health.

... I say that a woman has flesh that is more loosely textured and softer than that of a man, and, this being so, a woman's body attracts fluid from the belly <i.e. blood from nutriment> more quickly and in greater quantity than does a man's[1] ... when her body is full of blood and there is no evacuation from it, pain supervenes when the flesh becomes full and heated ....

[1] Our author illustrates this by a demonstration with wool and linen placed over a wide-mouthed vessel filled with water. The wool is revealed to absorb more liquid than the linen because it is looser and softer.

XVI.8. [Hippocrates], *Diseases of women* I.1 (VIII.10,1-5L)

A woman who has never given birth is held to suffer more painfully from menstruation than one who has.

The following concerns the diseases of women: I say that when a woman has not given birth she is affected by menstruation more painfully and more swiftly than one who has. For when she gives birth her vessels become more free-flowing for the menses. The lochial discharge and rupture within the body makes them become free-flowing ....

Herophilus

XVI.9. Soranus, *Gynaecology* I.27.2 (*CMG* IV, p. 17 IIb. = *Herophilus* Fr. 203 von Staden)

In the third century, however, Herophilus and others attacked this view that menstruation was universally beneficial for a woman's health and childbearing.

Some earlier physicians, as Herophilus also mentioned in his *Against common opinions*, say that menstruation is beneficial for health and for childbearing .... But Herophilus says that menstruation is helpful to the health of some women, but harmful to others.

XVI.10. Soranus, *Gynaecology* I.29.1 (*CMG* IV, p. 19 IIb. = *Herophilus* Fr. 204 von Staden)

Herophilus says that at one time menstruation is harmful for certain women; for some women, when they are not menstruating, are in a state of unimpeded health and often the opposite happens when they are menstruating and they become paler and thinner and contract the beginnings of diseases. At another time and in certain cases, it is beneficial so that women who were previously pallid and emaciated, later, after menstruation, have good colour and are well nourished ....

THE WANDERING WOMB

The Hippocratics considered that a major cause of women's diseases was the womb. It was believed that if it became dry it was liable to move itself from its natural position and attach itself to moister organs. The dislocated womb was responsible for a variety of ailments.

XVI.11. [Hippocrates], *Places in man* 47 (VI.344,3-22L)

Here some of the ailments caused by a dislocated womb are described.

Women's ailments: the womb is the cause of all ailments. For whenever the womb moves from its proper place, forwards or backwards, it causes illness. When the womb is displaced outwards but does not push its mouth forward and touch the labia, it is a very trivial complaint. When it moves forwards and does push its mouth forward to touch the labia, in the first place, it causes pain through contact; and, secondly, due to the womb's being blocked and obstructed by its contact with the labia the menstrual flow does not take place. This retention causes swelling and pain. If the womb descends and turns and then protrudes into the groin it will cause pain. If it ascends, turns and causes a blockage, here, too, it causes illness because of its porousness. When the womb has a malady from this cause, it causes pain in the hips and head. When the womb is full and swollen, there is no flow and it becomes replete. When it becomes full, it touches the hips. When the womb, full of moisture and distended, cannot contain that moisture and touches the hips, it causes pain both to hips and groin; its like having things like balls running around in the stomach that cause headache, sometimes in one side and sometimes all over according to the nature of the malady.

XVI.12. [Hippocrates], *Nature of woman* 8 (VII.322,11-324,9L)

Recommended treatment for a dislocated womb. (For treatment of dropsy in the womb see **XIII.7**.)

If her womb moves towards her hips, menstruation stops, and pain develops in her lower stomach and abdomen. If you feel with your finger, you will perceive the mouth of the womb is turned towards her hip.

When this condition occurs, wash the woman with warm water, make her eat as much garlic as she can, and drink undiluted ewe's milk after meals. Then fumigate and purge her. After the purge has taken effect, fumigate the womb again, with a mixture of fennel and absinthe. Immediately after fumigation, pull upon the mouth of the womb with your finger. Then insert a pessary made with squill; leave it in place for a while, and then insert a pessary made with opium poppies. If you think the position has been corrected, insert a pessary of bitter almond oil, and on the next day, a pessary of rose oil. She should cease inserting pessaries on the first day of her period, and start again the day after menstruation stops. The blood-flow during the period provides a normal interruption. If there is no flow, she should drink four cantharid beetles[1] with their legs, wings and heads removed, four dark peony seeds, cuttlefish eggs, and a little parsley seed in wine. If she has pain and an irregular flow, she should sit in warm water and drink honey mixed with water. If she is not cured by the first course of treatment, she should drink it again until menstruation begins. When it starts, she should abstain from food and have intercourse with her husband. During her period she should eat mercury plant, and boiled squid, and keep to soft foods. If she becomes pregnant, she will be cured ....

[1] According to Pliny (*Natural history*, 29.95) ground-up cantharid beetles were employed to induce menstruation.

XVI.13. [Hippocrates], *Places in man* 47 (VI.344,22-346,10L)

In order to attract the womb back to its proper place foul– and sweet-smelling substances were administered to repel and attract respectively. Here they were evidently applied to the vagina.

This is how these cases should be treated. If the womb has only moved forwards and it is possible to apply ointment to it thoroughly, employ any foul-smelling substance you like, either cedar or myssotos[1] or any other substance with a rather heavy and foul smell. Fumigate but do not use a vapour bath. Do not prescribe food or diuretic drinks at this time, or wash her in hot water. If the womb has moved upwards and is not diverted apply sweet-smelling pessaries that are also warming. These are myrrh, perfume, or any other aromatic and warming substance. Use these in pessaries, and from below apply fumigations of wine-vapour, and wash with hot water, and employ diuretics. Clearly, if the womb is not diverted and has moved upwards, a menstrual flow ensues. If it is diverted, a flow called the 'menses' does not take place.

[1] A savoury dish made with cheese, honey and garlic.

XVI.14. [Hippocrates], *Nature of woman* 3 (VII.314,14-21L)

On other occasions, however, they were applied both to nose and vagina. The treatment applied here seems to entail that the female body was regarded as a hollow tube connecting two orifices and affording the womb passage from the bottom of the body to the top.

When her womb moves towards her liver, she suddenly loses her voice, her teeth chatter and she turns a dark colour. This condition can occur suddenly, while she is in good health. The problem particularly affects old maids and widows – young women who have been widowed after having children.

When this condition occurs, push downwards with your hand away from her liver, and bind her with a bandage beneath her abdomen. Draw apart the os <uteri> and pour in most fragrant wine and apply evil-smelling things as fumigation to her nostrils. Put sweet-smelling things under her womb.

XVI.15. [Hippocrates], *On sterile women = Diseases of women* III.214
(VIII.416,3-5L)

A test to determine whether or not conception is possible. This test seems to entail
the above conception of the female body.

... clean thoroughly a head of garlic, snip off the head and insert it into the
womb; and on the following day see whether she smells of garlic through
her mouth; if she smells of it, she will conceive; if not she won't.

There is a very close parallel to this procedure in Egyptian medicine. See the
Carlsberg Papyrus VIII.4 (Iverson, 1939, pp. 21-2).

XVI.16. Plato, *Timaeus*, 91C

Plato develops upon this idea of the wandering womb and uses it to explain female
sexual desire.

In women, again, for the same reason, whenever what is called the matrix
or womb, a living-creature within them with a desire for child-bearing, is
long unfruitful beyond due season, it becomes vexed and irritated, and,
wandering everywhere throughout the body blocking the channels of
the breath and preventing respiration, brings extreme distress upon
the sufferer and causes all sorts of other diseases.

THE WANDERING WOMB DENIED

XVI.17. Aristotle, *Generation of animals* 720a12-14

Despite his contention here that wombs must have a fixed location, Aristotle
believed that the womb, when empty, could be pushed upwards causing a stifling
sensation (*History of animals* 582b22-6).

... both the seminal passages in males and the uterus in females must
have a fixed position and not wander about ....

XVI.18. Galen, *On the dissection of the uterus* 5 (II.895-6K = *CMG* V.2,1,
pp. 42-4 Nickel = *Herophilus* Fr. 114 von Staden)

Herophilus's dissection of human females enabled him to identify the 'membranes'
that support the womb.

<Herophilus> was not only competent in other branches of the art <of
medicine> and had attained the highest level of accuracy of what was
being learned through anatomy and had obtained the greatest amount of
his knowledge, not from irrational animals, like many researchers, but
from human beings themselves. Thus he asserts that the vessels that
nourish the uterus, and from which I said it is suspended, are clothed in
membranes[1] and that the membranes become constantly thicker and
harder and more callous in women who have been pregnant several times.

197

[1] Herophilus seems to be describing here the broad ligaments. See, too, Galen, *On the semen* 2,1 (IV.596-8K = *Herophilus* Fr. 61 von Staden) where Herophilus mentions arterial and venous connections between uterus and ovaries.

XVI.19. Soranus, *Gynaecology* I.8 (= *CMG* IV, p. 7 IIb.)

It seems likely that Soranus has been influenced here by Herophilus; but, like Aristotle, he was prepared to allow the womb a certain limited movement.

The uterus is connected by thin membranes to the parts above the bladder, to the parts beneath the rectum, and to the sides and the rear by excrescences from the hips and the *os sacrum*. When these membranes are contracted through inflammation, the uterus is drawn up and inclines sideways, but it prolapses when they are weakened and relaxed. So, then, the uterus is not a living-creature (as it appeared to some), but it is similar in certain respects as it has a sense of touch, and, on account of this, it is contracted by cooling agents, but loosened by rarefying ones.

*

In the fifth century BC Presocratic philosophers increasingly began to extend their interests in the conception and development of humans and the theories they put forward with regard to embryology in general and the sexual differentiation of the foetus in particular[1] came to exercise a considerable influence upon later medical beliefs. These and kindred biological inquiries thus became incorporated within a tradition that sought for its answers in terms of purely natural causes without recourse to supernatural explanations. The nature of our evidence of the work of these Presocratic philosophers, unfortunately, makes it extremely difficult to reconstruct any comprehensive system of human physiology from the few fragments and later testimonies that preserve their views upon these matters.[2] Although it is clear that philosophers like Diogenes, Democritus, and, most especially, Empedocles, reveal a keen interest in some matters, at least, germane to gynaecology, our earliest evidence of any extended investigations in this field is provided by the Hippocratic *Corpus*. Of the sixty or so treatises which comprise this collection ten are gynaecological in nature (viz. *On diseases of women* in two books; *On sterile women; On the nature of woman; On diseases of young girls*; *On the excision of the foetus; On superfoetation*; *On generation*; *On the nature of the child*; *On the eight-month child* and *On the seven-month child*).[3] In addition, other treatises, notably *Aphorisms* and *Coan prenotions*, include quite short sections dealing with such gynaecological questions as menstruation, conception, pregnancy, childbirth and miscarriage and the *Epidemics* provide valuable evidence regarding the medical treatment of women and reveal to what extent differences between male and female physiology and pathology were recognised and taken into account.

It has been claimed that some of these gynaecological works are probably the oldest in the *Corpus* and may be representative of the Cnidian school of medicine. While a reasonably persuasive case might be made in support of the former claim, most scholars nowadays would regard the distinction between Coan and Cnidian treatises as a false dichotomy of later invention constructed to explain the rivalry that developed in the Hellenistic period between the Empiricists and the Dogmatists. These works are best regarded as belonging, together with the other treatises in the *Corpus*, to a single tradition characterised by the same motivation to explain human physiology and the diseases and ailments to which the human organism is prone in terms of purely natural causation.

The quality of the gynaecological treatises is generally regarded as inferior and no scholar who does not regard Hippocrates as the universal author has claimed that they were actually written by him. One reason for their low esteem and comparative neglect until recently may be found in the fact that they contain, to a far higher degree than elsewhere in the *Corpus,* folk-beliefs, manifested in the practical remedies that make up a large proportion of their contents. It has been suggested that this particular peculiarity may have been the result of the incorporation of a female oral tradition. Other scholars, however, have stressed that these treatises speak with a male voice and that certain of their assumptions are unequivocally male. However, as Demand has pointed out,[4] the choice between a male and female tradition here is unnecessary: although the doctors were undeniably male, there is abundant evidence that they consulted women and so were able to record much information about women's experience that would ordinarily have been confined to the female sex. Thus, while the bulk of the material contained in the gynaecological treatises consists of women's-lore, this material was itself controlled, qualified, rationalised and redefined by male Hippocratic doctors.

The author of *Diseases* I observes as a general rule that the outcome of diseases may differ according to the sex as well as the age of the patient [XVI.1]. Again, in *Airs, Waters, Places* 3-4 [XVI.2] it is suggested that even when men and women catch the same disease the symptoms they manifest are quite different. Here we are given a classification of different types of environment and their endemic diseases. In the case of cities exposed to hot winds men are described as afflicted by dysentery, diarrhoea, ague, fever, frequent pustules, and piles, whereas the women suffer barrenness and miscarriages. In the case of a city exposed to cold winds, the men experience pleurisies, internal lacerations, inflamed eyes, and epistaxis, whereas the women are again barren, their periods are scanty and bad, childbirth is rare, and miscarriages frequent. (The strong antithesis shows that the author intends a distinct differentiation of symptoms between the sexes.) Here we have an early foreshadowing of what was to become a vigorous debate among doctors, namely whether or not women were affected differently by disease from men. At a later date Soranus reviews the main protagonists in this controversy [XVI.4] and concludes that, apart from conception, parturition and lactation, the female has illnesses in common with the male and does not require a specialised branch of medicine. This, however, does not appear to have been the case within the Hippocratic *Corpus* where many authors hold the view later rejected by Soranus and believe that a woman did require separate treatment, and consider that virtually any illness she suffered should be treated as a specifically female complaint. They regard gynaecology essentially as the treatment of the female reproductive system, which was held to be of central importance whenever she fell ill. This attitude is clearly apparent in *Diseases of women* I.62 [XVI.3]. Here, it is true, women's diseases are not set apart from a universal medicine dealing with both sexes, but rather opposed to a medicine dealing with the male sex. However, since no such 'andrological' medicine, no such specialist treatment exclusive to males, appears to exist anywhere else, it may be that our author means by *ta andrika nosêmata* all diseases that are not specifically *gynaikeia* and has coined this particular expression to make his argument more forceful.[5]

Although this Hippocratic view advocating different treatment for men and women is, as we have seen, rejected by several later eminent physicians [XVI.4], it should be noted that it reflects the earlier cultural belief that men and women were affected differently by disease. This belief that the effect of disease is gender-specific is first encountered in a passage in the *Works and Days* **[I.13]**. Here Hesiod, in describing the impact of the plague sent by Zeus, tells us that 'the men perish, the women are barren'. (The same viewpoint appears in the later description of the plague at Selinus, which was allegedly eradicated by Empedocles (Diogenes Laërtius, VIII.70 DK 31A1).[6] Here, we learn, the disease 'destroyed the men and caused the women painful childbirth'.) Thus, just as many of the therapeutic remedies contained in the gynaecological treatises are derived from earlier folk-lore, so the view of disease put forward here as gender-specific can similarly be traced back to earlier mythology.

Since the female body is more loosely textured and softer than that of the male, it attracts more fluid in the form of blood from the stomach than its male counterpart **[XVI.7]**. Whereas a man could counter a humid constitution and maintain his health by following a corrective regimen of diet and exercise (see *Regimen* I.35 (VI.512L)), a woman with her inherently spongier and softer flesh, coupled with a generally less active life-style, was unable to utilise all the food she ingested and, if she was to remain healthy and avoid a serious range of illnesses which included headaches, gout, fever, haemorrhoids, pains in the hips and loins, consumption, suffocation, and delusions, she needed a monthly evacuation of this excess blood. No amount of care over diet and life-style could overcome this innate weakness of the female body (*On the seven-month child* 9 (VII.450.10L)). Whatever the regimen followed, the normal mature female accumulated an excess of blood and she had to menstruate to maintain a healthy balance of her bodily humours. For a woman, then, menstruation provided the mechanism to ensure protection and relief from disease. Any break-down in this process resulted in ill-health. Accordingly, many Hippocratic physicians tended to regard virtually any disease a woman suffered as gynaecological in origin, as a malfunction in her reproductive system and due to the retention of menstrual blood. A woman who had never given birth was believed to suffer more painfully from menstruation than one who had **[XVI.8]**. Thus sexual intercourse was frequently advocated to facilitate the evacuation of menstrual blood and motherhood was widely regarded as the best solution for many women's health-problems since parturition resulted in her vessels becoming more free-flowing **[XVI.8]**. It was seen above **[II.24]** that in the case of young girls suffering from suicidal delusions due to the retention of blood, the treatment recommended by the physician was that the girls should marry as soon as possible on the grounds that they would regain their health upon becoming pregnant. Our author adds here that among married women it is the sterile who are the more prone to suffer from similar conditions.

The womb was regarded as the predominant cause of women's diseases **[XVI.11]**. It was believed that, if the womb became dry, it was liable to remove itself from its natural position and attach itself to moister organs. (This belief may have originated from observation of cases of prolapse of the uterus.) The Hippocratics sought to account for this movement of the womb by the explanation that, if, through lack of the moisture provided by intercourse, it became dry or was not anchored in its place by pregnancy, it became attracted to such moister organs as the heart, liver, brain, bladder or rectum. A womb full of menstrual blood or a foetus was less inclined to move about the body in this way. The wombs of women denied regular sexual intercourse, of young widows, who had borne children, and of older women, however, were particularly prone to dislocation **[XVI.14]** – the last group especially so, since, after the menopause, the production of menstrual blood had ceased.

In order to attract the womb back to its proper place the Hippocratic doctor administered foul-smelling substances to the nostrils and sweet-smelling perfumes to the vagina **[XVI.13 & 14** and see **XIII.7]**, or *vice versa*, depending upon the direction of the movement. Such treatment seems to entail that they regarded the female body as a tube connecting two 'mouths' and affording the womb passage from the bottom of the body to the top. The Hippocratic method of determining whether or not conception was possible offers support for this view. This test required the woman to sit above some strong smelling substance such as garlic or have it inserted in her womb **[XVI.15]**. If the smell could be detected through her mouth, she could conceive; if not, then her tube was blocked and efforts had to be made to unblock it.

This concept of a mobile womb was not confined solely to the Hippocratics. Plato seems to have further developed this idea and used it to account for female sexual desire by regarding the womb as the counterpart of the male organ and investing it with a life of its own **[XVI.16]**. Aristotle, too, despite his contention that the womb must have a fixed position **[XVI.17]**, nevertheless elsewhere declares his belief that, when empty, it could be pushed upwards and cause a stifling sensation (*History of animals* 582b22-6). Even after dissection of the human female in third-century Alexandria had enabled Herophilus to confirm that the human uterus was suspended from 'vessels that nourish it and are clothed in membranes' **[XVI.18]**, it was still widely believed that the womb was capable of moving and causing discomfort due to its displacement in all directions **[XVI.19]**.

Herophilus had a particular interest in obstetrics and gynaecology. His book, *Midwifery,* the first such treatise produced in antiquity, subsequently exercised a powerful influence. This work, of which scant evidence has survived, seems not to have been exclusively concerned with pathological conditions, but evidently also contained some of his physiological views. It is possible, too, that some of his detailed descriptions of aspects of female anatomy, e.g. of the uterus, ovaries and fallopian tubes, may also have belonged to this work rather than to one of his books on anatomy. It is apparent from this evidence that Herophilus rejected and demythologised the Hippocratic view that women suffer different diseases from men. He maintained that 'no disease is peculiar to women' **[XVI.5]**. He did, however, accept that there were certain conditions peculiar to women, viz. menstruation, conception, childbirth, breast-feeding, 'concocting' mother's milk, and 'the opposites of these'; and it is with these exceptions that the surviving testimonies of *Midwifery* are concerned. The only surviving fragment preserves verbatim his views on the reason for difficult labour **[XVI.6]**. Another instance where Herophilus apparently takes issue with Hippocratic medicine concerns menstruation. Our evidence in this case comes, not from *Midwifery*, but from his treatise, *Against common opinions,* where he sought to refute prevalent conceptions he believed to be mistaken. Here he attacks the view that menstruation is beneficial both for a woman's general health and for childbearing, maintaining that, while it is helpful to some women, it is harmful to others **[XVI.9 & 10]**.

See, especially, Dean-Jones, 1994; Demand, 1994.

---

[1] For an account of these theories see, especially, Lesky, 1951.

[2] For an attempt to do so see Longrigg, 1993a, Ch. 3.

[3] *On generation* and *On the nature of the child* belong together. *On diseases* IV is their sequel and the whole constitutes a single work which describes the formation and development of the human body and the genesis of disease (see, especially, Lonie, 1981). The two works, *On the eight-month child* and *On the seven-month child,* edited separately in ancient editions, in reality form a single treatise.

[4] Demand, 1994, p. 65.

[5] With Dean-Jones, 1994, p. 113.

[6] See Longrigg, 1993b, pp. 37-42.

Chronological Table[1]

The chronology of this period is very uncertain. There is still much controversy among scholars regarding the dates of the life-times of several of those listed below. Since their dates cannot be determined with any high degree of precision, approximations are given. In some cases it is only possible to provide a rough guide to the *floruit* of the individual concerned, i.e. the time at which we may presume he did his chief work. Whenever it is possible to give precise dates these are provided in bold type.

Date BC

c. 800	Homer
c. 700	Hesiod
Floruit c. 648	Archilochus of Paros
c. 625-547	Thales of Miletus
c. 610-540	Anaximander of Miletus
c. 585-525	Anaximenes of Miletus
Floruit c. 580	Alcaeus of Lesbos
Floruit c. 532	Pythagoras of Samos
c. 570-478	Xenophanes of Colophon
Floruit c. 525	Democedes of Croton
Floruit c. 500	Heraclitus of Ephesus
Floruit c. 470	Alcmaeon of Croton
c. 500-428	Anaxagoras of Clazomenae
c. 492-432	Empedocles of Acragas
Floruit c. 435	Herodicus of Selymbria
469-399	Socrates
c. 460-380	Hippocrates of Cos
431-404	Peloponnesian War
c. 430-350	Hippocratic *Corpus*[2]
430-427	Great Plague of Athens
Floruit c. 435	Diogenes of Apollonia
Floruit c. 435	Leucippus of Miletus
428-347	Plato
Floruit c. 420	Democritus of Abdera
Floruit c. 385	Philistion of Locri
c. 385	Foundation of the Academy
384-322	Aristotle
c. 371-287	Theophrastus of Eresus
c. 335	Foundation of the Lyceum
Floruit c. 330	Diocles of Carystus
323	Death of Alexander the Great
Floruit c. 320	Praxagoras of Cos

c. 300	Foundation of Museum & Library at Alexandria
Floruit c. 290	Strato of Lampsacus
Floruit c. 290	Herophilus of Chalcedon
Floruit c. 280	Erasistratus of Ceos

1. The Egyptian medical papyri cited in Chapter 1 seem to date from the Eighteenth and Nineteenth Dynasties, i.e. between 1550-1295 BC (Ebers) and 1295-1186 (Hearst and Papyrus Medicus Londinensis). However, the bulk of the medical knowledge they contain seems to have been drawn from as far back as the third millennium BC.

Most of our knowledge of Mesopotamian medicine has been preserved in cuneiform writing upon clay tablets which were part of a larger collection from the library of Assurbanipal buried when Ninevah was destroyed in 612 BC. Although these tablets are comparatively late, the texts themselves, which have been copied and re-copied by generations of scribes, are probably a millennium earlier.

2. The dates of individual treatises contained in the Hippocratic *Corpus* cannot be determined precisely. The majority of them seem to have been composed between *c.* 430 and 350 BC. Some, however, have been dated earlier than 430 and others, e.g. *Precepts* and *On the heart*, are almost certainly later.

Glossary of Technical Terms

anaglyphê kalamou, cavity in rear portion of floor of cerebellum likened by Herophilus to that in pens used at Alexandria. See *calamus scriptorius* & *calamus Herophili* below.

antiperistasis, term used by Aristotle to describe the 'circular thrust', the rhythmical reversal of the currents of air postulated by Plato to account for respiration. See, too, 'circular thrust' and *periôsis* below.

aorta, largest artery arising from the left ventricle of the heart and passing through the thorax and abdomen.

apeiron, Anaximander's first-principle.

artêria phlebôdês, arteria venalis, the pulmonary vein.

artêria, wind-pipe, then artery (as distinct from a vein).

astragalus, irregular bone of the foot with articular surfaces forming part of the inner series of the bones of the *tarsus*.

auscultation, monitoring the internal organs by listening to the sounds which they themselves emit.

bregma, front part of the top of the head, where the skull remains open longest.

calamus scriptorius, calamus Herophili, Latin translations of *anaglyphê kalamou*, listed above.

causus, a bilious remittent fever.

cerebellum, lesser brain situated in posterior cranial fossa of the skull, below the *cerebrum* and above the *medulla oblongata*.

cerebrum, largest part of the brain, consisting of right and left cerebral hemispheres and occupying the anterior and middle *fossae* of the skull.

chorioid, term employed by Herophilus to describe both the three membranes of the brain and the second tunic of the eye because he thought they resembled the chorionic membrane surrounding the foetus.

chorion, membrane surrounding the foetus.

circular thrust, the rhythmical reversal of currents of air postulated by Plato to account for respiration. See *antiperistasis* above.

clepsydra, water-clock, instrument used by Herophilus to measure pulsation.

clyster, rectal injection.

corona, the rim of the cornea where it joins the sclerotic.

critical days, those days on which diseases were held to come to a crisis.

deontological works, those works in the Hippocratic *Corpus* prescribing rules of behaviour in medical practice.

diadosis, a process of absorption through fine pores (*kenômata*) in the walls of the capillary veins.

didymoi, 'twins', term applied to both the the the testicles and the ovaries.

Diocles's spoon, a device for the extraction of the larger type of missiles.

diploê, the porous substance between the double plates in the bones of the skull.

dôdekadaktylos ekphysis, the 'growth of twelve fingers' breadth', i.e. the duodenal process.

dorkadizôn, 'capering like a gazelle', term coined by Herophilus to describe a certain type of abnormal pulse. See *myrmekizôn* below.

dura mater, 'thick membrane' (*pacheia mêninx*), strong fibrous membrane forming the outer covering protecting the brain.

dystocia, difficulty in childbirth.

ecrhythmic pulse, term employed by Herophilus to describe a pulse revealing the greatest deviation from the norm. See *heterorhythmic* & *pararhythmic* below.

embryotome, 'embryo-cutter', instrument used in abortion.

empyêma, agglomeration of pus in the pleural cavity.

enkephalos, fore-brain, term applied by Herophilus to the *cerebrum*.

epencranis, term applied by Erasistratus to the *cerebellum*.

epididymis, narrow convoluted structure lying on the outer surface of the testis (hence its name), created by the union of the seminiferous tubules and forming the commencement of the seminal duct or *vas deferens*.

epistaxis, bleeding from the nose.

Fallopian tube, uterine tube, which collects ova discharged from the ovary and passes them towards the cavity of the uterus.

female 'testicles', i.e. ovaries.

glandular assistants (*parastatai adenoeideis*), name given by Herophilus to the two seminal vesicles (*vesiculae seminales*). See below *s.v.*

haematopoeic function of liver, belief that the liver possessed the capacity to manufacture the blood.

heterorhythmic pulse, term employed by Herophilus to describe a pulse revealing a greater deviation from the norm. See, too, *ecrhythmic* & *pararhythmic*.

'horns', i.e. the Fallopian tubes.

horror vacui, attraction of the void. See *pros to kenoumenon akolouthia* below.

iamata, 'cures', description of successful treatments recorded in temples of Asclepius.

isonomia, term employed by Alcmaeon of Croton to describe the equality of the constituent powers within the body – a state of equilibrium producing health. See *monarchia* below.

kalamos, type of pen used in Hellenistic Alexandria. See *anaglyphê kalamou* above.

kenômata, extremely fine pores in the walls of the capillary veins contained with the bodily organs.

lênos, trough or reservoir of a wine-press. See *torcular Herophili* below.

loimos, plague, epidemic disease.

menses, periodic discharge from the womb.

miasma, pollution.

miqtu, term used in Babylonian medicine for diurnal epilepsy.

monarchia, term employed by Alcmaeon of Croton to describe the supremacy of any one of the constituent powers within the body – a state disruptive of health. See *isonomia* above.

myrmêkizôn, 'crawling like an ant', term coined by Herophilus to describe a certain type of abnormal pulse. See *dorkadizôn* above.

natrum, sodium carbonate used in Egypt for embalming. (Greek: *nitron* or *litron*.)

neuron, originally a sinew then also used for a nerve.

os sacrum, triangular bone articulated above with the fifth lumbar vertebra (forming the lumbo-sacral angle) and below with the coccyx.

os uteri, orifice of the womb.

pangenesis theory, reproductive theory holding that seed was drawn from all parts of the bodies of both parents.

pararhythmic pulse, term employed by Herophilus to describe a pulse revealing a small deviation from the norm. See *ecrhythmic* & *heterorhythmic* above.

paremptôsis, the transfusion of blood from veins into arteries.

parenkephalis, term applied by Herophilus to the *cerebellum.*

periôsis, term used by Aristotle to describe the 'circular thrust', the rhythmical reversal of the currents of air by which Plato accounted for respiration. See, too, *antiperistasis.*

pharmakapôlai, drug-sellers.

phlebotomy, venesection, blood-letting by opening a vein.

phleps artêriôdês, vena arterialis, the pulmonary artery.

pia mater, innermost layer of the membranes of the brain.

plêthôra, the flooding of the veins with a superfluity of blood engendered by an excessive intake of nourishment.

pneuma, breath, air, held by Praxagoras and Erasistratus to be contained in the arteries.

portal vein, the vein which grows from the portal fissure and extends obliquely downwards.

pros to kenoumenon akolouthia, lit. 'following towards what is being emptied', attraction of the void, see *horror vacui* above.

rhizotomoi, 'root-cutters', gatherers of herbs.

scamnus, Hippocratic bench used for the reduction of dislocations.

seminal ducts, i.e. the Fallopian tubes.

seminal vesicles (*vesiculae seminales*), reservoirs on each side of the male reproductive tract for the external secretion of the testes. See also *glandular assistants* above.

sêpsis, putrefaction.

sphygmology, study of the pulse.

succussion, the practice of violently shaking a patient while strapped to a ladder or bed in an attempt to cure such ailments as curvature of the spine or prolapse of the uterus.

sunanastomôses, fine capillaries, closed under normal circumstances, held by Erasistratus to connect the veins and arteries.

talipes varus, type of club-foot in which the outer border of the foot touches the ground.

tetractys of the decad, sacred symbol of the Pythagoreans representing the number ten by an arrangement of dots in triangular form.

torcular Herophili, the depression in the occipital bone where the sinuses of the *dura mater* meet which was likened by Herophilus to the trough or reservoir (*lênos*) of a wine press. This Latin translation is still in use.

trepanation, practice of cutting holes in the skull.

trephine, a hollow cylindrical instrument with a serrated lower ring and a fixed pin in the middle used for cutting out a circular piece of bone.

tricuspid valve, lit. 'three-barbed' valve at the entrance of the right ventricle of the heart which allows the blood to enter but not to relapse into the right auricle and *vena cava.*

varicose assistants (*parastatai kirsoeideis*), dilations of the *vasa deferentia* which assist in the production and transportation of the semen.

vasa deferentia, vessels for the conveyance of the secretions from the *epididymis* up the spermatic cord to its opening in the prostatic part of the urethra.

vein-like artery, *arteria venalis, artêria phlebôdês,* the modern pulmonary vein.

venae cavae, the two large veins which return the venous blood to the right auricle.

ventricle of the brain, hollow in the central portion of each hemisphere of the brain.

vesiculae seminales, see seminal vesicles above.

vis mediatrix naturae, the healing power of nature.

Bibliography

The bibliography aims to provide details of all the books and articles cited in the text. Other works relevant to the issues raised in the discussion are also cited here.

Abel, K. 1958. 'Die Lehre vom Blutkreislauf im Corpus Hippocraticum', *Hermes*, 86, pp. 192-219 (repr. with a 'retractatio' in Flashar, 1971, pp. 121-64).

Adair, M. 1996. 'Plato's view of the "wandering uterus" ', *Classical Journal*, 91.2, pp. 153-63.

Adcock, F. 1973. *Cambridge Ancient History*, vol. 5, Cambridge.

Alexanderson, B. 1963. *Die hippokratische Schrift Prognostikon*, Stockholm, Göteborg & Uppsala.

Allbutt, T.C. 1921. *Greek Medicine in Rome*, London (repr. New York, 1970).

Allen, R.E. & Furley, D.J. (edd.) 1970 & 1975. *Studies in Presocratic Philosophy*, 2 vols., London.

Amundsen, D.W. 1978. 'Images of physicians in classical times', *Journal of Popular Culture*, 11, 642-55.

Arnim, H. von, 1903-24. *Stoicorum Veterum Fragmenta*, 4 vols. (vol. 4 ed. M. Adler), Leipzig (repr. Stuttgart, 1964).

Aselli, G. 1627. *De lactibus siue lacteis uenis quarto uasorum mesaraicorum genere nouo inuento Gasparis Asellii Cremonensis anatomici Ticinensis dissertatio*, Milan.

Baldry, H.C. 1932. 'Embryological analogies in early Greek cosmology', *Classical Quarterly*, 26, pp. 27-34.

Balme, D.M. 1991. *Aristotle: Historia Animalium. Books VII-X*, Cambridge, Mass.

Bardong, K. 1954. 'Praxagoras', Pauly-Wissowa, *Real-Encyclopädie der klassischen Altertumsʹvissenschaft*, 22,2, Stuttgart, cols. 1735-43.

Barnes, J. 1979. *The Presocratic Philosophers*, 2 vols. (rev. edn. 1982), London.

Baumann, E.D. 1925. 'Die heilige Krankheit', *Janus*, 29, pp. 7-32.

—— 1937. 'Praxagoras of Kos', *Janus*, 41, pp. 167-85.

Beloch, K.J. 1904. *Griechische Geschichte*, Strasburg/Berlin/Leipzig (2nd. edn. 1927).

Bendz, G. 1990-3. *Caelius Aurelianus*, *CML* VI. 1, 2 vols., Berlin.

Bernhard, O. 1928. 'Ueber Malariabekämpfung im klassischen Altertum', in *Neuburger's Festschrift*, Vienna, pp. 44-6.

Bidez, J. & Leboucq, G. 1944. 'Une anatomie antique du coeur humain', *Revue des Études Grecques*, 57, pp. 7-40.

Booth, N.B. 1960. 'Empedocles' account of breathing', *Journal of Hellenic Studies*, 80, pp. 10-15.

Bourgey, L. 1953. *Observation et expérience chez les médecins de la Collection Hippocratique*, Paris.

Bourgey, L. & Jouanna, J. (edd.) 1975. *La Collection Hippocratique et son rôle dans l'histoire de la médecine: Colloque de Strasbourg*, Leiden.

Breasted, J.H. 1930. *The Edwin Smith Surgical Papyrus*, 2 vols., Chicago.

Bibliography

Brisson, L. 1987. *Platon: Lettres*, Paris.

Brock, A.J. 1916. *Galen: On the natural faculties. Books I-III* (Loeb Classical Library), London & Cambridge, Mass. (2nd. ed. 1952).

—— 1929. *Greek Medicine*, London.

Bruins, E.M. 1951. 'La Chimie du Timée', *Revue de Métaphysique et Morale*, 56, pp. 269-82.

Burnet, J. 1930. *Early Greek Philosophy*, 4th edn., London.

Burguière, P., Gourevitch, D. & Malinas, Y. 1988. *Soranos d'Éphèse: Maladies des femmes*, 3 vols., Paris.

Bynum, W.F. & Nutton, V. (edd.) 1981. *Theories of Fever from Antiquity to the Enlightenment, Medical History*, Supplement 1, London.

Capelle, W. 1931. 'Straton von Lampsakos', 13, Pauly-Wissowa, *Real-Encyclopädie der klassischen Altertumswissenschaft*, 4,1, Stuttgart, cols. 278-315.

Capriglione, J.C. 1983. *Prassagora di Cos*, Naples.

Cardini, M. Timpanaro, 1957. 'Respirazione e la clessidra', *Parola del Passato*, 12, pp. 250-70.

Chéhadé, A.-K. 1955. *Ibn al-Nafis et la découverte de la circulation pulmonaire*, Damascus.

Cherniss, H. 1935. *Aristotle's Criticism of Presocratic Philosophy*, Baltimore.

Clarke, E. 1963a. 'Apoplexy in the Hippocratic writings', *Bulletin of the History of Medicine*, 37, pp. 301-14.

—— 1963b. 'Aristotelian concepts of the form and function of the brain', *Bulletin of the History of Medicine*, 37, pp. 1-14.

Clarke, E. & Stannard, J. 1963. 'Aristotle on the anatomy of the brain', *Journal of the History of Medicine*, 18, pp. 130-48.

Cochrane, C.N. 1929. *Thucydides and the Science of History*, London.

Cohen, M.R. & Drabkin, I.E. 1958. *A Source Book in Greek Science*, Cambridge, Mass.

Cohn-Haft, L. 1956. *The Public Physicians of Ancient Greece*, Northampton, Mass.

Conrad, L., Neve, M., Nutton, V., Porter, R. & Wear, A. 1995. *The Western Medical Tradition*, Cambridge.

Cornford, F.M. 1937. *Plato's Cosmology*, London (repr. 1948).

—— 1952. *Principium Sapientiae*, Cambridge.

Crawfurd, R. 1914. *Plague and Pestilence in Literature and Art*, Oxford.

Crombie, I.M. 1963. *An Examination of Plato's Doctrines*, 2 vols., London.

Daremberg, C.V. 1865a. *La Médecine dans Homère*, Paris.

—— 1865b. Études d'archéologie médicale sur Homère', *Revue Archéologique*, n.s. 12, 95-111, 249-67, 338-55.

—— 1869. *État de la médecine entre Homère et Hippocrate*, Paris.

Daremberg, C.V. & Bussemaker, C. 1851-76. *Oribasius: Oeuvres*, 6 vols., Paris (repr. Amsterdam, 1962).

Daremberg, C. & Ruelle, C.E., 1879. *Oeuvres de Rufus d'Éphèse*, Paris (repr. Amsterdam, 1963).

Dawson, W.R. 1953. 'Egypt's place in medical history' in *Science, Medicine and History: Essays in Honour of Charles Singer*, 2 vols., Oxford.

Dean-Jones, L.A. 1991. 'The cultural construct of the female body in Classical Greek science' in *Women's History and Ancient History*, ed. S.B. Pomeroy, Chapel Hill.

—— 1992. 'The politics of pleasure: female sexual appetite in the Hippocratic Corpus', *Helios*, 19, pp. 72-91.

—— 1994. *Women's Bodies in Classical Greek Science*, Oxford.

Deichgräber, K. 1930. *Die griechische Empirikerschule: Sammlung und Darstellung der Lehre*, Berlin.

Bibliography

—— 1933. *Die Epidemien und das Corpus Hippocraticum*, Berlin.

Deichgräber, K., Schubring, K. & Schwyzer, E. 1935. *Über Entstehung und Aufbau des menschlichen Körpers*, Leipzig and Berlin.

Delatte, A. 1922. *Essai sur la politique Pythagoricienne*, Liège.

Demand, N. 1994. *Birth, Death, and Motherhood in Classical Greece*, Baltimore & London.

Demont, P. 1988. 'Hérodote et les pestilences', *Revue de Philologie*, 62, pp. 7-13.

Derenne, E. 1930. *Les Procès d'impiété intentés aux philosophes à Athènes au Ve et au IVe siècles avant J.C.*, Liège and Paris.

Diehl, E. 1925. *Anthologia Lyrica Graeca*, vol. 1, Leipzig.

Diels, H. 1879. *Doxographi Graeci*, Berlin.

—— 1893a. *Anonymi Londinensis ex Aristotelis Iatricis Menoniis et aliis Medicis Eclogae*, Berlin.

—— 1893b. 'Über die Excerpte von Menons Iatrika in dem Londoner Papyrus 137', *Hermes*, 28, pp. 407-34.

—— 1893c. 'Ueber das physikalische System des Straton', *Sitzungsberichte der Königlich preussischen Akademie der Wissenschaften zu Berlin 1*, pp. 101-27.

—— 1899. *Elementum*, Leipzig.

Diels, H. & Kranz, W. 1956. *Die Fragmente der Vorsokratiker*, 8th edn., 3 vols., Berlin.

Diepgen, P. 1937. 'Die Frauenheilkunde in der alten Welt', *Handbuch der Gynäkologie*, Bd. 12, Teil 1, Munich.

—— 1949. *Geschichte der Medizin*, Berlin.

Dietz, F.R. 1834. *Scholia in Hippocratem et Galenum*, 2 vols., Königsberg.

Diller, H. 1932. Ὄψις ἀδήλων τὰ φαινόμενα, *Hermes*, 67, pp. 14-42 (repr. in his *Kleine Schriften zur antiken Literatur* (Munich, 1971), pp. 119-43).

—— 1934. *Wanderarzt und Aitiologe (Philologus Suppl. Bd. 26,3)*, Leipzig.

—— 1941. 'Die philosophiegeschichtliche Stellung des Diogenes von Apollonia', *Hermes*, 76, pp. 359-81.

—— 1952. 'Hippokratische Medizin und attische Philosophie', *Hermes*, 80, pp. 385-409.

—— 1959. 'Stand und Aufgaben der Hippokratesforschung', *Jahrbuch der Akademie der Wissenschaften und der Literatur*, Mainz, pp. 271-87 (repr. in *Antike Medizin*, ed. H. Flashar, Darmstadt, 1971, 29-51).

—— 1962. *Hippokrates Schriften: Die Anfänge der abendländischen Medizin*, Hamburg.

—— 1970. *Hippokrates. Über die Umwelt (= CMG I. 1,2)*, Berlin.

—— 1973. *Kleine Schriften zur antiken Medizin*, Berlin.

—— 1975. 'Das Selbstverständnis der Griechischen Medizin in der Zeit des Hippokrates', in Bourgey & Jouanna, 1975, pp. 77-93.

Dittenberger, W. 1915-24. *Sylloge Inscriptionum Graecarum*, 3rd edn., Leipzig.

Dobson, J.F. 1925. 'Herophilus', *Proceedings of the Royal Society of Medicine*, 18, pts. i & ii, pp. 19-32.

—— 1926-7. 'Erasistratus', *Proceedings of the Royal Society of Medicine*, 20, pp. 825-32.

Dodds, E.R. 1951. *The Greeks and the Irrational*, Berkeley.

Dover, K.J. 1975. 'The freedom of the intellectual in Greek Society', *Talanta*, 7, pp. 24-54.

Drabkin, I.E. (ed. & tr.) 1950. *Caelius Aurelianus on Acute Diseases and on Chronic Diseases*, Chicago.

Drachmann, A.G. 1948. *Ktesibios, Philon and Heron*, Copenhagen.

Ducatillon, J. 1977. *Polémiques dans la Collection Hippocratique*, Paris.

Bibliography

Duminil, M.-P. 1983. *Le sang, les vaisseaux, le coeur dans la Collection Hippocratique*, Paris.

During, I. & Owen, G.E.L. 1960. *Aristotle and Plato in the Mid-Fourth Century*, Göteborg.

Ebbell, B. 1937. *The Papyrus Ebers, the Greatest Egyptian Medical Document*, Copenhagen.

Ebstein, E. 1931. 'Klassische Krankengeschichten: II. Der Mumps bei Hippokrates', *Kinderärtzliche Praxis*, 2, pp. 140-1.

Edelstein, E.J. & Edelstein, L. 1945. *Asclepius*, 2 vols., Baltimore.

Edelstein, L. 1931. *Περὶ ἀέρων und die Sammlung der hippokratischen Schriften*, Berlin.

―――― 1931. 'Antike Diatetik', *Die Antike*, 7, 1931, pp. 255-70, (repr. in *Ancient Medicine*, edd. O. & C.L. Temkin, Baltimore, 1967, pp. 303-16 as 'The dietetics of antiquity').

―――― 1932. 'Die Geschichte der Sektion in der Antike' in *Quellen und Studien zur Geschichte der Naturwissenschaften und der Medizin*, Bd. III, Hft. 2, Berlin, pp. 50-106 (repr. in *Ancient Medicine*, Baltimore, 1967, pp. 247-301 as 'The history of anatomy in antiquity').

―――― 1935. 'Hippokrates', Pauly-Wissowa, *Real-Encyclopädie der klassischen Altertumswissenschaft, Nachträge* 6, Stuttgart, cols. 1290-1345.

―――― 1937. 'Greek medicine in its relation to religion and magic', *Bulletin of the History of Medicine*, 5, pp. 201-46 (repr. in *Ancient Medicine*, Baltimore, 1967, pp. 205-46).

―――― 1939. 'The genuine works of Hippocrates', *Bulletin of the History of Medicine*, 7, pp. 236-48 (repr. in *Ancient Medicine*, Baltimore, 1967, pp. 133-44).

―――― 1940. Review of Jaeger, *Diokles von Karystos*, in *American Journal of Philology*, 61, pp. 483-9 (repr. in *Ancient Medicine*, Baltimore, 1967, pp. 145-52).

―――― 1943. 'The Hippocratic oath', *Supplement to the Bulletin of the History of Medicine* 1 (repr. in *Ancient Medicine*, Baltimore, 1967, pp. 3-63).

―――― 1952a. 'The relation of ancient philosophy to medicine', *Bulletin of the History of Medicine*, 26, pp. 299-316 (repr. in *Ancient Medicine*, Baltimore, 1967, pp. 349-66).

―――― 1952b. 'Recent trends in the interpretation of ancient science', *Journal of the History of Ideas*, 13, pp. 573-604 (repr. in *Ancient Medicine*, Baltimore, 1967, pp. 401-39).

―――― 1956. 'The professional ethics of the Greek physician', *Bulletin of the History of Medicine*, 30, pp. 391-419 (repr. in *Ancient Medicine*, Baltimore, 1967, pp. 319-48).

―――― 1966. *Plato's Seventh Letter*, Leiden.

―――― 1967a. *Ancient Medicine*, edd. O. & C.L. Temkin, Baltimore.

―――― 1967b. 'Hippocratic prognosis' from Chapter II, *Περὶ ἀέρων und die Sammlung der hippokratischen Schriften*, Berlin, 1931 (repr. in English translation in *Ancient Medicine*, Baltimore, 1967, pp. 65-85).

―――― 1967c. 'The Hippocratic physician' from Chapter III, *Περὶ ἀέρων und die Sammlung der hippokratischen Schriften*, Berlin, 1931 (repr. in English translation in *Ancient Medicine*, Baltimore, 1967, pp. 87-110).

Eijk, Ph.J. van der, 1990. 'The "theology" of the Hippocratic treatise *On the Sacred Disease*', *Apeiron*, 23, pp. 87-119.

―――― 1991. '*Airs, Waters, Places* and *On the Sacred Disease*: two different religiosities?', *Hermes*, 119, Hft. 2, pp. 168-76.

―――― 1996. 'Diocles and the Hippocratic writings on the method of dietetics and the limits of causal explanation', in *Hippokratische Medizin und antike Philosophie*, Verhandlungen des VIII Internationalen Hippokrates-Kolloquiums in

Bibliography

Kloster Banz/Staffelstein vom 23 bis 28 September 1993, edd. R. Wittern & P. Pellegrin, Hildesheim, pp. 229-57.

Fåhraeus, R. 1958-9. 'L'Air dans les artères', *Proceedings of the Fifteenth International Congress for the History of Medicine, Madrid, 1957*, 2 vols., Madrid, 1, pp. 151-3.

Farrington, B. 1961. *Greek Science* (rev. edn. Penguin), London.

Fasbender, H. 1897. *Entwicklungslehre, Geburtshilfe, und Gynäkologie in den Hippokratischen Schriften*, Stuttgart.

Festugière, A.J. 1948. *Hippocrate: L'Ancienne Médicine*, Paris.

Finlayson, J. 1893. 'Herophilus and Erasistratus: a bibliographical demonstration', *Glasgow Medical Journal*, 39, pp. 321-52.

Flashar, H. 1971 (ed.) *Antike Medizin*, Darmstadt.

Fränkel, H. 1925. 'Xenophanesstudien I und II', *Hermes*, 60, pp. 174-92 (repr. in *Wege und Formen frühgriechischen Denkens*, 2nd. edn., Munich, 1960, pp. 335-49 & Part II as 'Xenophanes's empiricism and his critique of knowledge (B34)' in *The Presocratics*, ed. A.P.D. Mourelatos, New York, 1974, pp. 118-31).

——— 1962. *Dichtung und Philosophie des frühen Griechentums*, 2nd. edn., Munich.

——— 1975. *Early Greek Poetry and Philosophy* (trans. by M. Hadas & J. Willis of *Dichtung und Philosophie*, 2nd. edn., Munich, 1962), Oxford.

Fraser, P.M. 1969. 'The career of Erasistratus of Ceos', *Rendiconti del Istituto Lombardo*, 103, pp. 518-37.

——— 1972. *Ptolemaic Alexandria*, 3 vols., Oxford.

Frazer, R.M. 1972. 'Pandora's diseases, *Erga*, 102-4', *Greek, Roman and Byzantine Studies*, 13, pp. 235-8.

Fredrich, C. 1899. *Hippokratische Untersuchungen* (Philologische Untersuchungen 15), Berlin.

French, R.K. 1978. 'The thorax in history', *Thorax*, 33, pp. 10-18, 153-66, 295-306, 439-56, 555-64, 714-27.

Fritz, H. von. 1971. *Grundprobleme der Geschichte der antiken Wissenschaft*, Berlin & New York.

Fuchs, R. 1892. *Erasistratea*, Diss. Leipzig.

——— 1894a. 'Anecdota medica graeca', *Rheinisches Museum*, 49, pp. 532-58.

——— 1894b. 'De Erasistrato capita selecta', *Hermes*, 29, pp. 171-203.

——— 1897 'Lebte Erasistratos in Alexandreia?', *Rheinisches Museum*, 52, pp. 377-90.

Furley, D.J. 1957. 'Empedocles and the clepsydra', *Journal of Hellenic Studies*, 77, pp. 31-4 (repr. in Allen & Furley, vol. II, 1975, pp. 265-74).

——— 1985. 'Strato's theory of the Void' in *Aristoteles Werk und Wirkung*, vol. I, ed. J. Wiesner, Berlin/New York, pp. 594-609 (repr. in *Cosmic Problems*, Cambridge, 1989, 13, pp. 149-60).

Furley, D.J. & Wilkie, J.S. 1972. 'An Arabic translation solves some problems in Galen', *Classical Review*, 22, pp. 164-7.

——— 1984. *Galen On Respiration and the Arteries*, Princeton.

Garofalo, I. 1988. *Erasistrati Fragmenta*, Pisa.

Gask, G.E. 1939-40. 'Early medical schools I-III', *Annals of Medical History*, I (1939), pp. 128-57, & II (1940), pp. 15-21 & 383-92.

Gatzemeier, M. 1970. *Die Naturphilosophie des Straton von Lampsakos*, Meisenheim.

Gerarde, J. 1597. *The Herball or Generall Historie of Plants*, London.

Ghalioungui, P. 1968. 'The relation of Pharaonic to Greek and later medicine', *Bulletin of the Cleveland Medical Library*, 15.3, pp. 96-107.

213

────── 1973. *The House of Life: per Ankh. Magic and Medical Science in Ancient Egypt.* Amsterdam.

Gigon, O. 1935. *Untersuchungen zu Heraklit*, Leipzig.

Gomme, A.W. 1956. *A Historical Commentary on Thucydides ii*, Oxford.

Gomperz, H. 1943. 'Problems and methods of early Greek science', *Journal of the History of Ideas*, 4, pp. 161-76.

Gomperz, T. 1910. *Die Apologie der Heilkunst*, 2nd. edn., Leipzig.

Gossen, H. 1912. 'Herophilos', Pauly-Wissowa, *Real-Encyclopädie der klassischen Altertumswissenschaft*, 8,1, Stuttgart, cols. 1104-10.

Gottschalk, H.B. 1965. 'Strato of Lampsacus, some texts', *Proceedings of the Leeds Philosophical and Literary Society*, 11, pt. 6, pp. 95-182.

Gourevitch, D. 1984. *Le Triangle hippocratique dans le monde gréco-romain. Le malade, sa maladie, et son médecin*, Rome.

────── 1985. *Le Mal d'être femme*, Paris.

Grapow, H. von, Deines, H. & Westendorf, W. 1954-62. *Grundriss der Medizin in der alten Ägypter*, 7 vols. in 9, Berlin.

Green, P. 1990. *Alexander to Actium: The Historical Evolution of the Hellenistic Age*, London.

Greenhill, W.A. 1843. 'Professor Marx's Herophilus', *British and Foreign Medical Review*, 15, pp. 106-14.

────── 1873a. 'Erasistratus', *Dictionary of Greek and Roman Biography*, 2, London, pp. 42-4.

────── 1873b. 'Herophilus', *Dictionary of Greek and Roman Biography*, 2, London, pp. 438-9.

Grensemann, H. 1968a. 'Der Arzt Polybos als der Verfasser hippokratischer Schriften', *Abhandlungen der Akademie der Wissenschaften und der Literatur im Mainz (Geistes- u. soz. wiss. Kl.*, 1968), pp. 53-95, Mainz.

────── 1968b. *Die hippokratische Schrift 'Über die heilige Krankheit'* (*Ars Medica*, Abt. ii, Bd. i), Berlin.

────── 1982. *Hippokratische Gynäkologie*, Wiesbaden.

Griffiths, A. 1987. 'Democedes of Croton: a Greek doctor at the court of Darius', in *Achaemenid History, II: The Greek Sources*, edd. H. Sancisi-Weerdenburg & A. Kuhrt, Leiden, pp. 37-51.

Grmek, M.D. 1980. *Hippocratica* (Actes du Colloque Hippocratique de Paris, 4-9 Septembre 1978), Paris.

────── 1989. *Diseases in the Ancient World*, Baltimore & London.

Guthrie, W.K.C. 1957. 'Aristotle as a historian of philosophy', *Journal of Hellenic Studies*, 77, pp. 35-41.

────── 1962. *A History of Greek Philosophy*, vol. I, Cambridge.

────── 1965. *A History of Greek Philosophy*, vol. II, Cambridge.

────── 1975. *A History of Greek Philosophy*, vol. IV, Cambridge.

────── 1978. *A History of Greek Philosophy*, vol. V, Cambridge.

────── 1981. *A History of Greek Philosophy*, vol. VI, Cambridge.

Hahm, D.E. 1977. *The Origins of Stoic Cosmology*, Columbus, Ohio.

Halliday, W.R. 1910-11. 'A note on the θήλεα νοῦσος of the Skythians', *Annual of the British School at Athens*, 17, pp. 94-103.

Hankinson, R.J. 1992. 'Doing without hypotheses: the nature of *Ancient Medicine*' in J.A. López Férez (ed.) *Tratados Hipocráticos* (Actas del VIIe Colloque International Hippocratique, Madrid, 24-29 September 1990), Madrid, 1992, pp. 55-67.

────── 1995. 'Pollution and infection: an hypothesis still-born', *Apeiron*, 28.1, pp. 25-65.

Bibliography

Hanson, A.E. 1990. 'The medical writers' woman', ch. 9 in *Before Sexuality*, pp. 309-37, edd. D.M. Halperin, J.J. Winkler & F.I. Zeitlin, Princeton, N.J.

—— 1991. 'Continuity and change: three case studies in Hippocratic gynecological therapy and theory', pp. 73-110 in *Women's History and Ancient History*, ed. S. Pomeroy, Chapel Hill & London.

—— 1992. 'The logic of the gynecological prescriptions', in J.A. López Férez, (ed.) *Tratados Hipocráticos* (Actas del VIIe Colloque International Hippocratique, Madrid, 24-29 September 1990) Madrid, 1992, pp. 235-50.

Harig, G. 1980. 'Anfänge der theoretischen Pharmakologie im Corpus Hippocraticum', in *Hippocratica* (Actes du Colloque de Paris, 1978), ed. M.D. Grmek, Paris, pp. 223-45.

Harris, C.R.S. 1973. *The Heart and the Vascular System in Ancient Greek Medicine*, Oxford.

Harris, J.R. 1971. *The Legacy of Egypt*, 2nd. edn., Oxford.

Head, B. V. 1911. *Historia Numorum: A Manual of Greek Numismatics*, 2nd. edn., Oxford.

Heiberg, J.L. 1894. *Simplicii in Aristotelis De Caelo Commentaria* (*Commentaria in Aristotelem Graeca*, VII), Berlin.

—— 1927. (ed.) *Hippocratis Opera*, vol. I. 1 (*CMG* I .1), Leipzig & Berlin.

Heidel, W.A. 1906. 'Qualitative change in Presocratic philosophy', *Archiv für Geschichte der Philosophie*, 19, pp. 333-79.

—— 1910. Περὶ φύσεως: a study of the conception of nature among the Presocratics', *Proceedings of the American Academy of Arts and Sciences*, 45, pp. 77-133.

—— 1933. *The Heroic Age of Science*, Baltimore.

—— 1941. *Hippocratic Medicine: Its Spirit and Method*, New York.

Heinimann, F. 1945. *Nomos und Physis*, Basel.

—— 1955. 'Diokles von Karystos und der prophylaktische Brief an König Antigonus', *Museum Helveticum*, 12, pp. 158-72.

—— 1961. 'Eine vorplatonische Theorie der τέχνη', *Museum Helveticum*, 18, pp. 105-30.

Helmreich, G. 1893. *Scripta Minora*, vol. III, Leipzig.

—— 1907-9. *Galeni De usu partium libri XVII*, 2 vols., Leipzig (repr. Amsterdam, 1968).

Hershbell, J.P. 1974. 'Empedoclean influences on the *Timaeus*', *Phoenix* 28, pp. 145-66.

Herzog, R. 1899. *Koische Forschungen und Funde*, Leipzig.

—— 1931. 'Die Wunderheilungen von Epidauros', *Philologus Supplementband* 22, Hft. 3, Leipzig.

Hett, W.S. 1957. *Aristotle: On the Soul, Parva Naturalia, On Breath* (Loeb Classical Library), Cambridge, Mass.

Hill, G.F. 1903. *Coins of Ancient Sicily*, London.

Hölscher, U. 1953. 'Anaximander und die Anfänge der Philosophie', *Hermes*, 81, pp. 257-77 & 385-418.

Hooker, E.M. 1958. 'Buboes in Thucydides?', *Journal of Hellenic Studies*, 78, pp. 78-83.

Horine, E.F. 1941. 'An epitome of ancient pulse lore', *Bulletin of the History of Medicine*, 10, pp. 209-49.

Hurlbutt, F.R. 1939. '*Peri kardiês*: a treatise from the Hippocratic Corpus', *Bulletin of the History of Medicine*, 7, pp. 1104-13.

Huxley, T.H. 1880. 'On certain errors respecting the structure of the heart attributed to Aristotle', *Nature*, 21, pp. 1-5.

Ideler, I.L. 1834-6. *Aristotelis Meteorologicorum Libri IV*, vol. I, Leipzig.

Bibliography

Ilberg, J. 1927. *Sorani Gynaeciorum Libri IV. De signis fracturarum. De fasciis. Vita Hippocratis secundum Soranum* (*CMG* IV), Leipzig & Berlin.

Iverson, E. 1939. 'Papyrus Carlsberg No. VIII. With some remarks on the Egyptian origin of some popular birth prognoses', *Historisk-filologiske Meddelelser udgivet af det Kgl. Danske Videnskabernes Selskab*, 26.5, pp. 1-31.

―――― 1953. 'Wounds in the head in Egyptian and Greek medicine', *Studia orientalia Ioanni Pedersen Septuagenario*, Copenhagen, pp. 163-71.

Jackson, R. 1988. *Doctors and Diseases in the Roman Empire*, London.

Jaeger, W.W. 1913. 'Das Pneuma im Lykeion', *Hermes*, 48, pp. 29-74 (repr. in *Scripta Minora*, Rome, 1960, pp. 57-102).

―――― 1934. *Aristotle: Fundamentals of the History of his Development*, Oxford.

―――― 1938a. *Diokles von Karystos, die griechische Medizin und die Schule des Aristoteles*, Berlin.

―――― 1938b. 'Vergessene Fragmente des Peripatetikers Diokles von Karystos nebst zwei Anhaengen zur Chronologie der dogmatischen Aerzteschule', *Abhandlungen der Preussischen Akademie der Wissenschaften, Phil.-hist. Klasse*, no. 3, pp. 1-46 (repr. in *Scripta Minora*, II, Rome, 1960, pp. 185-241).

―――― 1939-45. *Paideia: The Ideals of Greek Culture* (Eng. trans. by G. Highet), 3 vols., Oxford. (See, especially, 'Greek Medicine as Paideia', ch. 1, vol. 4, pp. 3-45.)

―――― 1940. 'Diocles of Carystus: a new pupil of Aristotle', *Philosophical Review*, 49, pp. 393-414 (repr. in *Scripta Minora*, II, Rome, 1960, pp. 243-65).

―――― 1947. *The Theology of the Early Greek Thinkers*, Oxford.

―――― 1957. 'Aristotle's use of medicine as a model of method in his ethics', *Journal of Hellenic Studies*, 77, pp. 54-61 (repr. in *Scripta Minora*, II, Rome, 1960, pp. 491-509).

Joachim, H.H. 1922. *Aristotle on Coming-to-be and Passing-away*, Oxford.

Joly, R. 1960. *Recherches sur le traité pseudo-hippocratique Du régime*, Paris/Liège.

―――― 1964. *Médecine Grecque*, Paris.

―――― 1966. *Le Niveau de la science hippocratique*, Paris.

―――― 1967. *Hippocrate: Du régime* (Collection des Universités de France, VI.1 Budé edn.), Paris.

―――― 1970. *Hippocrate: De la génération, De la nature de l'enfant, Des maladies IV, Du foetus de huit mois* (Collection des Universités de France, XI, Budé edn.), Paris.

―――― 1972. *Hippocrate: Du régime des maladies aiguës etc.* (Collection des Universités de France, VI.2, Budé edn.), Paris.

―――― 1977. (ed.) *Corpus Hippocraticum* (Actes du Colloque Hippocratique de Mons, 1975), Mons.

―――― 1978. *Hippocrate: Des lieux dans l'homme etc.* (Collection des Universités de France, XIII, Budé edn.), Paris.

―――― 1984. *Hippocrate: Du Régime* (*CMG* I.2,4). Berlin.

Jones, W.H.S. 1923-31. *Hippocrates*, Loeb Vols. I-IV (vol. III with E.T. Withington), London & Cambridge, Mass.

―――― 1924. *The Doctor's Oath*, Cambridge.

―――― 1945. ' "Hippocrates" and the Corpus Hippocraticum', *Proceedings of the British Academy*, 31, pp. 103-25.

―――― 1946. *Philosophy and Medicine in Ancient Greece*, Baltimore.

―――― 1947. *The Medical Writings of the Anonymus Londinensis*, Cambridge.

Jouanna, J. 1961. 'Présence d'Empédocle dans la Collection Hippocratique', *Bulletin de l'Association Guillaume Budé*, pp. 452-63.

——— 1965. 'Rapports entre Mélissos de Samos et Diogène d'Apollonie à la lumière du traité hippocratique', *Revue des Études Anciennes*, 67, pp. 306-23.

——— 1966. 'La théorie de l'intelligence et de l'âme dans le traité hippocratique Du régime: ses rapports avec Empédocle et le Timée de Platon', *Revue des Études Grecques*, 79, pp. 15-19.

——— 1975. *Hippocrate: La Nature de l'homme* (*CMG* I.1,3), Berlin.

——— 1983. *Hippocrate: Maladies II* (Collection des Universités de France, X.2, Budé edn.), Paris.

——— 1988. *Hippocrate: Des vents, De l'art* (Collection des Universités de France, V. 1, Budé edn.), Paris.

——— 1990. *Hippocrate: De l'ancienne médecine* (Collection des Universités de France, II. 1, Budé edn.), Paris.

——— 1992a. 'La naissance de la science de l'homme chez les médecins et les savants à l'époque d'Hippocrate: problèmes de méthode', *Tratados Hipocráticos* (Actas del VIIe Colloque International Hippocratique (Madrid, 24-29 September 1990), ed. J.A. López Férez, Madrid, 1992, pp. 91-111.

——— 1992b. *Hippocrate*, Paris.

——— 1996. *Hippocrate: Airs, eaux, lieux* (Collection des Universités de France, II. 2, Budé edn.), Paris.

Kahlenberg, W. 1955. 'Die zeitliche Reihenfolge der Schriften περὶ γονῆς, περὶ φύσιος παιδίου, und περὶ νούσων 4 und ihre Zusammengehörigkeit', *Hermes*, 83, pp. 252-6.

Kahn, C.H. 1960. *Anaximander and the Origins of Greek Cosmology*, New York.

Kalbfleisch, K. 1943. 'Die verkannten Venenklappen', *Rheinisches Museum*, 92, pp. 383-4.

King, H. 1983. 'Bound to bleed: Artemis and Greek women,' ch. 18 in *Images of Women in Antiquity*, edd. A. Cameron & A. Kuhrt, Beckenham, pp. 109-41.

1987. 'The daughter of Leonides: reading the Hippocratic Corpus' in *History as Text*, ed. A. Cameron, London.

——— 1995. 'Medical texts as a source for women's history', ch. 9 in *The Greek World*, ed. A. Powell, London, pp. 199-218.

Kirk, G.S. 1951. 'Natural change in Heraclitus', *Mind* 60, n.s. 237, pp. 35-42.

——— 1954. *Heraclitus, the Cosmic Fragments*, Cambridge.

Kirk, G.S. & Raven, J.E. 1957. *The Presocratic Philosophers*, Cambridge. (2nd. edn. M. Schofield, Cambridge, 1983).

Körbler, J . 1973. *Geschichte der Krebskrankheit*, Vienna.

Körner, O. 1922. 'Wie entstanden die anatomischen Kentnisse in *Ilias* und *Odyssee*?', *Münchener medizinische Wochenschrift* 69, pp. 1484-7.

Kotrc, R.F. 1977. 'A new fragment of Erasistratus' Ἡ ΤΩΝ ῾ΥΓΙΕΙΝΩΝ ΠΡΑΓΜΑΤΕΙΑ', *Rheinisches Museum für Philologie*, 120, pp. 159-61.

Kraay, C. 1976. *Archaic and Classical Greek Coins*, London.

Krug, A. 1985. *Heilkunst und Heilkult*, Munich.

Kucharski, P. 1964. 'Anaxagore et les idées biologiques de son siècle', *Revue Philosophique*, 154, pp. 137-66.

Kudlien, F. 1962. 'Poseidonios und die Ärzteschule der Pneumatiker', *Hermes,* 90, pp. 419-29.

——— 1963. 'Probleme um Diokles von Karystos', *Sudhoffs Archiv für Geschichte der Medizin und Naturwissenschaften*, 47, pp. 456-64 (repr. in H. Flashar, *Antike Medizin*, Darmstadt, 1971, pp. 192-201).

——— 1964. 'Herophilus und der Beginn der medizinischen Skepsis', *Gesnerus*, 21, pp. 1-13 (repr. in *Antike Medizin*, Darmstadt, 1971, pp. 280-95).

——— 1967. *Der Beginn des medizinischen Denkens bei den Griechen*, Zurich & Stuttgart.

Bibliography

—— 1968a. 'Pneumatische Ärzte', Pauly-Wissowa, *Real-Encyclopädie der klassischen Altertumswissenschaft, Supp. Bd.* 11, Stuttgart, col. 1101.

—— 1968b. 'Anatomie' in Pauly-Wissowa, *Real-Encyclopädie der klassischen Altertumswissenschaft, Supp. Bd.* 11, Stuttgart, cols. 38-48.

—— 1969. 'Antike Anatomie und menschlicher Leichnam', *Hermes*, 97, pp. 78-94.

—— 1970. 'Medical ethics and popular ethics in Greece and Rome', *Clio Medica*, 5, 91-121.

—— 1971. 'Galens Urteil über die Thukydideische Pestbeschreibung', *Episteme*, 5, 132-3.

—— 1977. 'Das Göttliche und die Natur im Hippokratischen *Prognostikon*', *Hermes*, 105, 268-74.

—— 1979. *Der griechische Arzt im Zeitalter des Hellenismus*, Wiesbaden.

—— 1981. 'A new testimony for Erasistratus?', *Clio Medica*, 15, pp. 137-47.

Kühlewein, H. 1894-1902. *Hippocratis Opera Omnia* (= Bibliotheca Scriptorum Graecorum et Romanorum Teubneriana), 2 vols., Leipzig.

Kühn, C.G. 1821-33. *Claudii Galeni Opera Omnia*, 20 vols. in 22, Leipzig (repr. Hildesheim, 1965).

Kühn, J.-H. 1956. 'System- und Methodenprobleme im Corpus Hippocraticum', *Hermes Einzelschriften*, 11, Wiesbaden.

Kühn, J.-H. & Fleischer, U. 1986-9. *Index Hippocraticus*, Göttingen.

Lacy, P. de (ed., tr. & comm.) 1978-84. *Galen: De placitis Hippocratis et Platonis*, 3 vols. (*CMG* V. 4,1,2), Berlin.

—— (ed., tr. & comm.) 1992. *Galen: De semine* (*CMG* V. 3,1) Berlin.

Langholf, V. 1986. 'Kallimachos, Komödie und hippokratische Frage', *Medizinhistorisches Journal*, Bd. 21, Heft 1/2, pp. 3-30.

—— 1990. *Medical Theories in Hippocrates*, Berlin.

Lasserre, F. & Mudry, P. 1983. (edd.) *Formes de pensée dans la Collection Hippocratique* (Actes du IVe Colloque International Hippocratique, Lausanne, 1981), Geneva.

Lefebvre, G. 1956. *Essai sur la médecine egyptienne de l'époque pharaonique*, Paris.

Lefkowitz, M.R. & Fant, M.B. 1982. *Women's Life in Greece and Rome*, London.

Leitner, H. 1973. *Bibliography to the Ancient Medical Authors*, Bern, Stuttgart & Vienna.

Le Page Renouf, P. 1873. 'Note on the Medical Papyrus of Berlin', *Zeitschrift für ägyptische Sprache und Altertumskunde*, 11, pp. 123-5.

Lesky, E. 1951. *Die Zeugungs- und Vererbungslehren der Antike*, Wiesbaden.

Licthtenthaeler, C. 1948. *La Médecine Hippocratique, 1: Méthode expérimental et méthode hippocratique*, Lausanne.

—— 1965. *Thucydide et Hippocrate vus par un historien médecin*, Geneva.

—— 1979. 'οὔτε γάρ ἰατροὶ ἥρκουν τὸ πρῶτον θεραπεύοντες ἀγνοίᾳ', *Hermes*, Bd. 107, Hft. 3, pp. 270-86.

—— 1984. *Der Eid des Hippokrates*, Cologne.

Lieber, E. 1996. 'The Hippocratic "Airs, Waters Places" on cross-dressing eunuchs: "natural" yet also "divine" ' in *Hippokratische Medizin und antike Philosophie*, Verhandlungen des VIII Internationalen Hippokrates-Kolloquiums in Kloster Banz/Staffelstein vom 23 bis 28 September 1993, edd. R. Wittern & P. Pellegrin, Hildesheim, pp. 451-76.

Link, H.F. 1814/15. 'Über die Theorien in den Hippokratischen Schriften nebst Bemerkungen über die Echtheit dieser Schriften', *Abhandlungen Königlich Preussischen Akademie der Wissenschaften*, Berlin.

Littman, R.J. & M.L. 1969. 'The Athenian Plague: smallpox', *Transactions of the American Philological Association*, vol. 100, pp. 261-75.

Littré, E. 1839-61. *Oeuvres complètes d'Hippocrate*, 10 vols., Paris.

Lloyd, A.H. 1935. 'The coin types of Selinus and the legend of Empedocles', *Numismatic Chronicle*, 15, pp. 73-93.

Lloyd, G.E.R. 1963. 'Who is attacked in *On Ancient Medicine?*', *Phronesis*, 8, pp. 108-26.

―――― 1964. 'Hot and cold, dry and wet in Greek philosophy', *Journal of Hellenic Studies*, 84, pp. 92-106 (repr. in Allen & Furley, 1970, vol. I, pp. 255-80).

―――― 1966. *Polarity and Analogy*, Cambridge.

―――― 1968a. *Aristotle: The Growth and Structure of his Thought*, Cambridge.

―――― 1968b. 'Plato as a natural scientist', *Journal of Hellenic Studies*, 88, pp. 78-92.

―――― 1973. *Greek Science after Aristotle*, London.

―――― 1975a. 'A note on Erasistratus of Ceos', *Journal of Hellenic Studies*, 95, pp. 172-5.

―――― 1975b. 'Alcmaeon and the early history of dissection', *Sudhoffs Archiv für Geschichte der Medizin und Naturwisssenschaften*, 59, pp. 113-47 (repr. in *Methods and Problems in Greek Science*, Cambridge, 1991, pp. 167-93).

―――― 1975c. 'The Hippocratic question', *Classical Quarterly*, n.s. 25, pp. 171-92 (repr. in *Methods and Problems in Greek Science*, Cambridge, 1991, pp. 199-223).

―――― 1975d. 'Aspects of the interrelations of medicine, magic and philosophy in ancient Greece', *Apeiron*, 9, pp. 1-16.

―――― 1975e. 'The role of medicine in the development of early Greek science', *Lampas*, 8, pp. 327-33.

―――― 1978. (ed.) *Hippocratic Writings*, Pelican Books, Harmondsworth.

―――― 1979. *Magic, Reason and Experience*, Cambridge.

―――― 1983. *Science, Folklore and Ideology*, Cambridge.

―――― 1985. *Science and Morality in Greco-Roman Antiquity*, inaugural lecture, Cambridge.

―――― 1987. *The Revolutions of Wisdom*, Berkeley and Los Angeles.

―――― 1990a. *Demystifying Mentalities*, Cambridge.

―――― 1990b. 'Plato and Archytas in the Seventh Letter', *Phronesis*, 35, pp. 159-74.

―――― 1991a. *Methods and Problems in Greek Science: Selected Papers*, Cambridge.

―――― 1991b. 'The definition, status, and methods of the medical τέχνη in the fifth and fourth centuries', pp. 249-60 in A.C. Bowen (ed.), *Science and Philosophy in Classical Greece*, New York.

Longrigg, J. 1963. 'Philosophy and medicine: some early interactions', *Harvard Studies in Classical Philology*, 67, pp. 147-75.

―――― 1964. 'A note on Anaximenes Fragment 2', *Phronesis*, 9, pp. 1-4.

―――― 1965a. 'Galen on Empedocles (Fragment 67)', *Philologus*, Bd. 108, Hft. 3/4, pp. 297-300.

―――― 1965b, 'Empedocles's fiery fish', *Journal of the Warburg and Courtauld Institutes*, 28, pp. 314-15.

―――― 1966. 'The sun and the planets', *Apeiron*, 1, pp. 19-31.

―――― 1971. 'Erasistratus', *Dictionary of Scientific Biography*, 4, New York, pp. 382-6.

―――― 1972. 'Herophilus', *Dictionary of Scientific Biography*, 6, pp. 316-19.

―――― 1973. 'Darwinism and Presocratic philosophy', *Durham University Journal*, 65, pp. 307-15.

—— 1974. 'Nicholas of Damascus', *Dictionary of Scientific Biography*, 10, New York, pp. 111-12.

—— 1975a. 'Praxagoras', *Dictionary of Scientific Biography*, 11, New York, pp. 127-8.

—— 1975b. 'Thales', *Dictionary of Scientific Biography*, 13, pp. 295-8.

—— 1975c. 'Elementary physics in the Lyceum and Stoa', *Isis*, 66, no. 232, pp. 211-29.

—— 1976. 'The "roots" of all things', *Isis*, 67, no. 238, pp. 420-38.

—— 1980. 'The Great Plague of Athens', *History of Science*, 18, pp. 209-25.

—— 1981. 'Superlative achievement and comparative neglect: Alexandrian medical science and modern historical research', *History of Science* 19, pp. 155-200.

—— 1983. '[Hippocrates] Ancient medicine and its intellectual context', in Lasserre & Mudry, 1983, pp. 249-56.

—— 1985a. 'A seminal "debate" in the fifth century BC?', in *Aristotle on Nature and Living Things: Philosophical and Historical Studies presented to D.M. Balme*, ed. A. Gotthelf, Pittsburgh and Bristol, pp. 277-87.

—— 1985b. 'Herophilus and the arterial vein', *Liverpool Classical Monthly*, 10.10, pp. 149-50.

—— 1985c. 'Elements and after: a study in Presocratic physics of the second half of the fifth century', *Apeiron*, 19, pp. 93-115.

—— 1988. 'Anatomy in Alexandria in the third century BC', *British Journal for the History of Science*, 21, pp. 455-88.

—— 1989. 'Presocratic philosophy and Hippocratic medicine', *History of Science*, 27, pp. 1-39.

—— 1992. 'Epidemic, ideas and classical Athenian society', ch. 2 in *Epidemics and Ideas: Essays on the Historical Perception of Pestilence*, edd. T. Ranger & P. Slack, Cambridge, pp. 21-44.

—— 1993a. *Greek Rational Medicine: Philosophy and Medicine from Alcmaeon to the Alexandrians*, London.

—— 1993b. 'Empedocles and the plague of Selinus: a cock and bull story?', *Tria Lustra: A Festschrift in Honour of John Pinsent*, Liverpool, pp. 29-34.

—— 1997. 'Medicine in the Classical world', *Oxford Illustrated History of Western Medicine*, ed. I. Loudon, ch. 2, pp. 25-39, Oxford.

Lonie, I.M. 1964. 'Erasistratus, the Erasistrateans, and Aristotle', *Bulletin of the History of Medicine*, 38, pp. 426-43.

—— 1973. 'The paradoxical text "On the Heart" ', *Medical History*, 17, pp. 1-15, 136-53.

—— 1977. 'A structural pattern in Greek dietetics and the early history of Greek medicine', *Medical History*, 21, pp. 235-60.

—— 1981. *The Hippocratic Treatises 'On Generation', 'On the Nature of the Child', 'Diseases' IV (Ars Medica II.7)*, Berlin.

—— 1983. 'Literacy and the development of Hippocratic medicine', in *Formes de pensée dans la Collection Hippocratique* (Actes du IVe Colloque International Hippocratique, Lausanne, 1981), edd. F. Lasserre & P. Mudry, pp. 145-61, Geneva.

MacArthur, W.P. 1954. 'The Athenian Plague: a medical note', *Classical Quarterly* n.s. 4, pp. 171-4.

McDiarmid, J.B. 1953. 'Theophrastus on the Presocratic causes', *Harvard Studies in Classical Philology*, 61, pp. 85-156 (repr. in Allan & Furley, vol. I, London, 1970, pp. 178-238).

Magnus, H. 1901. *Die Augenheilkunde der Alten*, Breslau.

Bibliography

Majno, G. 1975. *The Healing Hand: Man and Wound in the Ancient World*, Cambridge, Mass.

Malinas, Y., Burguière, A. & Gourevitch, D. 1985. 'L'anatomie gynécologique dans Soranos d'Ephèse', *Histoire des sciences médicales*, 19, pp. 161-7.

Maloney, G. & Savoie, R. 1982. *Cinq cent ans de bibliographie hippocratique 1473-1982*, Quebec.

Manetti, D. 1989. 'Alcmaeon', *Corpus dei Papiri Filosofici Greci e Latini*, 1, pp. 149-51.

—— 1990. 'Doxographical deformation of medical tradition in the report of the Anonymus Londinensis on Philolaus', *Zeitschrift für Papyrologie und Epigraphik*, 83, pp. 219-23.

—— 1996. ' Ὡς δὲ αὐτος Ἱπποκράτης λέγει. Teoria causale e ippocratismo nell' Anonimo Londinense (VI 43ss.)' in *Hippokratische Medizin und antike Philosophie*, Verhandlungen des VIII Internationalen Hippokrates-Kolloquiums in Kloster Banz/Staffelstein vom 23 bis 28 September 1993, edd. R. Wittern & P. Pellegrin, Hildesheim, pp. 295-310.

Manetti, D. & Roselli, A. 1982. *Ippocrate: Epidemie libro sesto*, Florence.

Mani, N. 1959-67. *Die historischen Grundlagen der Leberforschung*, 2 vols, Basel.

Mansfeld, J. 1971. *The Pseudo-hippocratic Tract περὶ ἑβδομάδων chs. 1-11 and Greek Philosophy*, Assen.

—— 1975. 'Alcmaeon: "physikos" or physician?', *Kephalaion*, edd. J. Mansfeld & L.M. de Rijk, Assen, pp. 26-38.

—— 1980. 'Theoretical and empirical attitudes in early Greek medicine', *Hippocratica: Actes du Colloque Hippocratique de Paris, 4-9 Septembre 1978*, ed. M.D. Grmek, Paris, pp. 371-91.

Manuli, P. 1980. 'Fisiologia e patologia del femminile negli scritti ippocratici dell'antica ginecologia greca', in *Hippocratica*, Actes du Colloque Hippocratique de Paris, 4-9 Septembre 1978, ed. M.D. Grmek, Paris, pp. 393-408.

Manuli, P. & Vegetti, M. 1977. *Cuore, Sangue e Cervello*, Milan.

Marquardt, J., Müller, I. & Helmreich, G. 1884-1893. *Claudiii Galeni Pergameni Scripta Minora*, 3 vols., Leipzig.

Marx, F. 1915. *Auli Cornelii Celsi quae supersunt (CML 1)*, Leipzig and Berlin.

Marx, K.F.H. 1838. *Herophilus, ein Beitrag zur Geschichte der Medizin*, Karlsruhe/Baden.

—— 1840. *De Herophili celeberrimi medici vita scriptis atque in medicina meritis*, Göttingen.

May, M.T. 1958. 'Galen on human dissection', *Journal of the History of Medicine*, 13, pp. 409-10.

Mesk, J. 1913. 'Antiochus und Stratonike', *Rheinisches Museum*, 68, pp. 366-94.

Michler, M. 1968. *Die hellenistische Chirurgie, I. Die alexandrinischen Chirurgen*, Wiesbaden.

Mikalson, J.D. 1984. 'Religion and the Plague in Athens, 431-423 BC', *Greek, Roman and Byzantine Studies*, 10 (Studies presented to Sterling Dow on his 80th Birthday), Durham, N.C., pp. 217-25.

Miller, H.W. 1948. 'A medical theory of cognition', *Transactions of the American Philological Association*, 79, pp. 168-83.

—— 1952. 'Dynamis and physis in *On Ancient Medicine*', *Transactions of the American Philological Association*, 83, pp. 184-97.

—— 1953. 'The concept of the divine in *De morbo sacro*', *Transactions of the American Philological Association*, 84, pp. 1-15.

—— 1955. 'Technê and discovery in *On Ancient Medicine*', *Transactions of the American Philological Association*, 86, pp. 51-62.

Bibliography

—— 1960. 'The concept of dynamis in *De victu'*, *Transactions of the American Philological Association*, 90, pp. 147-64.

—— 1962. 'The aetiology of disease in Plato's *Timaeus'*, *Transactions of the American Philological Association*, 93, pp. 175-87.

Moisan, M. 1990. 'Les plantes narcotiques dans le Corpus Hippocratique', pp. 381-92 in *La Maladie et les maladies dans la Collection Hippocratique* (Actes du VI⁰ Colloque International Hippocratique), edd. P. Potter, G. Maloney and J. Desautels, Québec.

Moon, R.O. 1923. *Hippocrates and his Successors in Relation to the Philosophy of their Time* (Fitzpatrick Lectures), London.

Morrow, G. 1969. 'Qualitative Change in Aristotle's *Physics'*, in *Naturphilosophie bei Aristoteles und Theophrast*, Heidelberg, pp. 154-67.

Mourelatos, A.P.D. 1974. (ed.) *The Presocratics*, New York.

Mudry, P. 1982. *La Préface du 'De Medicina' de Celse* (Bibliotheca Helvetica Romana 19), Lausanne.

Mugler, C. 1963. *Les Origines de la science grecque*, Paris.

Müller, I. 1874. *Claudii Galeni De Placitis et Platonis Libri Novem*, Leipzig.

Müri, W. 1953. 'Melancholie und schwarze Galle', *Museum Helveticum*, 10, pp. 21-38.

—— 1986. *Der Arzt im Altertum*, Munich and Zurich.

Nelson, A.H. 1909. *Die Hippokratische Schrift Περὶ φυσῶν. Text und Studien*, Diss., Uppsala.

Nestle, W. 1942. *Vom Mythos zum Logos*, Stuttgart.

Neuberger, M. 1906. *Die Geschichte der Medizin*, Stuttgart.

Nicaise, F. 1890. (ed.) *La Grande Chirurgie*, Paris.

Nickel, D. 1971. (ed.) *Galenus: De uteri dissectione* (*CMG* V. 2,1), Berlin.

Norenberg, H.-W. 1968. *Das Göttliche und die Natur in der Schrift Über die heilige Krankenheit*, Diss., Bonn.

Nunn, J.F. 1996. *Ancient Egyptian Medicine*, London.

Nutton, V. 1979. *Galen: On Prognosis* (*CMG*, V. 8,1), Berlin.

—— 1981. *Galen: Problems and Prospects*, London.

—— 1983. 'The seeds of disease: an explanation of contagion and infection from the Greeks to the Renaissance', *Medical History*, 27, pp. 1-34.

—— 1988. *From Democedes to Harvey*, London.

—— 1992. 'Healers in the medical market place: towards a social history of Graeco-Roman medicine', *Medicine in Society*, ed. A. Wear, Cambridge, pp. 15-58.

—— 1993. 'Beyond the Hippocratic oath: the earlier historical setting of professional ethics' in *Doctors and Ethics*, edd. A. Wear, J. Geyer-Kordesch & R. French, *Clio Medica*, 24, pp. 10-37.

—— 1995. 'What's in an oath?', *Journal of the Royal College of Physicians of London*, vol. 29, no. 6, pp. 518-24.

O'Brien, D. 1969. *Empedocles' Cosmic Cycle*, Cambridge.

—— 1970. 'The effect of a simile: Empedocles' theories of seeing and breathing', *Journal of Hellenic Studies*, 90, pp. 140-79.

Ogle, W. 1882. *Aristotle on the Parts of Animals*, London.

Onians, R.B. 1951. *The Origins of European Thought*, Cambridge.

Orlandini, P. 1961. *Enciclopedia dell'Arte Antica, Classica e Orientale*, 4, Rome, pp. 291-4.

Page, D.S. 1953. 'Thucydides' description of the Great Plague at Athens', *Classical Quarterly*, n.s. 3, pp. 97-119.

Parker, R.C.T. 1983. *Miasma: Pollution and Purification in Early Greek Religion*, Oxford.

Bibliography

Parry, A. 1969. 'The language of Thucydides' description of the plague', *Bulletin of the Institute of Classical Studies*, 16, pp. 106-18.

Peck, A.L. 1926. 'Anaxagoras and the parts', *Classical Quarterly*, 20, pp. 57-71.

—— 1953. 'The connate pneuma: an essential factor in Aristotle's solution to the problem of reproduction and sensation' in *Science, Medicine and History: Essays in Honour of Charles Singer*, ed. E.A. Underwood, London, pp. 111-21.

—— 1965. *Aristotle. Historia Animalium Books I-III*, Cambridge, Mass.

—— 1970. *Aristotle. Historia Animalium Books IV-VI*, Cambridge, Mass.

Petrequin, J.E. 1877. *Chirurgie d'Hippocrate*, 2 vols., Paris.

Phillips, E.D. 1973. *Greek Medicine*, London.

Pigeaud, J.M. 1978. 'Du rhythme dans le corps. Quelques notes sur l'interprétation du pouls par le méthode Hérophile', *Bulletin de l'Association Guillaume Budé*, 3, pp. 258-67.

—— 1987. *Folies et cures de la folie chez les médecins de l'antiquité gréco-romaine*, Paris.

Pinault, J.R. 1983. *Biographical Fiction in the Lives of Hippocrates*, Diss., University of Pennsylvania.

—— 1986. 'How Hippocrates cured the plague', *Journal of the History of Medicine and the Allied Sciences*, 41, pp. 52-75.

—— 1992. *Hippocratic Lives and Legends*, Leiden, New York and Cologne.

Pinoff, J. 1847. 'Herophilos. Ein Beitrag zur Geschichte der Geburtshilfe', *Janus* 2, pp. 739-43.

Pohlenz, M. 1917. 'Zu den hippokratischen Briefen', *Hermes*, 52, pp. 348-53.

—— 1938. *Hippokrates und die Begründung der wissenschaftlichen Medizin*, Berlin.

—— 1953. 'Nomos und Physis', *Hermes*, 81, pp. 418-38.

Poole, J.C.F. & Holladay, A.J. 1979. 'Thucydides and the Plague of Athens', *Classical Quarterly*, 29, pp. 282-300.

Popper, K.R. 1951. *The Open Society and its Enemies*, vol. 1 (2nd. edn.) London.

—— 1952. 'The nature of philosophical problems and their roots in science', *British Journal for the Philosophy of Science*, 3, pp. 124-56 (repr. in *Conjectures and Refutations*, 5th. edn., London, 1974, pp. 66-96).

Potter, P. 1976. 'Herophilus of Chalcedon', *Bulletin of the History of Medicine*, 50, pp. 45-60.

—— 1988. *Hippocrates* (Loeb Vols. V & VI), Cambridge, Mass. and London.

—— 1995. *Hippocrates* (Loeb Vol. VIII), Cambridge, Mass. and London.

Prag, A.J.N., 1990. 'Reconstructing King Philip II: the "nice" version', *American Journal of Archaeology*, 94, pp. 237-47.

Prag, A.J.N., Musgrave, J.H., & Neave, R.A.H. 1984. 'The skull from Tomb II at Vergina: King Philip II of Macedon', *Journal of Hellenic Studies*, 104, pp. 60-78.

Preus, A. 1983. 'Aristotle and Hippocratic gynecology', in *Aristoteles als Wissenschaftstheoretiker*, edd. J. Irmscher & R. Müller, Berlin.

—— 1988. 'Drugs and psychic states in Theophrastus' *Historia Plantarum*, 9.8-20' in W.W. Fortenbaugh et al. (edd.) *Theophrastean Studies*, New Brunswick, pp. 76-99.

Raeder, J. 1928-33. *Oribasii collectionum medicarum reliquiae*, 4 vols. (*Corpus Medicorum Graecorum* VI), Leipzig and Berlin (repr. Amsterdam, 1964).

Ranger, T. & Slack, P. 1992. *Epidemics and Ideas: Essays on the Historical Perception of Pestilence*, Cambridge.

Rechenauer, G. 1991. *Thukydides und die hippokratische Medizin*, Hildesheim/ Zurich/New York.

Regenbogen, O. 1931. 'Eine Forschungsmethode antiker Naturwissenschaft', *Quellen und Studien zur Geschichte der Mathematik, Astronomie und Physik*,

Bibliography

Bd. 1,2, Berlin, pp. 131-82 (repr. in his *Kleine Schriften*, Munich, 1961, pp. 141-94).

—— 1937. 'Eine Polemik Theophrasts gegen Aristoteles', *Hermes* 72, pp. 469-75 (repr. in his *Kleine Schriften*, Munich, 1961, pp. 276-85).

Reinhardt, K. 1916. *Parmenides und die Geschichte der griechischen Philosophie*, Bonn.

Rhodes, P. J. 1988. *Thucydides: History*, II, Warminster.

Riddle, J.M. 1991. 'Oral contraceptives and early term abortifacients during Classical Antiquity and the Middle Ages', *Past and Present*, 132, pp. 3-32.

—— 1992. *Contraception and Abortion from the Ancient World to the Renaissance*, Cambridge, Mass.

Ridgway, B. 1970. *The Severe Style in Greek Sculpture*, Princeton.

Rivaud, A. 1956. *Platon: 'Timée', 'Critias'* (vol. 10 in *Platon: Oeuvres complètes*, 3rd edn., Paris).

Rose, V. 1863. *Aristoteles Pseudepigraphus*, Leipzig.

Roselli, A. 1975. *La Chirurgia Ippocratica*, Florence.

Ross, W.D. 1924. *Aristotle's Metaphysics*, Oxford.

Rüsche, F. 1930. *Blut, Leben und Seele*, Paderborn.

Rusten, J.S. 1989. *The Peloponnesian War Book II*, Cambridge.

Sallares, R. 1991. *The Ecology of the Ancient Greek World*, London.

Salway, P. & Dell, W. 1955. 'Plague at Athens', *Greece and Rome*, 24, 62-70.

Sambursky, S. 1956. *The Physical World of the Greeks*, London.

—— 1962. *The Physical World of Late Antiquity*, London.

Sandison, A.T. 1959. 'The first recorded case of inflammatory mastitis: Queen Atossa of Persia and the physician Democedes', *Medical History*, 3, pp. 317-22.

Sarton, G. 1952 & 1959. *A History of Science*, vols. 1 & 2, Cambridge, Mass.

Saunders, J.B. de C.M. 1963. *The Transition from Ancient Egyptian to Greek Medicine*, Lawrence, Kansas.

Scarborough, J. 1970. 'Thucydides, Greek medicine, and the Plague at Athens', *Episteme*, 4, pp. 77-90.

—— 1976. 'Celsus on human vivisection at Ptolemaic Alexandria', *Clio Medica*, 11, pp. 25-38.

—— 1978. 'Theophrastus on herbals and herbal remedies', *Journal of the History of Biology*, 11, pp. 353-85.

—— 1983. 'Theoretical assumptions in Hippocratic pharmacology' in *Formes de pensée dans la Collection Hippocratique* (Actes du IVe Colloque International Hippocratique, Lausanne, 1981), edd. F. Lasserre & P. Mudry, pp. 307-25, Geneva.

Schmekel, E. 1938. *Die positive Philosophie in ihrer geschichtlichen Entwicklung*, Bd. I, Berlin.

Schmitt, C.B. 1985. 'Aristotle among the physicians', ch. 1 in *The Medical Renaissance of the Sixteenth Century*, edd. A. Wear, R.K. French & I.M. Lonie, Cambridge.

Schmutte, J.M. & Pfaff, F. 1941. *CMG Suppl. III: De consuetudinibus*, Leipzig and Berlin.

Schöne, H. 1907. 'Markellinos' Pulslehre. Ein griechisches Anekdoton', *Festschrift zur 49 Versammlung deutscher Philologen und Schulmänner in Basel im Jahre 1907*, Basel, pp. 448-72.

Schöner, E. 1964. *Das Viererschema in der antiken Humoralpathologie* (*Sudhoffs Archiv für Geschichte der Medizin und der Naturwissenschaften*, 4), Wiesbaden.

Schumacher, J. 1940. *Antike Medizin: Die Naturphilosophischen Grundlagen der Medizin in der griechischen Antike*, Berlin.

Bibliography

———— 1965. *Die Anfänge abendländischer Medizin in der griechischen Antike*, Stuttgart.

Semeria, A. 1986. 'Per un censimento degli Asklepieia della Grecia continentale e delle isole', *Annali Scuola Normale Superiore di Pisa*, 16, pp. 931-58.

Senn, G. 1929. 'Über Herkunft und Stil der Beschreibungen von Experimenten im Corpus Hippocraticum', *Archiv für Geschichte der Medizin*, 22 , pp. 217-89.

———— 1930. 'Hat Aristoteles eine selbständige Schrift über Pflanzen verfaßt?', *Philologus*, 85, pp. 113-40.

———— 1933. *Die Entwicklung der biologischen Forschungsmethode in der Antike und ihre grundsätzliche Forderung durch Theophrast von Eresos*, Aarau & Leipzig.

———— 1956. *Die Pflanzenkunde des Theophrast von Eresos*, ed. O. Gigon, Basel.

Sharples, R.W. 1995 *Theophrastus of Eresus: Sources for his Life, Writings, Thought and Influence. Commentary*, vol. V (Philosophia Antiqua, vol. 64), Leiden, New York and Cologne.

Sherwin-White, S.M. 1978. *Ancient Cos, Hypomnemata*, Hft. 51, Göttingen.

Shrewsbury, J.F.D. 1950. 'The Plague of Athens', *Bulletin of the History of Medicine*, 24, 1-25.

Sigerist, H.E. 1924. 'Die Geburt der Abendländischen Medizin', *Essays on the History of Medicine. Presented to Karl Sudhoff*, edd. Charles Singer and H.E. Sigerist, London and Zürich, pp. 185-205.

———— 1951-61. *A History of Medicine*, 2 vols., New York (repr. New York, 1967/87).

Simon, B. 1978. *Mind and Madness in Ancient Greece*, Ithaca and London.

Simon, M. 1906. *Sieben Bücher Anatomie des Galen*, 2 vols., Leipzig.

Singer, C. 1925. *The Evolution of Anatomy*, London.

———— 1927. 'The herbal in antiquity and its transmission to later ages', *Journal of Hellenic Studies*, 47, pp. 1-52.

———— 1956. *Galen: On anatomical procedures. A translation of the surviving books with introduction and notes*. (Publications of the Wellcome Historical Museum n.s. V.7), London and New York.

Singer, C. & Underwood, E.A. 1962. *A Short History of Medicine*, 2nd. edn., London.

Singer, P.N. 1997. *Galen: Selected Works*, Oxford.

Smith, G. Elliott 1914. 'Egyptian mummies', *Journal of Egyptian Archaeology*, 10, pp. 189-96.

Smith, W.D. 1979. *The Hippocratic Tradition*, Ithaca and London.

———— 1980. 'The development of Classical dietetic theory', *Hippocratica: Actes du Colloque Hippocratique de Paris 4-9 Septembre 1978*, ed. M.D. Grmek, pp. 439-48.

———— 1982. 'Erasistratus's dietetic medicine', *Bulletin of the History of Medicine*, 56, pp. 398-409.

———— 1990. *Hippocrates: Pseudepigraphic Writings*, Leiden, New York, Copenhagen and Cologne.

———— 1994. *Hippocrates* (Loeb Vol. VII), Cambridge, Mass. and London.

Solmsen, F.S. 1950. 'Tissues and the soul', *Philosophical Review*, 59, pp. 435-68.

———— 1957. 'The vital heat, the inborn *pneuma* and the *aether*', *Journal of Hellenic Studies*, 77, pp. 119-23.

———— 1960. *Aristotle's System of the Physical World*, Ithaca and New York.

———— 1961. 'Greek philosophy and the discovery of the nerves', *Museum Helveticum*, 18, pp. 150-67 & 169-97 (repr. in *Kleine Schriften*, Hildesheim, 1968, pp. 536-82, and *Antike Medizin*, ed. H. Flashar, Darmstadt, 1971, pp. 202-79).

Bibliography

Solomon, J. 1985. 'Thucydides and the recognition of contagion', *Maia*, 37, pp. 121-2.

Spencer, W.G. 1935-8. *Celsus. De Medicina*, 3 vols., Loeb edn., London and Cambridge, Mass.

Sprengel, K. 1792. *Versuch einer pragmatischen Geschichte der Arzneikunde*, Halle (4th edn., Leipzig, 1846).

Staden, H. von. 1975. 'Experiment and experience in Hellenistic medicine', *Bulletin of the Institute of Classical Studies*, 22, pp. 178-99.

———— 1982. '*Hairesis* and heresy: the case of the *haireseis iatrikai*', in *Jewish and Christian Self-Definition, III: Self-Definition in the Graeco-Roman World*, edd. B.F. Meyer and E.P. Sanders, London, pp. 76-100 & 199-206.

———— 1989. *Herophilus: The Art of Medicine in Early Alexandria*, Cambridge.

———— 1992a. 'Jaeger's "Skandalon der historischen Vernunft": Diocles, Aristotle, and Theophrastus' in *Werner Jaeger Reconsidered* (Proceedings of the second Oldfather Conference, held on the campus of the University of Illinois at Urbana-Champaign, April 26-28, 1990), ed. W.M. Calder III, Atlanta, Ga., 1992, pp. 227-65.

———— 1992b. 'Women and dirt', *Helios*, 19, pp. 7-30.

Stannard, J. 1961. 'Hippocratic pharmacology', *Bulletin of the History of Medicine*, 35, pp. 497-518.

———— 1962. 'The plant called Moly', *Osiris*, 14, pp. 254-307.

Steckerl, F. 1958. *The Fragments of Praxagoras of Cos and his School* (*Philosophia Antiqua* 8), Leiden.

Stella, L.A. 1939. 'L'importanza di Alcmeone nella storia del pensiero greco', *Memorie della Reale Accademia Nazionali dei Lincei*, ser. 6, vol. 8, fasc. 4, pp. 233-87.

Steuer, R.O. 1948. *whdw: Aetiological Principle of Pyaemia in Ancient Egyptian Medicine*, Baltimore (*Supplement to the Bulletin of the History of Medicine*, no. 10).

Steuer, R.O. & Saunders, J.B. de C.M. 1959. *Ancient Egyptian and Cnidian Medicine*, Berkeley and Los Angeles.

Sticker, G. 1923. *Hippokrates, der Volkskrankheiten erstes und drittes Buch*, Leipzig.

Stückelberger, A. 1984. *Vestigia Democritea: Die Rezeption der Lehre von den Atomen in der antiken Naturwissenschaft und Medizin. Schweizerische Beiträge zur Altertumswissenschaft*, Hft. 17, Basel.

Susemihl, F. 1891. *Geschichte der griechischen Literatur in der Alexandrinerzeit*, 2 vols., Leipzig.

Tannery, P. 1887. *Pour l'histoire de la science hellène*, Paris.

Taylor, A.E. 1928. *A Commentary on Plato's Timaeus*, Oxford.

Temkin, O. 1933. 'Views on epilepsy in the Hippocratic period', *Bulletin of the History of Medicine*, 1, pp. 41-4.

———— 1945. *The Falling Sickness: A History of Epilepsy from the Greeks to the Beginnings of Modern Neurology*, Baltimore.

———— 1953. 'Greek medicine as science and craft', *Isis*, 44, pp. 213-25.

———— 1956a. *Soranus' Gynecology. Translation with an Introduction*, Baltimore.

———— 1956b. 'On the interrelationship of the history and the philosophy of medicine', *Bulletin of the History of Medicine*, 30, pp. 241-51.

———— 1977. *The Double Face of Janus and Other Essays in the History of Medicine*, Baltimore.

———— 1985. 'Hippocrates as the physician of Democritus', *Gesnerus*, 42, pp. 455-64.

———— 1991. *Hippocrates in a World of Pagans and Christians*, Baltimore.

Bibliography

Theiler, W. 1925. *Zur Geschichte der teleologischen Naturbetrachtung bis auf Aristoteles*, Zürich and Leipzig.

Thivel, A. 1981. *Cnide et Cos?*, Paris.

Thompson, R. Campbell. 1903-4. *The Devils and Evil Spirits in Babylonia*, 2 vols., London.

Torraca, L. 1965. 'Diocle di Carysto, il "Corpus Hippocraticum" ed Aristotele', *Sophia*, 33, pp. 105-15.

Tracy, T.J. 1969. *Physiological Theory and the Doctrine of the Mean in Plato and Aristotle*, The Hague and Paris.

Trapp, H. 1967. *Die hippokratische Schrift De natura muliebri*, Diss. Hamburg.

Tuke, Sir J.B. 1910-11. 'Hippocrates', *Encyclopaedia Britannica*, 11th. edn., vol. 13, Cambridge, pp. 517-19.

Unger, F.C. 1923a. *Liber Hippocraticus de corde editus cum prolegomenis et commentario*, Diss. Utrecht.

——— 1923b. 'Liber Hippocraticus ΠΕΡΙ ΚΑΡΔΙΗΣ', *Mnemosyne*, 51, pp. 1-101.

Valk, M. van der 1971-87. *Eustathii Commentarii*, 4 vols., Leiden.

Vallance, J.T. 1990, *The Lost Theory of Asclepiades of Bithynia*, Oxford.

——— 1993. 'The medical system of Asclepiades of Bithynia' in W. Haase, *Aufstieg und Niedergang der Römischen Welt*, Bd. 37, Teil 1 *Wissenschaften (Medizin und Biologie)*, Berlin and New York, 1993, pp. 693-727.

Verbeke, G. 1945. *L'Évolution de la doctrine du pneuma*, Paris and Louvain.

Verdenius, W.J. 1962. 'Science grecque et science moderne', *Revue Philosophique*, 87, pp. 319-36.

Villaret, O. 1911. *Hippocratis De natura hominis liber ad codicum fidem recensitus*, Diss. Göttingen and Berlin.

Vitrac, B. 1989. *Médecine et philosophie au temps d'Hippocrate*, Paris.

Vlastos, G. 1947. 'Equality and justice in early Greek cosmologies', *Classical Philology*, 42, pp. 156-78 (repr. in Allen and Furley, vol. I, 1970, pp. 56-91).

——— 1950. 'The physical theory of Anaxagoras', *Philosophical Review*, 59, pp. 31-57 (repr. in Allen and Furley, vol. II, 1975, pp. 323-53).

——— 1952. 'Theology and philosophy in early Greek thought,' *Philosophical Quarterly*, 2, pp. 97-123 (repr. in Allen and Furley, vol. I, 1970, pp. 92-129).

——— 1953. 'Isonomia', *American Journal of Philology*, 74, pp. 337-66.

——— 1975. *Plato's Universe*, Oxford.

Wachtler, J. 1896. *De Alcmaeone Crotoniata*, Diss. Leipzig.

Wasserstein, A. 1972. 'Le rôle des hypothèses dans la médecine grecque', *Revue Philosophique*, 162, pp. 3-14.

Waszinck, J.H. (ed. & comm.) 1947. *Tertullian De Anima*, Amsterdam.

Waterlow, S. 1982. *Nature, Change and Agency in Aristotle's Physics*, Oxford.

Wehrli, F. 1950. *Straton von Lampsakos (Die Schule des Aristoteles)*, Hft. 5, Basel.

Weidauer, K. 1954. *Thukydides und die Hippokratischen Schriften*, Heidelberg.

Wellmann, M. 1888. 'Zur Geschichte der Medicin im Alterthume', *Hermes*, 23, pp. 556-66.

——— 1898. 'Das älteste Kräuterbuch der Griechen', *Festgabe F. Susemihl*, Leipzig, pp. 1-31.

——— 1900. 'Zur Geschichte der Medizin im Alterthum', *Hermes*, 35, pp. 349-84.

——— 1901. *Fragmentsammlung der griechischen Ärzte*, Bd. 1. *Die Fragmente der Sikelischen Ärzte*, Berlin.

——— 1903. 'Diokles', Pauly-Wissowa, *Real-Encyclopädie der klassischen Altertumswissenschaft*, 5,1, Stuttgart, cols. 802-12.

——— 1906-14. *Pedanii Dioscuridis De materia medica libri quinque*, 3 vols., Berlin.

Bibliography

———— 1907. 'Erasistratos', Pauly-Wissowa, *Real-Encycyclopädie der klassischen Altertumswissenschaft*, 6,1, Stuttgart, cols. 333-50.

———— 1922. 'Der Verfasser des Anonymus Londinensis', *Hermes*, 57, pp. 396-430.

———— 1929a. 'Spuren Demokrits von Abdera im Corpus Hippocraticum', *Archeion*, 11, pp. 297-330.

———— 1929b. 'Die Schrift Περὶ ἱρῆς νούσου des Corpus Hippocraticum', *Sudhoffs Archiv für Geschichte der Medizin und Naturwissenschaften*, 22, pp. 290-312.

———— 1930. 'Die pseudohippokratische Schrift Περὶ ἀρχαίης ἰατρικῆς', *Archiv für Geschichte der Medizin und Naturwissenschaften*, 23, pp. 299-305.

Wenkebach, E. & Pfaff, P. 1956. *Galeni in Hippocratis Epidemiarum librum VI commentaria I-VIII Berlin* (*CMG* V.10,2,2).

Wightman, W.P.D. 1971. *The Emergence of Scientific Medicine*, Edinburgh.

Wilamowitz-Moellendorff, U. von. 1901. 'Die hippokratische Schrift Περὶ ἱρῆς νούσόυ', *Sitzungsberichte der Königlich preussischen Akademie der Wissenschaften*, Berlin, pp. 2-23.

———— 1902. *Griechisches Lesebuch*, vol. II, Berlin.

Willerdings, G.K.F. 1914. *Studia Hippocratica*, Diss. Göttingen.

Williams, E.W. 1957. 'The sickness at Athens', *Greece and Rome*, 4, pp. 98-103.

Wilson, J.V. Kinnier & Reynolds, E.H. 1990. 'Translation and analysis of a cuneiform text forming part of a Babylonian treatise on epilepsy', *Medical History*, 34, pp. 185-98.

Wilson, L.G. 1959. 'Erasistratus, Galen and the Pneuma', *Bulletin of the History of Medicine*, 33, pp. 293-314.

Withington, E.T. 1921. 'The Asclepiadae and the priests of Asclepius', in *Studies in the History and Method of Science*, ed. C. Singer, vol. II, Oxford.

Wittern, R. 1974. *Die hippokratische Schrift De morbis I*, Hildesheim, Zürich and New York.

Wittern, R. & Pellegrin, P. 1996. (edd.) *Hippokratische Medizin und antike Philosophie*. Verhandlungen des VIII Internationalen Hippokrates-Kolloquiums in Kloster Banz/Staffelstein vom 23 bis 28 September 1993. Hildesheim.

Wöhrle, G. 1990. *Studien zur Theorie der Antiken Gesundheitslchre*, Hermes Einzelschriften, 56, Stuttgart.

Wright, M.R. 1981. *Empedocles: The Extant Fragments*, New Haven and London.

Zeller, E. 1856-81. *Die Philosophie der Griechen*, 2nd. edn., Tübingen.

———— 1920. *Die Philosophie der Griechen*, I.1 (7th. edn., 1923) and I.2 (6th. edn., 1920) edited and enlarged by W. Nestle, Leipzig.

Zeller, E. & Mondolfo. R. 1932-. *La filosofia dei Greci nel suo sviluppo storico*, Florence.

Concordance of Quoted Passages

Aelian
Nature of animals IX.33.1, **I.23**
Aëtius
On the opinions of the philosophers II.20.1, **II.9**; II.24.2, **II.10**; II.25.1, **II.11**;
    II.29.1, **II.12**; III.3.1 & III.3.2, **II.8**; III.4.1, **II.6**; IV.5.6-8, **VI.36**, **XIV.11**;
    IV.5.7, **XIV.12**; V.3.6, **III.23**; V.22.1, **III.15**; V.30.1, **III.2**; V.30.5, **IX.13**
Alcaeus Fr. 4, **II.1**
Anonymus Londiniensis 5.35-7.40, **IV.9**; 9.20-33, **XII.6**; 20.25-37, **III.5**; 20.25-50,
    VI.16; 33.43-51, **VII.22**
Anonymus Parisinus 3, **II.19**, **IX.17**; 4, **II.23**, **IX.18**; 17, **II.31**; 20, **IX.16**
Archilochus 74.3, **II.4**
Arctinus
Sack of Troy (scholium on *Iliad* 15.515), **XV.6**
Aristophanes, *Plutus* 659-738, **I.28**
Aristotle
Generation of animals 720a12-14, **XVI.17**; 726b1-11, **VI.32**; 735b32ff., **VI.33**;
    736a13, **VI.34**; 743a4ff., **VI.31**; 764a6ff., **III.24**; 777a7ff., **VI.7**
History of animals 494b25-495a18, **XIV.10**; 496a4ff., **XIV.9**; 512b1ff., **VI.11**
Meteorologica 365b6ff., **II.7**
Motion of animals 703a13ff., **VI.27**
On coming-to-be and passing-away 330a30-b6, **VI.25**
On respiration 471b30ff., **III.21**; 472b12ff., **VI.23**; 473a15ff., **VI.6**; 475b16ff.,
    VI.28
On sensation 437b23ff., **III.16**
On the soul 405b1ff., **VI.10**
Parts of animals 646a8-24, **VI.26**; 650a3ff., **VI.30**; 668b33ff., **VI.29**
Politics 1326a13-16, **IV.2**
Athenaeus
Scholars' banquet 15.687e, **VI.43**
Caelius Aurelianus
On chronic diseases I.5, **II.29**; III.4, **XV.19**
Chalcidius
Commentary on Plato's Timaeus 246, **XIV.4**
Clement
The teacher I.6.48, **VI.12**
Cornelius Celsus
On medicine Proem 3-4, **XII.2**; Proem 8, **IV.7**; Proem 14, **IX.19**; Proem 23-4,
    VII.2; Proem 26, **VII.3**; Proem 74-5, **VII.4**; III.9.2, **XII.15**; III.26, **II.20**; V.1,
    XIII.13; VII.5.3, **XV.18**
Corpus of Inscriptions at Delphi (Inv. 6687A&B & 8131), **I.29**
Decree of the Athenians, **IV.5**

229

Diodorus Siculus
  World history XII.45, 58, **X.7**; XIV.70.4-71, **X.8**
Diogenes Laërtius VIII.59, **III.11**; VIII.62, **III.12**; VIII.83, **III.7**; VIII.86, **VI.14**
Dioscorides
  On medical materials IV.75, **XIII.11B**
Ebers papyrus 1, **I.1**
Eustathius
  Commentaries on Homer's Iliad 11.514, **XII.3**
Galen
  On anatomical procedures 1.2, **VII.24**; 9.3, **VII.8**; 9.5, **VII.7**
  On diagnosing the pulses 4.3, **XI.12**
  On dissection of the uterus 5, **XVI.18**; 9, **VII.15C**
  On fullness 6, **IX.21B**
  On habits, **XII.18**
  On natural faculties 2, **IX.14**; 2.6, **VII.21**; 2.8, **VI.44**
  On the differences of fevers 2.18, **IX.15**
  On the differences of the pulses 4.2, **XI.10, XI.18**; 4.3, **XI.11**
  On the doctrines of Hippocrates and Plato 1.6, **VI.41**; 6.5, **VII.11**; 6.6, **VII.17**; 7.3,
    VII.16; 8.5.24, **IX.20**
  On the method of medicine 1.1, **VI.2**; 7.3, **VI.35**
  On the semen 1.16, **VII.15A**
  On the use of respiration 1, **VI.17**
  On the use of the parts 6.10, **VII.12**; 8.11, **VII.6**; 9.6, **VII.10**; 14.11, **VII.15B**
  On theriac to Piso 16, **X.10**
  On trembling, convulsions and cramps 5, **XI.9**
  On venesection against Erasistratus 3, **VII.18, VII.19**
  On venesection against the Erasistrateans at Rome 7, **IX.22**
  Synopsis of his own books on the pulses 8, **XI.16**; 14, **XI.14**
  Thrasybulus or Whether the art of health is part of medicine or gymnastics 33,
    XII.4; 38, **XII.19**
  Whether blood is contained naturally in the arteries 2, **VII.20**
Gerarde, John, *The Herball or Generall Historie of Plants* p. 281, **XIII.17**
Hearst Papyrus 85, **I.2**
Herodotus
  Histories 1.105, **II.25**; 2.86-7, **VII.1**; 3.129-30, **XV.7**; 3.131, **VI.1**; 3.133-4, **XV.8**
Hesiod
  Works and Days 100-4, **I.14**; 238-45, **I.13**
[Hippocrates]
  Affections 1, **IX.8**
  Airs, Waters, Places 1, 3, 4, 5, 6, **IX.4**; 3, **II.17**; 3-4, **XVI.2**; 5, 6, **IX.5**; 22, **II.26**
  Ancient medicine 1, 2, **V.1**; 3, **XII.9**; 9, **V.5**; 12, **V.2**; 14, **III.3**; 20, **IV.11, V.3, V.4**
  Aphorisms I.1, **VIII.2**; III.1, 19-23, **IX.2**; III.24-31, **IX.6**; VI.38, **VIII.4**
  Breaths 2, 4, **IX.7**; 3, 4, 5, 7, **IV.10**; 4, 5, **V.9**; 6, **X.4**; 13, **II.21**
  Decorum 7, 11-14, 16, 18, **VIII.7**
  Diseases I.2, **IX.1**; I.22, **XVI.1**; II.21, **II.22**; II.43, **XIII.6**; II.47, **XI.6, XI.7, XV.15**;
    II.48, **XI.8**
  Diseases of women I.1, **XVI.7, XVI.8**; 1.62, **XVI.3**
  Diseases of young girls 1, **II.24**
  Epidemics I.1, **X.9**; I.5, **VIII.3**; I.10, **XI.2**; I.12, **XI.5**; III, Case 16, **V.6**; VI.3.18,
    XII.7
  Humours 2, **XI.3**
  In the surgery 2-4, **XV.16**
  Law 2, **VIII.5**

230

Nature of man 2, **V.7, V.8**; 4, **III.4**; 7-8, **IX.3**; 9, **X.3, X.5**
Nature of the child 31, **V.17**
Nature of woman 2, **XIII.7**; 3, **XVI.14**; 8, **XVI.12**
Nutriment 18, 19, 21, 22, 23, 24, **V.12**
Oath, **VIII.1**
On anatomy 1, **XIV.7**
On fleshes 5, **XIV.6**; 19, **V.15**
On generation 2, **II.27**; 8, **V.16**
On joints 51, **XV.10**; 62, **XV.12**; 69, **XV.13**; 70, **XV.11**; 72, **XV.17**
On sterile women, **XVI.15**
On the art 11, **XI.4**
On the heart 1, 4-8, 10, **XIV.14**
On wounds in the head 1-2, **XIV.5**; 21, **XV.14**
Physician 1, **VIII.6**
Places in man 39, **XIII.5**; 47, **XVI.11, XVI.13**
Precepts 4, 6, 8, 10, 12, **VIII.8**
Prognostic 1, 2, 25, **XI.1**
Regimen I.2, **IV.12, XII.11**; I.4-5, **V.13**; III.74, **IV.13**
Regimen in acute diseases 1, **XII.10**
Regimen in health I.1, **XII.12**; I.2-3, **IX.9**
Sacred disease 1, **II.13, II.14, II.28**; 2-3, **II.15**; 14, **V.10**; 16, **V.11**; 18, **II.16**
Sevens 5, **V.14**
Homer
Iliad 1.46-53, **I.8**; 4.210-19, **XV.3**; 5.65ff., **XIV.1**; 5.114-22, **I.16**; 5.455-8, **I.17**;
    5.900-4, **XIII.2**; 11.397-400, **XV.1**; 11.504ff., **XV.5**; 11.822-36, **XV.2**; 11.842-8,
    XIII.1; 16.345ff., **XIV.2**; 16.527-31, **I.18**; 20.56-8, **II.2**; 21.198-9, **II.3**; 21.483-4,
    I.10; 22.322ff., **XIV.3**; 24.605-7, **I.11**; 24.758-9, **I.9**
Odyssey 4.220ff., **XIII.3**; 5.394-8, **I.19**; 9.407-11, **I.12**; 11.171-3, **I.15**; 13.286ff.,
    XIII.4; 19.455-8, **I.20**
Iamblichus
Life of Pythagoras 163, **XII.8**
Inscriptiones Graecae II².4960a, **I.27**; IV².1 Nos. 121-2, **I.24, I.25, XV.9**; VII.235,
    I.21
Marcellinus
On pulsation 11, **XI.17**; 31, **XI.15**
Marcellus
Letter of Cornelius Celsus On remedies, **XIII.14**
Oribasius
Medical collections 3.168ff., **XII.14**; 24.25.1-6, **VII.13**
Palatine Anthology VI.330, **I.26**
Papyrus Medicus Londiniensis 22, **I.3**
Pindar
Pythian III.46-55, **I.22**
Plato
Phaedrus 270C-D, **IV.8**
Protagoras 311B-C, **IV.1**
Republic III.406A-C, **XII.5**
Timaeus 70A-D, **XIV.8**; 70C-D, **VI.21**; 73C-D, **VI.20**; 79A-E, **VI.22**; 80D-E,
    VI.24; 81E-82A, **VI.18, IX.10**; 82A, **III.6**; 82B-83A, **IX.11**; 82B-E, **VI.19**;
    84C-E, **IX.12**; 85A-B, **II.18**; 86B-E, **II.30**; 88B-C, **XII.13**; 89B-D, **XIII.8**; 91C,
    XVI.16
Pliny
Natural history 25.23.57-8, **XIII.15**; 29.2, **IV.6**; 29.4-5, **VI.3**

Plutarch
  Table talk V.8.2, p. 683E, **VI.9**
Porphyry
  Homeric enquiries (on *Iliad* 11.515), p. 165, **XII.1**
  On the Styx, **VI.5**
Ps.-Galen
  Introduction or the Doctor 8, **XII.17**; 13, **IX.21A**
  On the humours **III.18**
Ps.-Plato
  Second letter 314D, **VI.15**
Ps.-Rufus
  On the anatomy of the parts of man 9, **VII.14B**
  Synopsis on the pulses 4, **XI.13**
Ps.-Soranus
  Life of Hippocrates according to Soranus 5, **IV.4**; 8, **IV.3**
  Medical questions 61, **VI.39**
Rufus
  On the naming of the parts of man 10, **VII.23**; 149-50, **VII.9**; 153, **VII.14A**
Sakikku 12-26, **I.7**
Scholium on Pindar, *Pythian odes* 1.51ff., **XV.4**
Seneca
  Natural questions III.14, **II.5**
Sextus Empiricus
  Against the mathematicians VII.49ff., **III.8**; XI.50, **XII.16**
Shakespeare
  Romeo and Juliet Act IV, Scene 3, **XIII.16**
Simplicius
  Commentary on Aristotle's Physics 24.13, **III.1**; 32.3, **III.14**; 152.18, **III.19**;
    300.19, **III.13**; 371.33, **VI.8**
Sophocles
  Oedipus Tyrannus 22-30, **X.1**; 169-83, **X.2**
Soranus
  Gynaecology I.8, **XVI.19**; I.27.2, **XVI.9**; I.29.1, **XVI.10**; III Proem 2, **XVI.4**; III
    Proem 3.4, **XVI.5**; IV.1.4-5, **XVI.6**
Stobaeus
  Physical extracts 1.8.2, **III.9**
Sumerian incantations, **I.4, I.5, I.6**
Tertullian
  On the soul 10, **VII.5**; 15.5, **VI.42**; 35.5, **XV.20**
Theodoret V.22.6 (= Aëtius, *On the opinions of the philosophers* IV.5.6-8), **VI.36**
Theophrastus
  History of plants 9.5, **XIII.9**; 9.6, **XIII.10**; 9.8, **XIII.11, XIII.12A**; 9.10, **XIII.12B**
  On the senses 10, **VI.4**; 25, 26, **III.10**; 43, **III.17, III.20**; 60, **III.22**
Thucydides
  History of the Peloponnesian war II.47-54, 58, III.87, **X.6**
[Vindicianus]
  On the seed (= *Fragmentum Bruxellense de semine*) 1, **VI.45**; 2, **VI.40**; 3, **VI.13**;
    41, **VI.37**; 44, **VI.38; XIV.13**

General Index

absinthe, 195
Achilles, 16, 134, 165, 168, 178, 188
Achilles tendon, 158
Acron of Acragas, 62
Aeneas, 10, 15
Aeschines, 13
Aesculapius, 42
Agamemnon, 134, 146, 154
Agave, 29
ague, 22, 109, 191, 199
ailments, caused by dislocated womb, 195
air, vector of epidemic disease, 124-5, 133-4
Ajax, 29
Alcmaeon of Croton: first doctor to reveal influence of Ionian Natural Philosophy, 31; theory of health, 31, 38, 59, 155; empirical approach to medicine, 33, 39, 53; researches into nature of sense organs, 34, 38; locates seat of intellect in head, 70; pioneer of rational medicine, 79; philosophical influence upon, 107; regards disease as due to seasonal and environmental factors, 107-8; disease as part of nature, 117; first to employ human dissection (?), 169, 176; also mentioned, 61, 83
Alexander, i.e. Paris of Troy, 179
Alexandria, human anatomy at, 84, 98-100
Alexandrian technology, 189
Alexandrians: views on nature of semen, 79, 83; employ treatment by contrary remedies, 152, 156; interest in healing properties of drugs, 164, 167; anatomical researches of, 84-100
Alfred of Sareshel, 166
almond oil, 195
Ambrosia of Athens, 12, 181, 188

Ammianus, 19
Amphiaraus, cult of, 11, 16
Amyntas III, King of Macedon, 81
anaglyphê kalamou (calamus scriptorius or calamus Herophili), 86-7
Anatomai, Dissections, 81
anatomy of heart, 94
Anaxagoras: influence on *Regimen* I, 56, 60
Anaximander, on the cause of thunder, lightning etc., 19; of sun's eclipse, 20; of moon's eclipse, 20; attitude to world around him, 28; conceives universe as balance between opposing forces, 31, 38; declares first principle *apeiron*, 31; influence on Alcmaeon, 59
Anaximenes: rejects belief that Zeus sends rain, 19; attributes earthquakes to natural causes, 19; attitude to world around him, 28
Andreas of Carystus: preserves evidence of Alexandrian pharmacology, 164, 167; Herophilus's pupil & personal physician of Ptolemy IV, 186; credited with invention of instrument for reducing dislocations of larger joints, 186, 189
'andrological' medicine, 199
Anonymus Londinensis, 45, 47-8, 112
Antiochus I, 41
aorta, 24, 115, 170, 172-3, 176
apeiron, 31
Aphrodite, 15, 25
Apollo, 8, 10, 15, 17, 101, 123, 131, 134; Apollo Nomius, 27, 29
Apollonius of Citium, 189
Apollonius Mus, 164, 167
apoplexy, 23-4, 29, 108, 115, 120

adviser to Dionysius, 67, 80; date of medical activity, 66-7, 80; visit to Athens (?), 67, 80; belief that respiration cools innate heat, 68, 80; influence on Diocles, 114; influence on Plato, 119

Philoctetes, 179, 188

philosophical intrusion into medicine: attacked in *Ancient medicine*, 118; attacked in *Nature of man*, 118

phlebotomy, 99, 122

physicians of Croton: considered best in Greece, 61, 79

phithsis, 192 (see, too, consumption)

pia mater, 173

Pindar, 188

Piraeus, 11, 127

plague: at Troy, 8, 15, 123, 134; at Thebes, 123-4, 134; at Athens, 16, 41, 125-31, 133-5; at Selinus, 200; sent by Apollo, 8, 15, 123, 134; sent by Zeus, 9, 15, 123, 134, 191, 200

Plato: on cause of epilepsy, 22, 29; on cause of madness, 27, 29; adopts four element theory, 33, 38, 68, 80, 119; ethical theory of pleasure and pain, 38; accounts for diseases on basis of geometrical atomism, 68-9; influenced by 'Sicilian' medicine, 68, 80; but rejects belief in primacy of heart, 69-70; and locates intellect in head, 69-70; adopts theory of cutaneous respiration, 64, 70-1; respiration for cooling purposes, 70; blood as agent of nutrition, 71-2; first visit to Magna Graecia, 80; tripartite classification of diseases, 112-13, 120; on origin of dietetics, 147, 154; hostile to use of drugs, 160, 166; knowledge of internal anatomy, 171, 177; description of heart, 171-2, 177; tripartite psychology of, 171, 177

plêthôra: origin of, 116, 121; starvation recommended as treatment for, 117, 122

pleural cavity, 184, 189

pleurisy, 44, 109, 120, 191, 199

Plutus, God of Wealth, 13, 14

pneuma, 45, 60, 94-6, 115-16, 120-1, 169-70, 173

Podalirius, 146, 154, 178-9, 188

Polycleitus, 40

Polycrates, tyrant of Samos, 61

Polydamna, 157

Polyphemus, 9, 15

portal vein, 88

Poseidon, 18, 19, 27, 29, 179

Praxagoras: on epilepsy, 23, 29; on apoplexy, 24, 29; on madness (*mania*), 28, 29; believes respiration a strengthening of soul, 68, 78, 82-3, 114; rejects belief that respiration cools innate heat, 68, 78, 82-3, 114, 120; regards heart as seat of intellect, 77-8; accepts some, but rejects other 'Sicilian' theories, 78, 82-3, 120; holds digestion effected by transformation of nutriment into blood, 78; differentiates between veins and arteries, 88; holds arteries contain *pneuma*, 95; teacher of Herophilus, 99; subscribes to variation of humoral theory, 114, 120; influenced by Diocles, 120; considers digestion to be effected by innate heat, 121; credited with distinction between veins and arteries, 121; first to assign a diagnostic role to pulse, 140; believes arteries possess power to pulsate independently of heart, 140, 144; discovery that only arteries pulsate, 144; credited with bringing dietetic medicine to perfection, 146-7, 155

Presocratic philosophers, 38-9, 198

prognosis, 136, 139, 143-4

pros to kenoumenon akolouthia, 96-7, 121 (see, too, *horror vacui*)

Protagoras, 40

Proteus, 16

Pseudo-Apuleius, 166

psoriasis, 108, 120

psychic disorders, due to physical causes, 120

Ptolemies: encouragement of medical research, 100

pulsation, 140-5

pulse-rate as diagnostic aid, 99

pulse: ant-like (*myrmekizôn*), 142; gazelle-like (*dorkadizôn*), 142

purgative, 159, 195

pustules, 22

Pythagorean Brotherhood, 106